THE HISTORY IN LITERATURE:
ON VALUE, GENRE, INSTITUTIONS

HERBERT LINDENBERGER

The History in Literature: On Value, Genre, Institutions

COLUMBIA UNIVERSITY PRESS

New York

Columbia University Press
New York   Oxford
Copyright © 1990 Columbia University Press

Library of Congress Cataloging-in-Publication Data

Lindenberger, Herbert Samuel, 1929–
The history in literature on value, genre, institutions
Herbert Lindenberger.
p.   cm.
Includes bibliographical references.
ISBN 0-231-07252-X (alk. paper)
1. Literature and history.
2. History in literature.
3. Literary form.
4. Values in literature.
5. Canon (Literature)
I. Title.
PN50.L55 1990
809'.93358—dc20   90-1679
CIP

Casebound editions of Columbia University Press books are Smyth-sewn
and printed on permanent and durable acid-free paper

∞

Printed in the United States of America

c 10 9 8 7 6 5 4 3 2 1

In memory of my cousin
Hanni Lindenberger Meyer,
active in the Herbert Baum resistance group,
executed in Plötzensee Prison, Berlin,
4 March, 1943,   age 22

CONTENTS

ACKNOWLEDGMENTS

This project began, innocently enough, as a grant proposal entitled "Social and Historical Factors in Modern Literary Criticism" and submitted to the National Endowment for the Humanities and the Stanford Humanities Center, the funding from both of which enabled me to spend the academic year 1982–83 at the center. Although the only part of the present volume I completed that year was the first section of essay 9, the reading and the conversations during this, the center's first year of operation, helped determine the shape that this book was to take. I decided during the year not to attempt a single, sustained argument, but to write a series of closely related essays that could supply some theoretical grounding, together with practical examples, and also a measure of polemic, for the turn (not, I contend, a return) to history that was taking place in British and American criticism during the 1980s.

In the years that followed my sabbatical, the topics I chose when responding to invitations to speak at conferences and conventions and to contribute to collections were always designed with this book in mind. The Prologue was published in *Scandinavian Studies* (1990); essay 1 in *The Wordsworth Circle* (1985); essay 4 in *Idee/ Gestalt/Geschichte: Festschrift Klaus von See* (Odense University Press, 1988); essay 7 in *Comparative Criticism* (Cambridge University Press, 1989); essay 8 in *Genre* (University of Oklahoma Press, 1987); and the first part of essay 9 in *Profession 84* (Modern Language Association, 1984). I thank the editors of these journals and books for permission to use these essays here. All have been revised (some quite substantially) except for the earliest one I wrote, "Toward a New History in Literary Study," for which I have instead supplied an afterword. Essays 2, 3, 5, 6, and the afterword to 9 are published here for the first time. Translations, unless otherwise indicated within the list of works cited, are my own.

A book such as this, which seeks to engage with current controversies, is more dependent than others on the interchange of ideas with colleagues and students. My gratitude extends to many more than I can name here. I cite first the various members of Stanford's faculty seminar on interpetation, which, during its nine-year tenure from 1979 to 1988, brought together people from such diverse fields as anthropology, religious studies, and law, with the literary contingent quickly learning that it had no monopoly on matters of interpretation. I feel especially grateful for the discussions with students that took place in those seminars I used as testing grounds for some of these essays, especially the seminars entitled "Theories of Romanticism," "Romanticism and History," and "Literature and Institutions."

Parts of all these essays were read as lectures at other universities, and the discussions after these lectures were often decisive for the expansion and revision of individual essays. I thank the following institutions for giving me the opportunity to present the material of this book: California State University, Chico; Columbia University; Cornell University; Emory University; Georgia Institute of Technology; the Grasmere Wordsworth Conference; Harvard University; Humboldt State University; the Ohio State University; the State University of New York, Albany; the University of California, Los Angeles; the University of California, Santa Barbara; the University of Georgia; the University of Washington; and Western Michigan University. I am also grateful to the Arnold Schoenberg

Institute at the University of Southern California for allowing me to examine Schoenberg's autograph of his play *Der biblische Weg* as well as other documents.

Let me single out the following persons, all of whom commented in detail on most and, in some instances, on all these essays and who often forced me to rethink and better formulate my positions: Marshall Brown, Richard Hooker, Anne K. Mellor, Marjorie Perloff, Adena Rosmarin, Clifford Siskin, and William Mills Todd III. Any author would feel grateful to have such demanding yet also friendly critics. In addition I wish to acknowledge the criticism and advice that the following colleagues at Stanford and other universities have given me on particular essays related to their areas of specialization: Thomas A. Bauman, Edward J. Brown, Caryl Emerson, Lazar Fleishman, Gregory Freidin, Regenia Gagnier, Barbara Charlesworth Gelpi, Alan Liu, Charles R. Lyons, Nicholas V. Riasanovsky, Paul Robinson, and Egon Schwarz. I also thank my family—my wife Claire and children Michael and Elizabeth—for listening to me think out this book, showing skepticism toward still inchoate arguments and often, as well, taking issue with my positions.

Stanford, California
September, 1989

IN PLACE OF THE USUAL PREFACE:
A GLOSSARY OF KEY TERMS

CANON: a term we ignore when its referent remains in stable condition but that we invoke incessantly whenever it is threatened with change. If this were an ordinary glossary, it would remind its readers that the term derives from the word *reed*, that reeds were used in classical times as measuring rods, that, in the course of time, the means for measurement transformed itself into the object measured. This glossary is less concerned with the history of its terms than with their function in the present-day critical marketplace. Canons here take the form of banners by means of which particular movements, nations and regional constructs such as the so-called West establish pedigrees, define an identity, and present themselves to the world. Four of the essays in this book focus specifically on the processes of canon construction and change. Essay 1 explores how the canon of English romantic poetry defined itself over the years, above all how it accommodated itself to, indeed even served as an expression of, fundamental changes in the function and mission of criticism. The following essay looks at the critical fortunes of a single poem, Wordsworth's "Resolution and Independence," to describe the tactics employed by critics since the poet himself to assure and maintain its canonical status. Essay 6 looks at canon making (more precisely canon change) in a more general sense, while essay 7 presents a case study of a recent battle over what precisely should be "the" canonical texts of Western culture, whether there should even *be* such a list, indeed whether the whole concept of Western culture that this list purportedly represents is still viable today.

ESSAY: a term that, ever since the originary, authorizing examples set by Montaigne and Bacon, has allowed writers to package their wares within small, self-sufficient confines and by means of tentative, non-authoritarian stances. The present volume takes this long-standing license to pursue several styles of inquiry—for example, historical case studies of individual works (essays 2, 4, and 5), institutional analysis (essays 1, 7, and 8), ideological critique (Prologue and essay 3), overt polemic (essays 6 and 9), and dialogue (Epilogue). Yet all the essays, like moths hovering about the same light, focus upon the nouns within the book's title, all five of which they seek to elucidate and reassess as well as to expand these words' meanings and to suggest new relationships among them.

GENRE: a term that arouses expectations that the reader never quite expects to see met. Going back as it does to Plato (1:656–61), genre analysis could be called the most ancient genre within criticism, and for much of its history it remained notable for its prescriptiveness and its insensitivity to the particularities of history. Indeed, the phrase "Genre in History," which serves as the title of part II, might seem a contradiction in terms, at least to the extent that the term *genre* suggests timeless forms resistant to historical pressures. Yet the tension between timelessness and temporality, between the constancy of the expectations that readers entertain and the unexpected contingencies to which they can expect to see them subjected, has made the study of genre a fertile ground for a historically oriented criticism. Within this book, genre appears not simply as an aesthetic term, but also includes theoretical constructs such as the theories of and about romanticism to which essay 3 is directed. It can also include what is sometimes classified as a "medium," for example opera, which in essays 4 and 8 is juxtaposed, respectively, with historical drama and visual art. Genres from supposedly alien forms of discourse such as literature and history become aligned in essay 5, which examines a single, canonical work from literature in relation to the earlier historical texts it absorbed and to the later historical texts it helped generate.

HISTORY: a term that gave no trouble as long as it referred to things that, at one time or another, simply happened. In literary studies today history serves not so much as a backdrop or even as an object of inquiry than as a special way of thinking—a way that assumes, for instance, that phenomena long taken to be timeless or grounded in nature are rooted in particular times and places, indeed, that these roots are often ignored or suppressed in the interest of making these phenomena appear to be timeless and natural. It is this attitude that guides all the essays in this book, including those not overtly concerned with historiographical matters. Three essays, however, address themselves specifically to the methods with which we approach history. The Prologue seeks to uncover some ways in which the nineteenth century "experienced" history. Essay 5 scouts the borderlines between those entities customarily labeled literature and history. The final essay, together with its afterword, tries to define, account for, and assess the turn to history in recent literary criticism.

INSTITUTIONS: a term that for much of its history evoked those domiciles to which persons deemed to be insane or dangerous were relegated. Within literary study the term has emerged, ever since the recent turn to history, as a tool for examining the means by which research in this field is produced. Indeed, the selfconsciousness attendant upon such an examination may sometimes work to question, even to redirect the activities in the field. The term *institutions*, when applied to literary studies, functions like a set of Chinese boxes, each one smaller than and contained within the other. Thus, an understanding of contemporary literary study would involve first that commodious box we might label the American university system, then a smaller box referring to a particular type of university (public or private, large or small, prestigious or not), then humanistic study within the contemporary university, after which one would uncover ever smaller, more specialized boxes such as literary study in the larger sense and finally the study of national literatures, periods, and theoretical perspectives. These smallest entities can be described according to such institutional attributes as the conferences and journals they sponsor and the critical vocabulary they employ in their classes and their writings. Though much of what this book has to say about institutions is centered around a set of categories such as these, it is also concerned with other institutional forms such as the opera house (essays 4 and 8), the art museum (essay 8), and the various modes of art—theater, novel, architecture—developed during the nineteenth century to popularize history (Prologue). Indeed, it is through the study of institutional structures that we can understand the often suppressed relationships between the creation of art and its subsequent consumption and canonization. If we look at an institution, to cite a recent definition, as "an objectified social activity with established roles and functions" (Todd 45), it is evident that an examination of both art and criticism from an institutional point of view is obviously at odds with those older definitions of literary and reading activity that celebrate unmediated, spontaneous creation and reception. Although part 3 is specifically labeled "Institutions," the term pervades the book as a whole. Moreover, this book has been fully implicated in the activities of that continuing institution the university, which, through its salary, its research funds, and the institutes it sponsors, through the students it supplies for trying out the ideas that follow, through the journals, books and conferences that first sponsored some of the essays, through the press that is printing and disbursing these ideas, has obviously left its imprint (sometimes not readily discernible) on the very process with which the author has questioned the role of institutions.

LITERATURE: a term that lost its innocence about two centuries ago when it ceased referring simply to a loosely organized collection of writings and revealed itself instead as a magical body. Although written in full awareness that the honor accruing to this term has provided the institutional means that made its writing possible in the first place, this book seeks above all to problematize the term. To play upon the words of its title, it will observe, among other matters, the relationships that literature entertains with that other form of textual production we know as history; or the ways that values shift within the body of literature as well as the ways that literature itself confers value upon that which assumes its name; or how any magical claims that literature might make become encumbered through an understanding of the institutional procedures by means of which it is evaluated and transmitted.

OPERA: a term that, doubtless because of the extravagance of its referent, has offered special allures for compilers of dictionaries ever since its definition by Rousseau as a "dramatic and lyric spectacle striving to reunite all the enchantments of the fine arts in the representation of an impassioned action" (*Dictionnaire* 339), and by Johnson as "an exotick and irrational entertainment, which has been always combated and always has prevailed" (2:160). The present glossary, though resisting these allures, is concerned with the term's use in this book, where it functions as an expanded and problematic version of the term *literature*. Poised uncomfortably between music and literature, opera tests the boundaries between these forms of expression and also between the academic and artistic enterprises associated with each of them. To the extent that music has often claimed a universality by virtue of its non-verbal nature, opera can affect a timelessness not easily conceded to non-musical drama. Yet through its extravagance and its penchant for swaying its audiences by overtly non-rational means, opera has rarely been granted the dignified status that most other forms of literature and music have enjoyed over the years. Two essays within this book, 4 and 8, use opera as a focal point for exploring the form's historical and institutional dimensions at particular times. The first of these essays looks at three operas from widely distinct periods to demonstrate opera's often unacknowledged entanglements with history—for example, its ability to give voice to theories of history and to political tensions coincident with the time an opera was composed. The second of these essays examines the aesthetic conservatism of the present-day operatic repertoire and, by means of a comparison between the opera house and the art museum, analyzes the pressures that govern the interpretation and the consumption of works within these institutions.

ROMANTICISM: the most controversial of the grand period terms—controversial, among other reasons, for when precisely it began, thrived, and ended; if, in fact, it ever ended; whether its politics should be classified as left or right; what its guiding ideas were; indeed, if it was a good thing that it even happened at all. Although writings associated with the so-called age of romanticism are central to most of these essays (all, in fact, except the last four), this book does not address itself directly to questions of this sort. Rather, it employs examples drawn from the period as a means of demonstrating such matters as the processes of canon making, the historicity of historical thinking, and the framing effects of institutions. Yet the connections between these matters and what we call romanticism are something more than accidental, for, as essay 3 suggests, certain notions associated with the period—for example, notions concerning the stages of human and cultural development—are themselves implicated in the institutionalization of literary study, indeed in the very concept of literature that legitimates this study.

THEORY: another Chinese-box term that, in its smallest manifestation, refers to certain ideas promoted so successfully by several Yale professors during the 1970s that this has remained the indicated meaning whenever an English department in the hinterland searches for what it takes to be a theorist. A larger box would encompass a range of influential mid- to late-twentieth-century theories, each with its characteristic vocabulary, from the "critical theory" of the Frankfurt school to the "dialogism" of a Bakhtin. A still larger size would contain the long-standing tradition of a line of theories of and about literature from the Greeks to the present. The largest of all would link literary theory with those areas of inquiry called theory in the various scientific disciplines, which tend to demarcate a theoretical perspective by means of its difference from experimental work. The essays within this book assume the inadequacy of the traditional distinction between theory and practice in literary study, and, by their example, propose instead that whatever theoretical framework guides an essay is itself put into question by the supporting historical detail, which in turn suggests the need to rethink and revise this framework. Moreover, the book itself would resist being classified as theory, if only because (whichever of the Chinese boxes would seem to contain it) it seeks to treat theory and theories as historical artifacts that are themselves products of and responses to concrete historical situations.

VALUE: a term that straddles the material and spiritual realms, as a result of which it seems particularly useful for discussing phenomena that display their spiritual status while hiding whatever material processes have created and sustained them. The section of this book entitled "Value in History" is primarily concerned with the ways that the values attributed to texts, authors, and, indeed, to whole periods shift in the course of time. The second essay in this section charts these shifts in value by examining the critical history of a poem that overtly elaborates upon value in both its spiritual and material manifestations. As literary study becomes more conscious of its material foundations, it recognizes that, just as it shares the category of institutions with sociology, so it shares that of value with economics. It may also come to recognize the exchanges of value that go on continually, though also quite normally, within critical discourse. For many today, attaching the term *theory* to a piece of critical writing is itself an attribution of value (even when it refers to what any other discipline would label practice). To cite other value-laden terms from this book's title, literature has conferred value upon the works that lay claim to the term ever since the term itself became endowed with high value, while in recent years history has come to wear an aura that accords a special value to texts honored with this designation. Indeed, the attempt, within essay 4, to locate history within opera is itself a way of endowing an art form of traditionally questionable status with a value commensurate with that of literature.

THE HISTORY IN LITERATURE:
ON VALUE, GENRE, INSTITUTIONS

PROLOGUE

⁓ꝏ⁓

Experiencing History in the Age of Historicism

Perhaps the most efficient way of introducing this essay is to indicate the titles I discarded along the way. Since my aim is to examine the historicity implicit in the nineteenth century's perception of history, I recognized from the start that whatever title I chose would itself color, even limit the subject I sought to explore. For example, I might well have chosen the title "Constructing History," which would have underlined our contemporary notion that the external world is a construction we fabricate according to the biases of our own time and place. Or I might have hit upon the title "Rethinking History," which would have lent a selfconsciousness to my project without stressing the willfulness we hear in "Constructing History." I never seriously considered the title "Understanding History," for this might have suggested that I speak with the credentials of a professional philosopher who has decided

1

to aim the big analytical guns at his disposal on that often amorphous, none-too-well-demarcated territory we call history.

All these titles impose a typically cerebral twentieth-century perspective on history that differs markedly from the style with which the nineteenth century itself looked upon the subject. Had I been focusing on a period earlier than the nineteenth century, I would have done well to choose a title such as "Learning from History," and this would surely have proved apt for such diverse and temporally dispersed cultures as ancient Rome, Elizabethan England, and Enlightenment France, all of which attributed a high value to the moral lessons that a study of the past could offer the present. Such a title would also have stressed the fact that throughout most of history the various segments of the past were seen none too differently either from one another or from the present, for which these past times were meant to provide an ongoing series of lessons.

Yet if I wanted a title to approach the way the nineteenth century itself approached the past, surely the name I finally settled on, "Experiencing History," was the aptest among those I had tried out, for in the nineteenth century history had, to a degree it had never done before, come to serve as an experience, as a way of sensuously apprehending and trying to make sense of the world. When I say "as it had not done before," I am of course making a statement about origins, and this search for origins is typical of the way the nineteenth century experienced history. In earlier centuries one would rarely have asked when a particular way of thinking or experiencing began, and if one asked such a question, it would have been in a relatively casual manner—as when adding a descriptive adjective to a noun that might otherwise look too bare. As products of the nineteenth century's way of seeing the world, we find it natural, even necessary, to ask when—not to speak of why— a particular phenomenon came into being, when it reached its apogee, and when it was perceived to be on the wane, and, if we believe it over and done with, when it came to its end.

Although my present inquiry makes me suspicious of the naturalness and the need to pose such questions, I recognize that at least a tentative answer serves a rhetorical purpose, namely, a reader's quite understandable desire to know what a writer is focusing upon, what precisely the limits of his inquiry are. Ever since the revolution in historical thought that we attribute to the nineteenth century, we have become so accustomed to thinking historically that we expect temporal borders to be drawn in discussions of the past in order not to feel ourselves lost. I shall answer simply that I am demarcating a way of experiencing history that starts roughly (the word *roughly* being an attempt to ward off the more niggling sort of questioner) in the late eighteenth century and that lasted until well into our present century; indeed, many of its traces are still with us today. But I have no intention in this essay of presenting a formal history of this way of experiencing history: any such attempt would represent a falling back into the mental habits, the methods, and the assumptions that we have come to associate with that period. Rather, I want to use this opportunity to distance myself from some of these habits, methods, and assumptions, to stand back and to ask to what degree our own way of perceiving the world as well as of institutionalizing this knowledge may still be informed by the nineteenth-century's particular way of experiencing history.

To achieve this perspective I shall try to isolate some of the characteristic dichotomies that the nineteenth century used to classify its perceptions and judgments of the past. In examining the dichotomies that a culture sets up—for example, that of nature versus grace during the Renaissance, or of nature versus the social order during the eighteenth century—we are able to lay bare the forms within which the culture apprehends and judges the world. But before listing some key dichotomies by means of which the nineteenth century viewed the past, let me point to a deep tension central to that century's experience of history. On the one hand, one notes a desire to distance the present from the past, to see the past objectively, or, to use the famous phrase that Ranke established early in the century as the goal of historical writing, to see the past "wie es eigentlich gewesen"—"as it really was" (33–34:vii). On the other hand, despite this persistent attempt to gain a distance from the past, the nineteenth century felt the need to experience the past in all its presentness. No art form illustrates this tension as powerfully as historical drama. Quite unlike historical dramas written during earlier centuries, historical drama in the nineteenth century sought to capture not simply a narrative of past events, but above all to render the past in all its immediacy— which meant that the stage settings, the costumes, sometimes even earlier manners of speech, attempted to render a moment of the past with what the audience would believe to be a high degree of accuracy. This search for historical immediacy is evident both in nineteenth-century productions of earlier historical plays, above all those of Shakespeare, and in a multitude of new historical plays from Goethe's *Götz von Berlichingen* in the 1770s to the plays of Hauptmann and Strindberg well over a century later. Yet paradoxically the immediacy with which the audience sought to grasp the past served to decrease the temporal distance, in fact to bring the past into the present. At the very time that we leave our everyday world for some privileged spot of past time, this spot, embodied in the décor and above all in the actor impersonating a long-dead figure, comes back like a ghost from the past to establish its own direct presence.

Although historical drama, whether in the many nineteenth-century operas on historical themes or merely in spoken form, can illustrate this tension with special intensity, other art forms that purport to render history found their own ways to endow pastness with presence. Readers of a long historical novel by Scott or by one of his many followers would not of course see before them the battlements of a medieval castle or an actor in armor, as would the theater audience, yet these very readers were trained by these authors to lose themselves within the imagined past of the novel to the point that, as with that most famous reader Emma Bovary, this past implanted itself firmly within their imaginations. The very length of nineteenth-century historical novels served as a guarantee that their readers would have ample time to depart their present lives long enough for the rendered past to establish its presence and, indeed, to help reshape the readers' sense of their own present. Similarly, the many narrative histories of the nineteenth century—for example, those of Macaulay, Michelet, and Parkman, to cite examples from different national cultures—tended not only to cultivate length—a length often far greater than that of historical novels—but, as we have recently come to recognize, they consciously used literary devices to help their readers experience history in a manner not much different from what the historical novel gave them.[1]

The tension I am describing between the pastness and the presence of the past is by no means limited to verbal forms: it is central to the types of visual experience sought in the nineteenth century. Historical drama, of course, managed to embellish the verbal with a visual dimension. Indeed, the backdrops and costumes we view on the stage inhabit the same visual world that we associate with historical paintings of the time. Even without hearing the spoken word, those who attended the first public exhibitions of the great historical paintings from David to Delacroix may well have felt themselves transported to some great moment of the past familiar from their school reading of history or their personal knowledge of recent great events; as with the narrative histories and the historical novels that they read, these paintings, often very large in size and deliberately theatrical in manner, sought to overwhelm their viewers with a powerful presence that their often meticulously delineated past could establish in these viewers' own humdrum nineteenth-century lives.

One did not have to seek out paintings to experience this visual experience of the past. The characteristic architectural forms of the nineteenth century were quite consciously retrospective. The new buildings that the inhabitants of the rapidly growing nineteenth-century cities saw sprouting up around them were meant to repeat recognizable historical periods. The very names of the various period revivals in architecture—Neoclassical, Neogothic, Neoromanesque—that successively reshaped the citiscapes of Europe and America testify at once to the pastness of what was to be evoked and, in the ever-present "neo" prefix, to remind us that this pastness was establishing its presence during the new industrial age.[2] To create this presence, these revivals did not insist on simply repeating the original social functions of buildings, as they easily enough could in the construction of a Neogothic cathedral. But the Gothic style could manifest itself in the details of a small private domicile, just as the various capitals that once had graced pagan temples could now be experienced on the porches of Southern antebellum mansions, even in the decorative work of simple one-story cottages. At the same time those architectural artifacts that had survived the long ages in which experiencing history had not yet become a desirable activity now achieved the status of revered objects. Pilgrimages to famed Gothic cathedrals could now be made, not, as before, to visit a saint's relics, but to experience a great lost moment of time. Even those periods in which little had survived often proved powerful in imposing their past presence on the present, if only in the form of fragmentary ruins, the resurrection of which opened up the thriving new industry of classical Near Eastern archaeology.

The perceived need of confronting the past as it really was suggests one of the reigning dichotomies of the time, namely, the apparent conflict between an authentic and an artificially contrived experience. This conflict, deriving as it does from the eighteenth-century dichotomy between nature and the social realm, during the succeeding century manifested itself in a driving determination to recover what was authentic within a civilization perceived to be inimical to such authenticity of experience. In its approach to history the nineteenth century employed a variety of ways to recover the voices of what would otherwise be a lost past. To hear these voices as they really were, Ranke and the historians who followed in his wake pursued the archival method of digging up the past—much as their fellow archaeologists used picks and shovels to unearth fragments of pediments and limbless torsos. Since simple folk did not yet register the cultural changes of their more highly placed contemporaries, they too could serve as archival materials, as we can see in the work of the brothers Grimm and those who followed them in the emerging new fields of folklore, linguistics, and anthropology.

The dichotomy between an authentically revealed past and an artificially reconstituted one manifested itself in critical distinctions between the type of epic represented by the Homeric poems and the *Chanson de Roland,* on the one hand, and the more selfconsciously literary epic of a Virgil, a Tasso, or a Milton.[3] Until well into the eighteenth century one would not ordinarily have distinguished between Homer and Virgil on these grounds. Yet this distinction among epic poets was to become a persistent theme structuring literary works as well as the way that commentators came to speak about authors, works, and their relation to the world around them. Schiller's essay of 1795, *On Naive and Sentimental Poetry,* offers a bald distinction between poets like Homer, who supposedly retained a direct, unmediated relation with nature, and those more selfconscious ones, like Virgil, who, by dint of conscious effort, worked to restore this now-lost relationship. The dilemma that poets saw themselves facing could easily be transferred from the literary realm to the larger culture, which cultivated the notion that authentic experience could best be located somewhere in the past—a past, moreover, that manifested itself both in the childhood of the individual and in the earlier development of a whole people.

Yet the many attempts to uncover, to reexperience this purportedly once-authentic experience were themselves, we now recognize, compromised by the artificial contrivances necessary to mediate this experience. The authentic voice of earlier men that the brothers Grimm uncovered in their fairy tales or that Brentano and Arnim brought to light in their collection of folk lyrics, were, it turns out, heavily edited, modernized, reshaped to give their prospective readers a historical experience compatible with what these compilors thought could best communicate with their own contemporaries. And surely, despite our skepticism about their meddling, they judged correctly, for the illusion they created of a lost past exercised a hold over these readers that a more pedantically reconstructed past could never have accomplished. The various reconstructions of epics and romances from *Ossian* to the *Kalevala* and the *Mabinogion*, however authentic they may once have seemed, now strike us as more firmly rooted in the world of their editors and translators—and, in the case of *Ossian*, of its fabricator Macpherson—than in whatever lost past they claim to voice. Similarly, the historical experience that visitors to Carcassonne supposedly undergo has been badly compromised by reminders that the walled city owes more to the nineteenth-century restoration work of Viollet-le-Duc than to the ruins he found at the site. Indeed, we now have sufficient historical perspective on the historicizing efforts of the nineteenth century to place these efforts within the context of nineteenth-century culture. When we look at a nineteenth-century historical painting such as Ingres's *Joan of Arc*, with its tight Neoclassical lines, or when we read the long description of costumes and ceremonies in a novel such as *Ivanhoe*, we today are less aware of these works' medieval referents than of their creators' attempt to impose their own, peculiarly modern view of the Middle Ages on their materials. Whatever authenticity of experience they may have sought to give their audiences, with our own historical distance our attention remains directed to the historicity implicit in their very striving for such authenticity.

If the achievement of authenticity now strikes us as a more complex matter than the nineteenth century let on, we also recognize that the ways that history came to be classified were more problematic than they once seemed. In earlier centuries historical writings belonged to that general realm that was once dubbed "letters." What separated historical narrative from other forms such as epic and tragedy was largely a matter of generic classication. By the nineteenth century, however, literature had come to occupy its own realm, a realm that defined itself as art and that literature came to share with painting and music. Whereas letters could once accommodate such diverse genres as historical narrative, biography, and the scientific treatise, that new art-oriented classification called literature could absorb history only when the latter was subsumed within one of the reigning literary genres. Thus, historical drama and the historical novel could count as literature in a sense that historical narrative, now fast becoming an academic enterprise, no longer could. Yet historical fiction and historical drama remained among the most popular and also most prestigious literary forms during the nineteenth century just as historical painting—at least throughout the first half of the century—achieved a prestige unmatched by other genres of painting.

In the nineteenth century those artifacts and activities that came to be honored with the term "art" maintained a certain transcendental aura from which other artifacts and activities remained excluded. The term "history," when not specifically tied to an acknowledged artistic genre such as drama or painting, generally referred to a realm distinctly beneath anything that could be labelled transcendent. History was the place of contingency, of nasty power politics, of those lowly, often grubby forms of life that, in the course of the century, fought continuing battles to gain admittance to that sanctum that called itself art. Movements such as realism and naturalism can be seen in retrospect as attempts to represent the historicity of the contemporary world in a guise that could achieve the prestige of art. In the course of the century the gap separating those seemingly independent realms of art and history was subject to a constant reassessment about where precisely to draw the borderlines between them. Whenever the historical threatened to invade the artistic domain, rationalizations needed to be made to insure that the power struggles and the lowly detail we associate with history had been treated in such a way that they achieved a degree of universality to compensate for their contingent, temporal character. One notes this tendency to universalize in Ibsen's famous speech before the Norwegian League for Women's Rights when, in obvious reference to the conflicts engendered by the creation of his character Nora many years before, he stated, "I have been more the poet and less the social philosopher than people generally seem inclined to believe" (337). To defend his role as artist, Ibsen was forced to underplay the historicity inherent in his writing during his realist period. When he went on to say, "My task has been the *description of humanity*," he invokes a term typical of those who seek to absorb the temporal within a timeless framework. Whether one speaks of "the human," "humanity," or "the human condition," the human beings who people the canvases, plays and novels of representational art and literature achieve a universality, a timelessness, often even a transcendental quality to raise them above the mortality and the lack of significance to which they would ordinarily be subjected in so-called "real life." Art must, in effect, de-historicize itself to retain its status as art.

If the opposition of history and art engenders a conflict whereby the latter establishes its hegemony over the former, one can point to another dichotomy, history and myth, of which each member pretends to maintain its autonomy from the other. By myth I refer to a whole series of nineteenth-century attitudes, conventions, and devices that sought to give new significance to a variety of disparate phenomena such as dreams, symbols, literary romance and, for that matter, the traditional content of what had long counted as mainstream myth, namely, the mythology of the ancient world. Within the terms of this dichotomy, history was associated with the real, the worldly, the rational. Myth, on the other hand, occupied those territories that history seemed to disdain; when myth introduced the supernatural, it did so without ordinarily claiming any truth-value in the unearthly events it was representing.

It is significant to what degree certain nineteenth-century authors respected the borders they saw separating myth from history. The Balzac of *Séraphita* maintained an authorial presence separate from that of his novels on ordinary life in early nineteenth-century France. The Flaubert of the *Tentation*, on the surface at least, stands at a far remove from the Flaubert of *Madame Bovary*. Strindberg, in the first years of the present century, composed symbolic plays at the very time he was writing some of his major history plays. Myth and history provided two separate but not necessarily antithetical ways of producing certain truths cherished by the nineteenth century. For writers like Flaubert and Strindberg, who cultivated both paths, the literary production that belongs to one of these cannot achieve its full significance for us without our awareness of what came out of the other path.

Yet the division between history and myth was only an apparent one—the product, surely, of that new scientific mentality which limited historical research to what "really" was and relegated less real phenomena to some realm of the imagination. Though nominally maintaining their separate identities, the two paths of history and myth often sought to converge, as in that ubiquitous nineteenth-century genre called "historical romance." Note that history appears in this designation in the role of a modifying adjective, as though ceding primacy to the noun *romance*. Readers of Scott and his successors, as well as audiences attending the multitude of plays and operas on historical themes, must have recognized that the history they were witnessing was scarcely "real" in the newer scientific sense; yet they also knew that the imaginative resources available within these new genres gave them access to what must have seemed the very spirit of history. Thus, each of these paths worked in collusion with the other—and with a particularly striking effect in Flaubert's *Salammbô*, whose meticulous archaeological research would seem to compensate for the extravagance of its romance.

Among the dichotomies within which history forms one term, the second term tends to define itself according to what history is not. But within nineteenth-century culture one often sees history itself subdivided into antithetical or at least complementary categories. Among the most persistent of these divisions is national history as opposed to world history. In certain respects one can see these terms as less opposed than parallel to one another. Both national and world history define themselves in terms of development: thus, individual historical developments within each mode of history are linked to one another in narratives that build on metaphors of growth, decline, resurgence, and to the extent that these narratives are shaped in a specifically Hegelian manner, they depend on moments of crisis and dialectical turnings to provide high points along the way. It scarcely seems any wonder that history, whether national or international, easily lends itself to theatrical treatment in the nineteenth century. The distinctions between national and world history are perhaps analogous to those between an individual and the larger family to which he or she belongs. The history of each party can obviously be told separately, for each has its own identity, its particular configuration of events, even a larger governing structure—yet these histories also intersect with one another at crucial moments. Thus, although Strindberg kept his cycle of Swedish history plays separate from his world-historical cycle, there are memorable spots in the national plays in which he makes us aware of what is transpiring at that moment in the world-historical arena—for example, the reference to the execution of the British king, Charles I, in *Queen Christina* or to the fall of the Bastille in *Gustav III* (21, 263).

However distinct the various national histories that developed

during the nineteenth century attempted to remain from one another, from our present vantage point they often look strikingly
similar. Whether in long since unified France or Sweden, or in
recently unified Germany or Italy, each seeks to legitimate, often in
fact to glorify the life of a particular people—yet all the national
histories use similar modes of narration and often similar structuring principles. Although the timing may differ from country to
country, national histories ordinarily concentrate on matters such
as the formation and the consolidation of the state against an
outgoing feudalism, the dangers imposed on the new state by challenges to its legitimacy, and the progressive liberation of the populace against monarchical oppression. (If Germany and Italy could
not quite recapture the early stages in the way that the long unified
states could do, historians could represent these stages in the history of component parts such as Prussia and Tuscany.) Not only do
these stories sometimes seem interchangeable, but they follow patterns similar to those imposed upon world history. Thus Hegel's
theory of the progressive liberation of mankind as a whole since
the time of the Oriental despotisms is mirrored in the various
national histories that chart the stages of liberation within a particular people.

Since the individual events that make up national and world
history achieve their full meaning only in relation to the larger
narrative of which they form a part, those intent on translating
history into art often faced the dilemma of relating part to whole,
of finding devices to bridge the distance from these individual
events to the larger stories they are meant to imply. The literary
conventions to which a historical play or novel is committed force
a concentration upon micro- rather than macro-history, upon temporally constrained periods rather than upon larger time spans,
upon individual lives, whether of royalty or of common people,
rather than upon some collective entity—though the writer would
ordinarily find ways of reminding readers and audiences of the
macro-significance of his particular narrative. Only rarely, as in
the Hungarian dramatist Imre Madách's *Tragedy of Man*, which
encompasses world history from Adam and Eve to the nineteenth
century within the confines of a single play, do we find an attempt
at macro-history that seeks to bypass micro-history.

Some nineteenth-century writers developed a unique way of
moving from micro- to macro-history—namely, by proliferating
their micro-narratives to form a cycle. More often than not the idea

for a larger cycle emerged after the writer had tried his hand at one or more micro-texts. Certainly Strindberg could not have foreseen his national, let alone his world-historical cycle of plays when he wrote *Master Olof*—any more than Scott, when he started *Waverley*, knew he would run the gamut of medieval and modern Scottish and English history in what came to be known as the Waverley novels. The idea of a historical cycle is by no means limited to drama and fiction— as Victor Hugo demonstrated in *La Légende des siècles* by stringing together a vast collection of lyric poems each of which focused on a discrete moment of history. Hugo, like the historical novelists and dramatists, recognized that the ancient idea of epic could no longer be embodied in a single, long heroic poem, but rather in a cycle of brief works representing a number of subgenres. Each work, concentrating on a single or at least a few moments of micro-history, could serve as a fragment of macro-history. Even if the fully completed cycle would fail to encompass the whole of national or world history, the suggestive power of the individual fragments could at least imply the existence, even the structure, of the larger narrative. If we extend the notion of history to include the history being made during the author's own time, we recognize that the cycles produced by writers such as Balzac and Trollope present a special version of macro-history, with the epic breadth they suggest inhering not in its temporal extension, as it does in Scott's and Strindberg's historical cycles, but in a spatial breadth that encompasses many levels of the society in which they themselves lived.

The shifting ways in which one can define the relationship between micro- and macro-history during the nineteenth century are analogous to the ways writers sought to determine whether the proper locus of history was the world of ordinary people or of those who led them. This conflict could express itself either in political or aesthetic terms—or sometimes both at once. Could one best understand history by means of larger social forces or by the diplomatic maneuverings and personalities of those in high office? Was the proper language in which the past spoke to us that of everyday life, sometimes in fact some local or now-archaic dialect comprehensible to at best a few members of a potential audience, or was it the high literary language in which real-life figures, even of the recent past, were expected to speak in verse? (Strindberg's alternative prose and verse versions of *Master Olof* suggest alternative solutions to this problem.)

To a degree the difference between high and low history can be categorized in generic terms, with historical drama the genre for traditionally high matters and with the new genre of historical fiction for the more lowly ones. Georg Lukács attempted to pinpoint this distinction in his book on the historical novel by showing the differing roles that famous personages play in the two genres: whereas kings and figures of equivalent stature are placed at the center of a history play, they remain strictly on the sidelines in a historical novel, making at most brief appearances (Lindenberger, *Historical* 37–39, 127–28)— like Queen Elizabeth in *Kenilworth* or the Russian empress in *The Captain's Daughter*. Yet the history of historical drama in the nineteenth century reveals a persistent battle between high and low language, between high and low personages, for dominance of the form. Within specific national traditions certain works— for example, *Danton's Death* in Germany, *Boris Godunov* in Russian, *Master Olof* in Sweden— count as landmarks in which lowly people and/or lowly language successfuly invaded a form hitherto confined to higher matters. In his opera *Khovanshchina* Musorgsky presented a political struggle in which the warring royalty were kept wholly offstage and in which the common people, for whom music supplied a more easily communicable language than the varying archaic dialects in which they must have spoken, occupied the foreground. The conflict between the roles of high and low in historical drama were themselves indicators of power struggles for the control of history— at once in the way history was to be told, who should be telling it and for what purpose, and who should ultimately triumph on the real-life historical stage.

The conflicts depicted between persons of high and low station in nineteenth-century history plays extend to still another issue, this one less specifically political and more psychological, even metaphysical, in its import. I speak here of a conflict between the hero and his or her surrounding world. To the extent that the nineteenth century was obsessed with the genesis, the nature, and the fate of what Hegel called world-historical individuals (39–43), historical drama tended to set these individuals against a social framework that could work to support them, to impede their progress, to goad them on to significant action, often even to martyr them. The heroic figures of these plays are not necessarily world-historical in stature, but they may, like Kleist's Prinz Friedrich, Pushkin's Boris, or Strindberg's Erik XIV, occupy principally a national-historical role. Nor need they be royalty or even military leaders to assume heroic status: a king's minister, a tribune of the common people, even a famous artist or thinker (once the aesthetic and intellectual realms had become idealized as they were in the nineteenth century) can equally fit the bill. What matters is the interaction we see between hero and world and the questions this interaction is expected to raise for us: how is the hero shaped by his surrounding world, and how is this world, in turn, reshaped by the hero's action? How might the hero have turned out differently if he had lived in a different time or had not been forced to play the historical role imposed upon him? How might the world have turned out differently without the intercession of this hero? What are the borders behind the private and public realms? In what ways, for instance, are the hero's private idiosyncrasies a product of his public position, and how do these, in turn, affect the public world?[4] I state these issues as questions since historical dramatists of the nineteenth century generally are sparing in the answers they care to give. It is almost as though they set up this conflict between the individual self and external reality as a means of suggesting some ultimate inscrutability in history. In contrast with earlier centuries, in which the study of the past served to instruct us morally or to provide explanations for present ills, history now comes to display hidden depths that resist ultimate explanation. Like that emerging discipline that called itself the philosophy of history, nineteenth-century historical drama is notable for the mysteries, even the mystifications it sets up and also for the grandeur of scope that accompanies the kinds of questions it raises.

My own attempt in this essay to recreate an age that itself first set up an agenda of how one might recreate a past age could be seen as a product of that very model of thought I am trying to rethink. Certainly it was the nineteenth century that created the possibility of a period concept and that thus enables us today to isolate the biases and styles of argument peculiar to the nineteenth century as a period. And to the extent that the century's period thinking became institutionalized, it also became part of the common lore that large numbers of people could take for granted down to our own day. In the course of the century what were once taken to be individual schools of poets or painters became linked to larger period concepts that froze them within particular moments in the development of Western culture. Thus, the English Lake Poets eventually became part of that larger cultural complex we call romanticism, while the painters who decorated the Vatican during the papacy of Julius II came to define what we now call the High Renaissance. Periods achieved the status of cultures that grew organically—to use a typical nineteenth-century metaphor—out of the ruins of earlier periods and themselves ultimately died to make way for periods needing to be born. Describing a particular period became an interdisciplinary exercise, as we note from that great model for periodizing, Jakob Burckhardt's *Civilization of the Renaissance in Italy*, which includes sections not only on art and literature, but on "the state as a work of art" (39–120), on Renaissance festivals, on morality and religion.

When individual phenomena that we deem important do not easily fit the available period models, we have customarily generated new categories—for example, Mannerism to fit the art that separates High Renaissance from early Baroque or, if we are unable or unwilling to characterize a time-span with sufficient individualizing detail, we simply invent something we call an age of transition to fill in the space separating the death of one period and the birth of another. A whole series of prefixes and descriptive adjectives is ready at hand to chart the growth and decline of periods. Most any period, in fact, can be expected to move from "pre-" through "early" to "high" and thence downward to "late" or "decadent" and ultimately toward a stage designated as "post-" — at which point we look for signs of some emerging new period.

The educational and cultural institutions that developed during the nineteenth century enabled that period's period-thinking to be enshrined for later periods such as ours. The distinction I cited earlier between national and world history was itself institutionalized within school systems throughout the civilized world, with students ordinarily taking separate courses in each of the two areas. Though originally tied to the study of the history of individual languages, each nation's literary history, in turn, became a subject of serious inquiry and, above all, a means for instilling national identity and pride in a citizenry that was trained to locate examples of greatness in past writings in its native tongue.

It seems no accident, moreover, that the public art museum was a creation of the nineteenth century. Once the museum came to organize its holdings according to historical principles, it could offer its visitors a means of experiencing the whole of civilized (and eventually even of "uncivilized") history from the Greeks to whichever school it chose to count as modern; within a brief afternoon's visit one could move from room to room to witness, by means of immediate visual impressions, the unfolding of the various periods of art as they had only recently been defined. As diverse art forms became the objects of study in schools and universities, the historical focus became primary; the study of literature was defined as the study of literary history, of art as art history, of music (a relative latecomer to academic investigation) as music history. The framework within which one viewed and analyzed and judged an artifact was determined by the period concepts one had learned by means of poetry anthologies and museum- and concert-going; thus, one came to see a painting first of all as assuming the formal properties and subject matter of a *Renaissance* painting, or to read a lyric as an exemplar of the diction, rhyme scheme, and intellectual content of a *medieval* poem.

As the study of history itself became institutionalized, it developed its own means of implanting memorable images of the past into the minds of the newly literate masses. Images that had first been conceived as ideal types to typify the life of an age—the stoic Roman, the feudal baron, the Renaissance prince, the enlightened despot—became easily recognizable stereotypes as they made their way through the educational system and the cultural media. The new historical consciousness upon which the nineteenth century prided itself became a way of distinguishing its own world view from those earlier world views it had discovered—the very term "world view" or *Weltanschauung* being of course a product of this consciousness. An earlier period such as the Middle Ages or the Enlightenment could be criticized for its lack of historical consciousness, while occasional authors could be singled out for the prescience they showed in anticipating it. Despite his notorious anachronisms, Shakespeare allegedly proved himself a modern historian before his time by means of his empathy for ancient Rome or his ability to sense the difference between the medieval and Renaissance worlds in the contrast he offered between the courts of Richard II and Henry IV.[5] Similarly, anthropologists have sometimes sought evidence of historical consciousness in cultures that lacked significant contact with the European sources of this consciousness.[6]

Despite the tenacity with which nineteenth-century notions of history have persisted in our culture, a succession of thinkers in our own time has laid a groundwork—often with memorable tag-words—to question these notions. The most influential historical dramatist of our century, Bertolt Brecht, invented his vaunted alienation effect (191–95) as a means of preventing his audiences from indulging in the illusion that they were witnessing some authentically rendered real-life past. If the serious historical dramatists who followed Brecht felt themselves inhibited forever from evoking the world of the past, within the arena of mass culture the cinema—from the silent epics of Cecil B. De Mille down to the historical extravaganzas issued with regularity in the world's movie houses—has sought to guarantee audiences the illusion of an authentic historical experience.

If one sets up a list of those who have made us rethink the way we apprehend history during the last generation, one would cite, among several others, H. G. Gadamer, whose theory of historical understanding questions the possibility of objectively knowing the past; Gadamer's phrase "fusion of horizons" (273–74, 337, 358) suggests the interplay of two horizons—those of the past and of the present-day observer—that remain linked to one another in an epistemologically inextricable way. Foucault's image of what he called "epistemes" (xxii–xxiv, 344–87)—a new period concept that stresses the discontinuities between ages—works to undermine the nineteenth-century faith in historical continuity, even if that century's sense of continuity was achieved in the face of sharp contradictions that resolved themselves in an ongoing dialectical drama. Hayden White has created a fruitful historical distance between us and the great nineteenth-century historians and philosophers of history, whom he presents as masters of, though also men who were mastered by, the techniques and structural forms of literary discourse—with the obvious implication, almost a cliché these days, that history may well be little more than a fiction. Behind all these figures there hovers, of course, the powerfully skeptical critique of nineteenth-century historical thought in the work of Nietzsche (1:209–85), whose own life had ended precisely with the end of the century. Our current selfconsciousness about historical consciousness is perhaps best encapsulated for us by the distinction we now make between two distinct meanings of the word "history"—history as that which happened in the past and history as the narratives we ourselves create to grasp the past.

Yet the terminology we employ is still very much rooted in the historical thinking of the last century. Not only do we continue to use the period terms "classical," "medieval," "Renaissance," but a consensus has recently developed that the most serious art being practiced today can best be described by the word "postmodern." Thus, the rapid succession of visual styles from pop and op through minimalism and neo-expressionism have been lumped together as various manifestations of postmodernism, as have a number of poetic and musical styles such as the verse of the so-called "language" poets, the musical minimalism of a Philip Glass or Steve Reich, and the inter-media iconoclasm of John Cage. The postmodern buildings we visit and sometimes even inhabit these days allow us to experience a multitude of easily recognizable earlier architectural styles when, with a selfconscious ease that pokes fun at the very idea of historical periodization, they mix, say, an Egyptian column, Renaissance arches, and Gothic statuary under a Spanish-mission-style tile roof.

The word "postmodern" may well be emblematic of a shift in our relation to history: in view of the categories that emerged in nineteenth-century historical thought, it is only natural that the history of the arts— not to speak of culture as a whole— should culminate in modernism, which we now recognize as the dominant style of the first half of the present century and whose very name suggests that it stands at the end of the line among the historical periods projected by the nineteenth century. By that account, postmodernism must surely be an afterthought, a product following the end of time, the end of history— at least of time and history as they were once constituted.

To the extent that we have distanced ourselves from these categories created by that most historical-minded of times, the nineteenth century, perhaps we can learn to do history in inventive new ways without, for instance, the burden of those particular period designations that were themselves inventions of that time and without, as well, the need to embed our historical perceptions within the various binary pairs I have sketched out in the course of this essay. To advertise our distance from that earlier mode of thought, we might even consider labeling this newer way of doing history posthistoricist[7]— not, certainly, to suggest that we have passed the end of time, but to insist that time can return to the foreground of our thought without being vulnerable to the traps lurking within that older, historicist conception of history I have sketched out here. The essays that follow attempt a possible "post-historicist" approach by focusing on a variety of relationships between literature and history. The first two essays, for example, argue that the values we assign at any moment to particular works and styles, indeed to what we conceptualize as "literature" itself, are themselves historically contingent phenomena. The next three attempt to stretch our customary notions of genre—in the first, to show how a particular mode of theorizing displays some persistent generic attributes as it moves through history and, in the next two, how particular genres interact and differentiate themselves in diverse historical situations. The final group of essays focuses on an idea that in fact hovers over the whole volume— namely, that the ways we judge and experience literature, as well as the ways we organize, articulate, and disseminate our judgment and experience, result from institutional mediations that seek to obliterate their own traces. If I may return to the titles I toyed with at the start of this essay, a posthistoricist approach would stress not so much the "experience" of the past, whether of history or literature, but rather the processes by which we "construct" whatever pasts we deem serviceable.

I

VALUE
IN HISTORY

ONE

⌒∿⌒

Romantic Poetry and the Institutionalizing of Value

S ome sixty years ago, in an essay teasingly named "Wordsworth in the Tropics," Aldous Huxley challenged the long-accepted commonplace of Wordsworth's universality by speculating on how well the poet's notion of a unifying and generally benign nature would stand up under tropical heat. "A few weeks in Malaya or Borneo would have undeceived him," Huxley writes. "Wandering in the hothouse darkness of the jungle, Wordsworth would not have felt so serenely certain of those 'Presences of Nature,' those 'Souls of Lonely Places,' which he was in the habit of worshipping on the shores of Windermere and Rydal" (672–73). However antiquated Huxley's image of a nature-loving Wordsworth may seem to us today, his complaint about the poet's insensitivity to modes of being outside his native domain strikes a special chord in our own time, in which the experience of diversity—whether in culture or

23

in nature—has come to replace the experience of unity that we earlier sought in our reading.

Though a stint in the tropics might well have given Wordsworth a less ethnocentric view of the natural world than we find in his poetry, his attribution of universality to the nature he knew by no means deterred the reading and teaching of his poetry throughout the anglophone world, even in those locales whose natural vegetation Huxley dubbed "terrifying" and "sinister" (673). Indeed, Wordsworth and his fellow luminaries within the British literary canon remained standard fixtures in the educational systems of former colonial domains long after the dismemberment of the British empire and are still read today— one assumes with appreciation— by English speakers of the most diverse colors and geographical backgrounds.

By the same token, educated readers outside the anglophone world often experience considerable difficulty accepting Wordsworth's greatness even when the landscape and climate in which they are rooted are similar to his own. A distinguished German literary scholar to whom I once showed the Simplon Pass passage from *The Prelude* asked me what the fuss was all about: after all, as he put it despite my strong protests, the poet Haller had done this sort of thing many years before in his descriptive poem *Die Alpen.* Whenever I point out *The Ruined Cottage* or one of *The Prelude*'s so-called spots of time to foreigners unfamiliar with the Anglo-American literary tradition, they tend to show indifference, complain of prosiness, and, to cite a reaction I have heard on several occasions, remark that this "can scarcely be called *romantic* poetry."

What one concludes from comments such as these is that the universality we have long attributed to the art we revere is not quite so universal as we like to think. To the extent that the universality of literature derives from an author's ability to cross national borders, Byron and Scott, as we know, can make far more universal claims than can any of their British contemporaries; indeed, however much we may speak of the untranslatability of great literature, the fact remains that both these authors exercised a decisive effect throughout the Western world in foreign translation—and not necessarily through those writings for which we most respect them today. Doubtless there are many reasons one can give why Byron and Scott could claim the broad readership that Wordsworth never enjoyed—for example, the fact that they offered particular visions of life that their readers on the Continent were prepared to accept at that moment, or, to put it in more material terms, that their intermediaries on the Continent were able to convince these readers to accept. Or one might speculate that the peculiar values Wordsworth had to offer had already been offered by earlier writers on the Continent such as Rousseau and Goethe.

Let me approach the notion of a work's or an author's universality from still another angle: although we ostensibly use the word *universal* as a descriptive term to portray a work's ability to transcend the categories of time and space, we actually intend it as an evaluative term—just as we do words such as *truthful, great, powerful,* and *beautiful*. These terms, just like the various negative terms to which each of them stands in opposition, can be viewed as functioning to achieve certain ends within particular social contexts. Thus, terms such as *universal* and *great* often satisfy the need of readers to feel they are sharing a text with a multitude of other readers past and present, that this text belongs to a network of classical texts stretching back to the beginnings of what we call our culture and that these texts exert a continuing power on those still unwritten texts that later generations will presumably assimilate within this network.

One could, in fact, describe a classic within this culture as a binding mechanism that encourages readers out of their isolation to share, articulate, and propagate certain values that the culture has come to locate within particular authors and works. Goethe provided a compelling image of this binding process in that memorable moment within *Werther* when the ill-fated lovers stand alone at a window watching the end of a thunderstorm and feeling refreshed by the warm rain. Charlotte looks at the sky and at Werther, puts her hand on his, and tearfully pronounces the word *Klopstock* (*Sorrows* 41).[1] At the time Goethe wrote his novel, Klopstock was a cult figure among young people of sensibility—much as, in our own day, certain media personalities function as binding forces among youth. The pronouncement of Klopstock's name (which does not have the comic effect in German that it does in English) serves to encapsulate a whole range of feelings and values that bind the lovers to one another and that also bind the author to his readership, which, large though it may be, comes to form a closed community that presumably can pride itself on its ability to participate in these feelings and values. And just in case Goethe's readership should not be as fully aware as Werther himself was of the meaning latent in the name *Klopstock*, the narrator quickly mentions what

he calls "the magnificent ode" (assumed to be Klopstock's celebrated "Frühlingsfeier") in which meteorological happenings similar to those transpiring outside Charlotte's window had been enacted.

Once *Werther* had turned into the cult book it quickly became
among the young, one can well imagine couples bonding after a
storm with the name *Goethe* rather than *Klopstock* on their lips.
One can also imagine that, in the course of the nineteenth century,
as the English romantic poets became assimilated within their
literary tradition, many travelers uttered the name *Wordsworth* to
one another as they stopped to view deafening mountain streams,
or misty, sheep-filled hillsides, or solitaries wandering over lonely
moors. What passed between them would have amounted to something more than showing off their literacy or their literariness—
though these factors cannot be ignored—but, more important, it
would have defined a particular cultural space, a set of shared
attitudes, a new way of perceiving the world that had come to be
associated irrevocably with the awesome name they pronounced.
So irrevocably, in fact, that we have a difficult time imagining how
it was when this cultural space had not yet been cleared out, when
other, often quite foreign modes of perceiving the world prevailed.

Thus far I have sketched out some of the processes by which we
commit ourselves to and make value judgments about a body of
writing—whether of Wordsworth in particular, of romantic poetry
in general, or, indeed, of any form of what we call literature. My
central assumption is that our commitments and our evaluative
gestures do not come to us from nature (whether in a physical or
more abstract sense), but are mediated to us through the familial,
educational, and social networks within which we function in the
course of our lives. On one level this assumption seems so obvious
that it scarcely needs voicing. Yet the reigning theories of poetry
from the romantics onward have sought to impress us with the
notion that poetic texts somehow manage to speak for themselves,
that they can exercise their power, or magic, or some other type of
authority without the need for mediation. It thus seems especially
appropriate to focus a study of the evaluative process on our changing perceptions of the romantics themselves, for they were so successful in propagating theories to defend their own work that these
theories could claim a generalizing power to account for our experience of and devotion to, all literature and, for that matter, to
everything that we have come to classify as art in general. Whereas
essay 2 focuses on the shifting evaluations of a single romantic

poem, and essay 3 on the persistence of these romantic theories over a considerable stretch of time, the present essay concentrates on the ways that the English romantic poets as a group have been mediated to a succession of reading publics, and, above all, on the changing institutional forms that have been created to perpetuate not only their own writings but also the larger values to which these writings supposedly give voice.

When Barbara Herrnstein Smith, in her recent study of literary evaluation, writes, "We make texts timeless by suppressing their temporality" (50), she refers to a universalizing process that the romantics themselves set into motion. Although readers and critics over the years have worked in collusion with one another and with the poets themselves to suppress the temporality of romantic texts, one might also remember that Wordsworth, despite his alleged "denial of history" (see Liu *Wordsworth* 31, 39), himself sometimes showed a keen awareness of the historical processes by which a mode of writing enters and attempts to transform the world. In one of the less frequently quoted passages from the Preface to *Lyrical Ballads*, Wordsworth stresses the fact that, as he puts it, "metrical language must in different æras of literature have excited very different expectations: for example in the age of Catullus, Terence and Lucretius, and that of Statius or Claudian, and in our own country, in the age of Shakespeare and Beaumont and Fletcher, and that of Donne and Cowley, or Dryden, or Pope" (*Prose* 1:122). Wordsworth's sense of historical change, above all his stress on the reader's changing expectations from era to era, contains the germs of some far more elaborate, and also quite historically minded, theories of stylistic change that have entered critical discussion in recent years. I refer, for example, to E. H. Gombrich's demonstration of how styles of painting evolve over time as well as Jauss's notion of a "horizon of expectations" (*Toward* 3–45) that played so prominent a role in recent German studies of literary reception. If one sets this early statement by Wordsworth next to his pronouncement, in the supplement to the Preface of 1815, that "every author, as far as he is great and at the same time *original*, has had the task of *creating* the taste by which he is to be enjoyed" (*Prose* 3:80), then it is clear that however persuasively he sometimes stressed the ability of language to exert visionary power, he also retained a firm sense of the reader's need to be prepared, even to a degree manipulated, into a frame of mind that would allow him to receive and above all acknowledge this power.

Our usual way of tracing the history of Wordsworth's and his

contemporaries' reception is to stress a succession of phases starting with their initial failure to achieve their proper recognition, a
failure that resulted from the application of early critical criteria
inappropriate to their particular mode of writing—in short, what
we might call the "this-will-never-do" phase or the "Keats-and-
the-reviewers" tragedy. From here on we move to their eventual
triumph—not simply their acceptance within the literary canon,
but, even more fundamentally, the institutionalization of certain of
their guiding ideas within anglophone culture as a whole. If, by the
end of the nineteenth century, romanticism, together with its various aestheticist and pastoralist offshoots, had penetrated, indeed
had helped shape the cultural mainstream, by the early part of the
present century it entered a distinctly negative phase characterized
by a radical re-evaluation not only of what had come to seem its
canonical texts, but of the values for which it had stood. A final
phase that would give the narrative a happy ending is the rehabili-
tation of romanticism—at least within the walls of the university—during the last generation by means of an uneasy alliance of
historical reconstruction, thick verbal interpretation, and ahistorical deconstruction. Within this final phase even the negative thrust
of the early modernist attack on romanticism becomes neutralized
through the common assertion that modernism represents a continuation—though in disguised form—of many central romantic
tenets and forms.

As a narrative about the shifting fortunes of romanticism in
literary history, this account is probably not too far off the mark.
Yet it is only one type of story, one that, with its dramatic ups and
downs, its defeats and reconciliations, sometimes seems to em-
brace the form of literary romance. Let me propose another story,
though this one, if it takes the form of a story at all, would more
likely be termed a modernist narrative than the more linear one I
outlined above. I propose to examine some of the ways that the
evaluative procedures we use are embedded within larger institutional structures and situations. Thus, throughout more than a
century after that body of writing we call romantic came into
being, the evaluation and consumption of serious literature (the
distinction between serious and non-serious being of course a romantic one) took place within a large and essentially public realm
distinctly different in character from the academic realm that has
dominated literary dissemination for most of the present century.
For purposes of analysis I shall treat these two realms separately;

each of them, I shall suggest, functions in so distinct a way that the evaluative process itself assumes different forms within public and academic criticism.

The gap that separates our own academically mediated literary opinions from those generated during earlier times is especially evident whenever we look at the pronouncements of Matthew Arnold. Consider, for example, these words that Arnold uttered in 1883 on accepting the presidency of the Wordsworth Society:

> We live in a world which sometimes, in our morose moments, if we have any, may almost seem to us, perhaps, to have set itself to be as little poor as possible, and as little chaste as possible, and as little obedient as possible. Whoever is oppressed with thoughts of this kind, let him seek refuge in the Wordsworth Society. ("President's" 5)

This is an extreme statement, to be sure. Like the lovers in "Dover Beach," Arnold seeks refuge from a hostile, all-too-threatening world—not, as in the poem, through the consolations of private relationships, but through what, many years before, Arnold had labeled the "healing power" offered by Wordsworth's poetry (*Poetry* 161–62, 109). We may also remember that in another context Arnold chose that line from Wordsworth's Prospectus, "Of joy in widest commonalty spread," to evoke the bond that ties the poet at once to his divine source and to the readers whom he in turn binds together as he brings them in touch with this source (*CPW* 9:51). In his role as public critic Arnold in effect continues Wordsworth's own mediating function. Whether we choose to call Arnold's approach moral or religious, the role he assumes belongs to a world wholly foreign to our own, for, like a succession of English critics extending back to earlier centuries, he carries the publicly acknowledged authority that belongs to a spokesman for a large community. It is characteristic of critics within this tradition that sentiments of this sort can be uttered both within verse and critical prose. The lines I quote come at the end of an extended comparison that Arnold makes between entrance into the Wordsworth Society and entrance into a monastery; one could argue, moreover, that the extremity of the image he has chosen also reveals the extremity of stance he assumes as critic.

Yet the extremity of Arnold's stance also helps to foreground some of the central characteristics of public-style criticism. For one thing, evaluation remains an overt and overriding concern of any public critic. As spokesman for the community he must constantly instruct his readers on the best and the worst that are thought in his time; indeed, he sees his task as one that trains the reader as much as possible to make these distinctions within the framework that he himself has established. Moreover, for the public critic the writer under consideration functions not simply as a fabricator of literary works, but as a cultural force—someone who embodies a particular set of qualities and values distinct from those attached to any other author's name. Thus, if Arnold celebrates Wordsworth for his healing power, he casts Byron as a demonic force that defied a newly emerging middle-class philistinism (*CPW* 9:231–33); Keats, though consummately gifted, is cast as one who died before his talents had sufficiently ripened (*CPW* 9:214–15); and, in memorable phrases that challenged generations of academic laborers to disprove them and that, in fact, have never fully worn off, Arnold casts Shelley as the "beautiful and ineffectual angel" and Coleridge as "poet and philosopher wrecked in a mist of opium" (*CPW* 9:237).

However just or unjust these labels, it is significant that, for Arnold and other public critics of the nineteenth and early twentieth centuries, each of the romantics has his own carefully crafted role to play. Some critics may assign a poet a more positive role than Arnold does—as Pater, for example, does for Coleridge (143–70). What remains fundamental is that the great names composing the romantic pantheon are like literary characters—each as distinct from the others as the dramatis personae of a humour play, yet varied and complementary enough to add up to a cohesive plot. As one examines the particular role a poet plays, one notes that these roles range from the most salutary (a part usually assigned to Wordsworth) through the partially salutary down to the distinctly unsalutary—with the last-named role variously assigned to Byron or to Shelley. It is significant not only that poets were judged for their moral efficacy, but that the potentially dangerous poets were as necessary to the pantheon as those whose health-giving powers were obvious on the surface. Even when one was asked to close one's Byron, the act of confronting and then rejecting a dangerous force was a necessary part of the educational process. It is also significant that what had early emerged as a five-poet romantic pantheon has remained pretty much in place to this day—except for the addition of Blake, whom the Victorians had relegated to the minor part of pre-Raphaelite precursor.

Among the remarkable features of the romantic pantheon is the fact that up to our own day it has consisted wholly of poets—and male ones to boot. If the Augustan pantheon was able to contain a bitter, sometimes scatological prose satirist, its romantic successor excluded the novelists and essayists who were Wordsworth's and Shelley's contemporaries. Even the acceptance of Byron's satiric side came relatively late. One can doubtless ascribe many good reasons for the hegemony of poets within the pantheon, for example the fact that romantic theory elevated poetry above other forms (even when, as for Shelley, the best Roman poetry was to be found in Roman institutions [494]); or one can cite the fact that no prose writer of the time could assume the role of a cultural force as appropriately as Wordsworth or Byron—even if some, like Hazlitt and De Quincey, created a highly charged prose in the process of defining Wordsworth's and his contemporaries' peculiar force. Though attempts are made now and then to place Jane Austen within the romantic pantheon, the obvious difficulties of assimilating her style and her ideas to the reigning definitions of romanticism generally result in quibbling over how far these definitions can be stretched to accommodate her.

But the special status poetry enjoyed within the public critical sphere may also have had something to do with the need to keep a clear distinction going between the higher and lower forms of literature. Wordsworth himself keeps us aware of this distinction when, in the Preface of 1800, he complains that Shakespeare and Milton, as he puts it, "are driven into neglect by frantic novels, sickly and stupid German Tragedies, and deluges of idle and extravagant stories in verse" (*Prose* 1:128). However much Wordsworth may have drawn his diction and his themes from the lower ranges of literature, he was himself aiming for a lofty and higher art whose identity derived from the distance it could establish from those trivial, essentially non-serious genres he disparaged so vehemently in this passage. It is significant that one of these genres— the "idle and extravagant stories in verse"—displays the same external form as the higher type of poetry.

But in the nineteenth century poetry had itself become an evaluative term, one that became increasingly used to label the higher ranges, sometimes even those that were written in prose. Indeed, one can speak of a two-fold mode of evaluation—the first of which is concerned with the individual poem, the second with the status of the individual poet, whose work now becomes judged for whether it belongs to the more trivial forms or to that higher realm characterized by terms such as *poetic, visionary,* and *imagination.* As one reads through those public critics whose office it was to guard this higher realm, one notes that the individual poem is less important in itself than as a sign that its author can lay claim to that select company who assume the title *poet,* which no longer referred simply to a craft but had now become an honorific term. It is significant, for example, that the publication of *The Prelude* half-way through the century did little, one way or another, for Wordsworth's status within the English romantic pantheon.[2] Those who had embraced *The Excursion* as his sacred book maintained their adherence to that poem. Others, like Arnold, who located Wordsworth's greatness in the shorter poems of the great decade (*CPW* 9:42) could argue his status without recourse to his longer works— a critical tactic, I might add, that would have been unthinkable in earlier centuries, whose poetics assumed that a writer's claim to be a major poet depended on the completion of a successful long poem.

The aura that has customarily surrounded romantic poetry has often obscured from view the actual historical processes by which this aura has come to glorify particular poets. Although the scholarship on romanticism has not neglected the reception of the major poets, reception studies of the period generally belong to that older scholarly mode we call positivist. From this body of scholarship we can learn what the reviewers said about the poets or what later poets and public critics said about the impact that a particular poet or work exercised upon them. Today we are likely to analyze such statements in ways that the older scholarship never conceived—as well as to seek out other types of statement that it would doubtless not have found relevant.

How, for example, did the romantic view of poetry come to crowd out other views in the consciousness of readers? What precisely was the training process by which readers came to change those older expectations that Wordsworth, in the Preface of 1800, saw as barriers to the proper reception of his poetry? In the early decades after the publication of *Lyrical Ballads,* what mediating forces had enabled such novel claims for Wordsworth as that of Keats, who declared Wordsworth "deeper than Milton" (1:281), or that of John Stuart Mill, who ascribed a therapeutic power to his poems (*Autobiography* 88–90)? How was romantic poetry, in the course of the century, made to serve changing cultural needs? How did the aura exercised by

romanticism come to color and change the image of the literary and cultural past that had existed in preceding centuries?

To be more concrete, what communicative mechanisms made
all this possible? Much as we sometimes like to think that poetic
texts can communicate their magic on their own, what specific
actions and events enabled readers to believe that texts speak out
in this way? What precisely were the networks within which writers, publishers, and reviewers created a positive attitude toward
these particular texts as well as a negative attitude toward those
texts they sought to exclude or relegate to a lower place in the
canon? What roles, for instance, were played by certain influential
publishing houses and journals? Did the political motivations that
originally stood behind certain romantic works become distorted
in the process of transmission? What was the role of anthologies in
dispensing romantic literature to a large public? At what point did
romantic writing and its underlying values become institutionalized within the British and American school systems? To what
degree was the dispensing process accomplished by derivative
poets—in America, for example, by Bryant and Longfellow, both
of whom were easier to grasp and more comfortably local than
their English forebears?

Questions such as these are only now starting to be addressed by
scholarship.[3] In this essay and in the two that follow I attempt to
lay out the groundwork by means of which some of them may be
answered, while in the final section of this book I point out how
certain attitudes associated with romanticism have remained institutionalized within the university even in our own day. The distinction I make in the present essay between public and academic
criticism seeks to show how the evaluative process takes disparate
forms within different institutional and historical situations. Thus
the revolt of early modernist poets against romanticism was not
simply the revolt against romantic diction and romantic ideas that
their manifestos claimed it to be, but it was also a sign of a larger
cultural change that had taken place in the course of the nineteenth
century. By the time that the strong anti-romantic reaction had set
in early during the present century, many notions central to romanticism had already seeped down to those lower strata of culture from which the romantic poets and their greatest Victorian
advocates had carefully distanced themselves. The rebellion that T.
S. Eliot, Ezra Pound, and their fellow poets staged was essentially

an avant-garde reaction against those aspects of romanticism—its language and ideas grown stale through their dissemination within the new mass culture—from which they needed to distance themselves to create their own, more rarefied cultural territory.

Like Wordsworth and Coleridge before them, the early modernists sought to persuade readers to reconsider the expectations with which they customarily approached poetry, and to put their ideas into effect, these modernists still attempted to work within that mode of communication I have called public criticism. Yet the arena within which they exercised the role of public critic no longer included that wider public for which their nineteenth-century predecessors wrote. Instead of writing for broadly circulating monthlies or quarterlies, they were often forced to make their bold, iconoclastic pronouncements in what became known as little magazines. Much as Eliot was able to renew the critical rhetoric of Matthew Arnold, his audience at the time of his major statements must have constituted only a small fraction of those for whom Arnold spoke. In his later days, when his pronouncements had become canonical, sometimes in fact pompous, the audience most eager to hear what he had to say consisted of professors and graduate students of English. However problematic the role of public critic had become in the early modernist era, Eliot and his immediate followers, like the great public critics before them, engaged in the dramatic evaluative gestures that managed to knock down sacred reputations and to assign high status to neglected writers with whom they wished to be associated in that special and privileged group they linked together with the word *tradition*.

Despite their disparagement of romanticism, to some degree the early modernists kept intact the relative values that Arnold had assigned to the members of the romantic pantheon. Thus, although Eliot was willing to grant Wordsworth a certain cool respect (*Use* 67–81), he could reject Shelley with disdain (*Selected* 304, *Use* 87–100), as could F. R. Leavis (203–32), though the latter granted Wordsworth a more secure place than he had been assigned during earlier stages of the anti-romantic onslaught (154–202). It is as though the outright rejection to which romanticism was subjected demanded, by way of compensation, that at least some poet, or at least a few poems, be saved, even if grudgingly. Pound, unwilling to make any concessions to romanticism, went outside the pantheon altogether and voiced some kind words for Crabbe and Landor, both of whom he could praise for retaining certain non-romantic virtues (276–79, 286, 344). Yet no critic of stature has practiced as staunchly a negative and persistent anti-romanticism as Yvor Winters, who could dismiss Wordsworth with the usual relish he displayed in upsetting canons: "He is a very bad poet who nevertheless wrote a few good lines" (167).

However negative the attitude of Eliot and his compeers toward romanticism, they insisted, like their predecessors, on treating the romantics as cultural forces. The very fierceness of their attack, even when they pretended to be concerned only with matters of poetic diction, betrays their understanding of the power they knew that the romantics could exercise on those coming under their sway. What the Victorians had seen as salutary had now come to assume distinctly unsavory aspects—for poets who needed retraining in their craft and for readers who required weaning from expectations of verbal magic and visionary uplift.

Since I earlier proposed a sharp distinction between the realms of public and academic criticism, it may seem strange that I include among the public critics names such as Leavis and Winters, both of whom made their characteristic pronouncements while drawing university paychecks and both of whom trained generations of students to transmit their anti-romantic messages within the academic network. Yet both these figures, one at Cambridge, the other most of a hemisphere away at Stanford, represent what seems a belated attempt to maintain the prerogatives and the moral fervor of the public critic at a time that serious critical writing had become economically viable only within a university setting. The gap separating public and academic criticism is evident in the fact that both these men habitually complained in print of the discrimination and general hostility they met in the university world. Although Eliot was able to retain his independence from the academy, one might note that his most sustained confrontation with the romantics, *The Use of Poetry and the Use of Criticism*, took place in the Norton lectures that he delivered at Harvard in 1932–33, while his central critical perspectives later became systematized by his academic followers in the form of the New Criticism.

The New Criticism, however strong its origins in public criticism, was a thoroughly academic enterprise. If the values it borrowed from the early modernists dictated an anti-romantic bias, the heatedness and fervor that had traditionally marked the public arena gave way to method, consistency, and a shying away from

those ideas that might bring about too rapid a change in the way
we enshrine and consume the great works of the past. It remained
for Northrop Frye, in his so-called "Polemical Introduction" to
Anatomy of Criticism, to give the *coup de grâce* to the evaluative
procedures that had characterized Anglo-American criticism for
over two centuries. In that passage of his introduction in which he
enumerates antithetical reasons for promoting and demoting
Shakespeare, Milton, and Shelley, Frye trivializes these procedures
to the point that later students must have wondered how intelli-
gent people could once have fought as vigorously as they once
did over the relative merits of poets. Of Shelley, for instance, he
writes,

> The agenda would run: Demoting Shelley, on the ground that
> he is immature in technique and profundity of thought com-
> pared [to the other two poets]. . . . Promoting Shelley, on the
> ground that his love of freedom speaks to the heart of modern
> man more immediately than poets who accepted outworn
> social or religous values. (23–24)

If the evaluative gestures that Frye exposes so mercilessly sound
like intellectual foolishness, one should note that Frye addresses
his readers from an institutional vantage-point different from that
of the public critics whom he attacks. A bit later in his polemical
introduction he states baldly "that criticism has no business to
react against things, but should show a steady advance toward
undiscriminating catholicity" (25). The word *discriminating*, which
had served as a positive value term to describe the activity of
public critics, has for Frye become distinctly negative, for the act
of discriminating obviously prevents the achievement of that catholicity for which his ideal academic critic should aim.

Despite Frye's attack on evaluation, even the early readers of
Anatomy of Criticism noted the evaluative biases that stood behind
his own critical enterprise—for example, his impatience with the
more mimetic forms of art and his attempt to renew interest in
romance. Moreover, the various positive judgments that are to
comprise the catholicity of taste recommended by Frye were themselves mediated at one time or another by public critics. How, after
all, could a poet be remembered over the centuries without the
work not only of individual critics, but also of the editions, coffee-
house conversations, and allusions in later poets that kept his name

and his work alive long before the study of the modern literatures was institutionalized within the university?

Once this institutionalization had been completed at the end of the nineteenth century, first in Germany, then in America and in various other countries that imitated the German university system,[4] the trend toward "undiscriminating catholicity" that Frye advocated had already set in. In *The Use of Poetry* Eliot spoke against this trend from the standpoint of the public critic when he attacked the academic scholar for, as he put it, "demanding of poetry, not that it shall be well written, but that it shall be 'representative of its age' " (25). The academic bias that Eliot condemned is of course a product of that nineteenth-century theory of history I discussed in the prologue and according to which individual events, personalities and aesthetic artifacts are defined in relation to a general period concept. Although its roots go back to Herder and Hegel, this was still the reigning theory of history at the time that literary study entered the university. Moreover, despite the many changes in critical fashion within our own century, the notion that every age has produced literature representative of itself has persisted, though often quite unthinkingly.

Although Frye would not have called himself a historical critic of the sort that Eliot attacked, his argument for catholicity can be interpreted as an attempt to preserve the integrity of the whole literary tradition without regard to the fashions that come and go. The academic bias guiding Frye's enterprise becomes clear at the end of his introduction when he demands that criticism take the form of what he calls "a body of knowledge" in contrast to that traditional role in which it attempted to render, as he put it, "the direct experience of literature, where every act is unique, and classification has no place" (29). Frye's application of the phrase "body of knowledge" to literary study advertises the fact that all areas of inquiry within the modern university recognize the hegemony of science as a model.

If criticism must accommodate itself to a scientific model, the role of evaluation would have to be considerably different from what it was in public criticism. The academic critic can pretend, for instance, that he is not engaging at all in evaluation—so at least in their quite different ways did Northrop Frye and the older historical type of scholar. Or he can, as I am doing in the present essay, attempt to analyze the process of evaluation as a social and historical phenomenon. Or he can, as in the age of the New Criti-

cism, test some of the evaluative assumptions of the early modernist critics—with the result that the romantic urns turns out to be
better wrought and more paradox-laden than their detractors among
public critics had imagined. Certainly the hyperbolic judgments
and the expressions of moral fervor that traditional public criticism cultivated would seem indecorous in a setting where critics
are expected to call their activities "research" and to package their
work, as best they can, to conform to the packaging of physicists
and political scientists.

Within the academic setting, evaluative statements take relatively safe paths— as, for example, in the confrontation of classic
poems with obviously bad ones in Richards's *Practical Criticism.*
Similarly, value judgments become a means to demonstrate a critical method: during the New Critical era, for instance, a Keats ode
could illustrate organic form, while in more recent times the same
ode could be used to uncover the barely concealed gaps that con-
found the poet's attempt to achieve the organicism he has sought
in the first place. Those academics with a Leavisite turn of mind
could celebrate the humanity implicit in Wordsworth's depictions
of solitaries, or if a Marxist approach seemed timely, one could
expose the class ideology that blinded the poet into believing he
could ever use poetry to make contact with solitaries in the first
place. The sustained intellectual analyses that the university demands both in class presentations and in published writings allows, in fact encourages, the subordination of an individual critic's
evaluative concerns to a larger framework of ideas that can pass
for a body of knowledge. It was only by means of such sustained
analyses, for example, that the peculiar distinction of Blake's
prophecies became evident—with the result that the five-poet romantic pantheon that reigned in the era of public criticism was
able to absorb a sixth divinity only a generation or two ago.

Despite the fact that it succeeded in canonizing Blake, academic
criticism, to the extent that it mutes down and even inhibits the
evaluative process, has generally worked to stabilize the canon of
authors and texts. It would be hard to imagine an influential academic critic today speaking out, as Leavis did, when, over half a
century ago, he declared that "Milton's dislodgment, in the past
decade, after his two centuries of predominance, was effected with
remarkably little fuss" (42). Even a less flamboyant pronouncement such as Matthew Arnold's refusal to grant Chaucer (for lack
of high seriousness) a place among the truly great (*CPW* 9:177)

would not be taken very seriously within a contemporary academic setting. (Even the frequent accusations of a male poet's sexism one hears today are generally attributed to the poet's culture rather than to his person.) Whatever the merits of these evaluative recommendations, the Miltonists and Chaucerians throughout the anglophone world would feel forced to defend their professional turf. Nor can one imagine a whole period wiped out of the canon, as the young Pound and Eliot would doubtless have wiped out the romantic period if they had been given a free hand with the university curriculum.

Within a bureaucratic mode of organization such as the university too much is materially at stake to enable the displacement of established fields. The unspoken, usually unacknowledged constraints remain too powerful to encourage rapid, radical deviations from the prevailing model. Despite some recent changes, this model is surprisingly similar to what it was when the study of the modern literatures entered the university. At that time these literatures were subdivided into national and temporal segments. The predominant view of history early in the century dictated a division of literature according to national categories, for the nationalist impulses dominant in those days spilled over readily into literary scholarship. Despite its pretensions to scientific objectivity, early literary scholarship sought to trace the development of the national literature as a means of glorifying the nation-state through the recognition of a cultural heritage that could compete with those of ancient Greece and Rome. The separate national categories were further subdivided into temporal blocks, each of which was thought to represent a particular stage in the development of the national consciousness.

However much we have outgrown this view of history, it has shaped both the organization of the various literature departments and the direction of individual careers—and, once established, any establishment is likely to outlive those once-vital ideas that presided at its origins. One may remember Max Weber's analysis of the conservatism typical of bureaucracies:

> Once it is fully established, bureaucracy is among those social structures which are the hardest to destroy. . . . The individual bureaucrat cannot squirm out of the apparatus in which he is harnessed. In contrast to the honorific or avocational 'notable,' the professional bureaucrat is chained to his activ-

ity by his entire material and ideal existence. In the great
majority of cases, he is only a single cog in an ever-moving
mechanism . . . and is forged to the community of all the
functionaries who are integrated into the mechanism. (228)

Within the framework that Weber sets up, the older public critic,
even if his fees as a literary journalist gave him some professional
status, enjoyed the relative independence of Weber's pre-bureau-
cratic notable. By contrast, terms such as *Miltonist, medievalist,*
and *romanticism specialist* function more precisely as bureaucratic
job descriptions than as references to autonomous individuals or to
genuine intellectual categories.

   In recent years, as I shall show in more detail in essays 6 and 7,
university departments of literature have witnessed considerable
agitation about the legitimacy of the literary canons they have
inherited. Might not this agitation, coming as it does from groups
as diverse as feminists, Marxists, ethnical minorities, and those
who question traditional distinctions between high and popular
art, culminate in some radical dislodgment of the major figures out
of which our notion of literary traditon was built? Even if such
recently created job descriptions as *feminist critic, literary theorist,*
and *specialist-in-the-relation-between-literature-and-the-other-arts* come
to supplement the period- and author-based positions in national-
literature departments, one can be sure that the thirty-to-forty-year
contract that constitutes academic tenure is itself a guarantee against
major disruptions within the bureaucratic organization. Even these
new job designations, which one would expect to be characterized
by a method or point of view rather than by a time period, are still
often linked to openings in specific periods—with the result that
the typical feminist critic, for instance, practices her craft on, say,
romantic writers alone.[5]

   As in many areas of life, the mode of production within the
university helps to determine intellectual consciousness. And since
faculty members in fact determine the curriculum, they play the
central role in deciding not only which writings are to be taught,
but also which writings should be printed in the textbooks their
students will use as well as which will be explicated in detail in
scholarly journals as a continuing part of the canonization process.
If shifting student enrollments in recent years have shown a demand for new types of courses to compete with the traditional
period and major-author courses, this demand is itself the result of

certain new intellectual attitudes that faculty members, especially many younger ones, have succeeded in transmitting to students.

Although we have seen some changes, and although more will doubtless occur, one should not underestimate the ability of the modern bureaucratic organization to protect itself against too rapid and too disruptive a change. For one thing, within that system that Weber calls the bureaucratic machine a new challenge is far more likely to *extend* the canon than to allow its present membership to be shrunk. Frye's recommendation that critics cultivate "undiscriminating catholicity" is emblematic of the way the academic machine processes the challenges directed against itself. The feminist challenge has doubtless improved the critical fortunes of Dorothy Wordsworth and Mary Shelley, but there is no evidence thus far that it has decreased interest in their menfolk; indeed, one must remember that until recent years the memory of these women was kept alive largely through their relationship to their more celebrated male kin. A feminist analysis of the roles these women play in these poets' self-portraits— an analysis, for example, of the astronomical parts that Shelley assigned his women in *Epipsychidion*, or of the parts that Dorothy and Mary Wordsworth play in *The Prelude* as instruments in the author's growth—such an analysis does not so much dim the male writer's long-held glory, but rather lends a certain contemporary fascination to his work.

Anne Mellor has recently challenged the traditional romantic pantheon with the complaint that "the critical canonization of only six of the literally hundreds of male and female writers of the early nineteenth century reflects certain assumptions deeply imbedded in our political culture" (8). Similarly, Jerome McGann's claim that specialists in romanticism have read the poets uncritically within a framework that the poets themselves determined (see *Romantic* 1–31) not only suggests some striking new way of approaching their work, but it also opens up the possibility of taking a fresh look at writers who stand wholly outside that canonical framework.

If one examines the *Norton Anthology of English Literature*, that most canonical of indicators as to where the English literary canon stands at any given moment, one notes that between its first edition in 1962 and its latest update in 1986 the pantheon of what Mellor calls "six male poets" stands intact, though it has been carefully supplemented with reasonably generous helpings of Mary Wollstonecraft, Dorothy Wordsworth, and Mary Shelley. The section on romanticism in the first edition had included no writings by women except for two paragraphs from Mrs. Radcliffe's *The Italian* that were inserted, as their heading made clear, to illustrate "the evolution of the Byronic hero" (Abrams et al. 2:611). Although the new edition more or less retains the short selections from the minor poets and prose essayists of the period, it contains nothing that could be labeled "popular" literature, nor, except for its excerpts from *A Vindication of the Rights of Women,* does it include any texts belonging to that category "non-literary" discourse from which the romantics distinguished what they called literature.

Even within the six-poet pantheon itself the evaluative process continues as new versions of canonical poems are published and their relative value debated. Despite the disruptions that feminists and those with other new agendas may threaten, the cards in the traditional pack continue to undergo constant reshuffling. Previously neglected writings such as Wordsworth's later poems and Coleridge's massive prose works (including some that were projected but never written) are being treated to detailed interpretation and thus achieve a reassessment. Even if a poet's relative place within the canon remains fairly stable, the image with which he is presented to readers is subject to continual change. Within the academic bureaucracy one can always count on new critical perspectives, new texts, new interpretations to generate enough subsequent work so that the machine will keep on running. To put it another way, the machine's need for survival ultimately controls its members' interests and concerns. In order to survive, the academic machine, much like the makers of brand-name consumer products, needs to remind its customers that it is constantly doing something new—yet too precipitous an introduction of the new can also wreak havoc with its essential workings.

The machine's need for survival can also hide the fact that the newness it chooses to advertise—whether newness of interpretation, evaluation, critical method or the materials upon which the critic focuses—is not necessarily something that conveys a sense of discovery or that generates the intellectual excitement accompanying the most interesting discoveries. It so happens that significant intellectual action in the study of different literary periods and approaches takes place at varying and often unpredictable times. Those who started working on the English romantics, above all on Wordsworth, during the mid-1950s remember the exhilaration that came from the rediscovery and reassessment of what they saw as a neglected and often maligned body of literature, one that had fallen by default into the custodial care of learned, bureaucratically entrenched antiquarians from whom they sought to wrest it away.[6] For a considerable time romanticism served as the testing ground for such critical modes as the history of ideas, phenomenology, and, most famously, deconstruction. The publication of a collection called *Deconstruction and Criticism* (see Bloom, ed.) in 1979, in which the Yale critics of that time aimed their interpretive guns at a single Shelley poem, celebrates the compatibility of romanticism with the methodological category in the title, yet it also, we can now see with a decade's hindsight, marks the end of the period when romanticism stood at the forefront of literary study in America.[7]

Although the Renaissance became the primary testing ground for the so-called new historicist mode that has dominated the 1980s, serious romantic studies continue unabated, with the work in this mode, as I shall indicate in essay 3 and in the final essay, here taking its own characteristic directions to accommodate itself to the historical events and concerns of this period. In view of the present essay's focus, one may ask how well the romantic pantheon to which we have so long been accustomed will fare in the current critical marketplace. Will the skepticism toward the notion of a poet's universality—so tentatively stated by Huxley, yet so earnest an enterprise today—inhibit the rhetoric that critics and teachers have traditionally exercised to persuade others to bond with them in revering a canonical figure? Will some future edition of the *Norton Anthology* radically cut back its selections from Wordsworth and Coleridge to leave room for texts representing a discourse different from what the romantics taught us to call literature? If my analysis of the workings of academic bureaucracy is correct, one may feel assured that the changes will come slowly enough to allow ample time for accommodation.

TWO

Evaluation as Justification and Performance: The Leech Gatherer as Testing Ground

A little more than half way through the critical history of "Resolution and Independence," A. C. Bradley defined the problems that readers have characteristically encountered with this poem. As Bradley puts it, "Resolution and Independence" is "probably the most Wordsworthian of Wordsworth's poems, and the best test of ability to understand him." The test to which Wordsworth puts his readers for Bradley derives from an uncomfortable mixture of "lines of extraordinary grandeur" and, "mingled with them, lines more pedestrian than could be found in an impressive poem from any other hand." Bradley does not question the success of the poem, of which, as he declares, "there can be no sort of doubt." Yet he marvels at the fact that a successful poem can contain elements that in themselves one would scarcely deem worthy of great poetry, and then, to provide a concrete reminder of how low this poet could sink, he cites what he terms the "helpless reiteration of a question ['How is it you live, and what is it you do?'], which in other poems threatens to become ludicrous, and on which a writer with a keener sense of the ludicrous would hardly have ventured" (136). Bradley's complaints about pedestrian and ludicrous elements in "Resolution and Independence" achieve a special force when we recognize that these elements have continually put Wordsworth's readers to the test, not simply of their ability to understand him, as Bradley phrases it, but also of their willingness, in spite of these flaws, to acknowledge his greatness as well as the success of this particular poem.

The use of "Resolution and Independence" as a test of the poet's, as well as of this poem's, value is central to the history of Wordsworth's reception. Coleridge, in *Biographia Literaria*, quotes large chunks of the poem to illustrate what he saw as one of Wordsworth's characteristic defects, namely, "the INCONSTANCY of the *style*" (2:121)—yet Coleridge also ends his discussion not only by calling "Resolution and Independence" a "fine poem" but labeling it as "*especially* characteristic of its author" (2:126). In fact the poem does not simply illustrate the first of the defects Coleridge cites, but, as Coleridge puts it, "There is scarce a defect or excellence in [Wordsworth's] writings of which it would not present a specimen" (2:126).[1]

In statements such as these, that "Resolution and Independence" achieves greatness in spite of, perhaps even because of, its defects, we recognize that this poem is not merely, as Bradley claims, a test of our ability to understand Wordsworth, but that the fluctuations in the assessment of the poem, together with the ways that certain issues have become obsessive within the poem's interpretive history, can also help us understand some of the processes with which the values of poems in general are made and remade in the course of time. To what precisely are we assigning value when we call a poem "fine" or "great," or, as with "Resolution and Independence," "uneven"? Is it the words and stanzas that make up the entity we are assessing? Or the larger vision of life we associate with the poem, what Bradley refers to when he calls "Resolution and Independence" the most Wordsworthian of poems? Or are we locating value in a certain moral attitude with which we happen to sympathize and that we think we discern in the poem? Or in a certain theory of poetry or of literature as a whole that seems to be embodied, even validated for us, by the poem? And why do certain issues—in the case of "Resolution and Independence," the proper

mix of lofty and commonplace language and subject matter—come
to dominate the interpretation and evaluation of the poem for
much of its critical history?

The evaluation of "Resolution and Independence" does not begin with Coleridge or even with its earliest printed reviews—it was
mentioned far less than many other poems in *Poems, in Two Volumes*, in which it first appeared[2]—but with the poet's own justifications of the choices he made during the process of composition
and revision. Indeed, an issue central to the quotations I cited from
Coleridge and Bradley, namely, the gap separating the poem's commonplace elements from those of a more lofty kind, is evident in
what we know about the early stages of the poem. For example, in
a much-quoted letter to his future sister-in-law, Sara Hutchinson,
Wordsworth shows himself defensive about the Hutchinson sisters'
evident complaint of the tediousness they found in the leech gatherer's extensive speeches within the version of the poem that they
had been sent during the spring of 1802. This version was of course
quite different from the one that Wordsworth published for the
first time five years later and even more different from that final
version that we still encounter today in the standard anthologies.[3]
This early version, as far as one can piece it together from its
partially destroyed manuscript, contains a goodly amount of the
leech gatherer's direct speech—while it does not yet include the
celebrated comparisons of the old man, successively, to a stone,
sea-beast, and cloud. It is significant that Wordsworth does not
here, as in many other places, specifically defend his use of lowly
language; in fact, when he insists that the poem must be read, as
he puts it, "with the feelings of the Author," he acknowledges that
the poem may not work for every reader. The basis for his defense
of the poem, among other grounds, is the plight of the leech gatherer himself, whose situation should itself move the reader. "Such
a figure," Wordsworth exclaims, "in such a place, a pious self-
respecting, miserably infirm, and [   ] Old Man telling such a
tale!" (*Letters* 1:366). And the poet goes on to beg Sara Hutchinson
to read more subtly and carefully if she hopes to experience the old
man's situation in the proper way. If we take Wordsworth's defense
literally, it is clear that he asks his reader to assent to his own
feelings about the old man whether or not she can also assent to
the linguistic means he employed to make his point.

Yet Sara Hutchinson's criticism—and perhaps also whatever
criticism Coleridge made at that point in the poem's composition—

exercised a powerful effect on the extensive revisions to which Wordsworth subsequently subjected "Resolution and Independence." It is as though the poet recognized he had not encoded the poem with the proper instructions for reading it. Thus, in an evident attempt to keep the reader from finding the old man tedious, at least one of his subsequent versions eliminated the leech gatherer's words altogether and instead rendered his speech by means of indirect discourse alone, though the first printed version, five years later, allowed the old man his own voice for three lines near the end of the poem. As one examines Wordsworth's revisions, one recognizes that the poet was constantly tinkering with the balance between the commonplace and the more lofty forms of language. For example, one stanza of "Resolution and Independence" detailing the leech gatherer's dress—

He wore a Cloak the same as women wear
As one whose blood did needful comfort lack;
His face look'd pale as if it had grown fair,
And furthermore he had upon his back
Beneath his Cloak a round & bulky Pack,
A load of wool or raiment as might seem
That on his shoulders lay as if it clave to him
                    (Curtis 191, 193)

—these lines, which echo the description of the old man in Dorothy Wordsworth's journal, were eliminated at the galley-proof stage just before the first printing in 1807. Here, as in his subsequent revisions for later editions, Wordsworth was constantly reworking the poem's balance between higher and lower modes of language. As late as 1820, for instance, he pushed this balance in the direction of the lofty by dropping the lines

He answer'd me with pleasure and surprize;
And there was, while he spake, a fire about his eyes

in favor of the now quite familiar

He answer'd, while a flash of mild surprise
Broke from the sable orbs of his yet-vivid eyes.
                    (*Poems* 127)

Yet the poet's reassessments are not embodied simply in his revisions, but also in those comments he left about "Resolution and Independence." For example, his citation, in the Preface of 1815, of the similes of stone/sea-beast/cloud to exemplify the "powers of the Imagination" works both to underline the sublime side of the poem and to give "Resolution and Independence" a privileged place in the history of poetry alongside such other examples of imaginative power as the passages he cites from Virgil, Shakespeare, and Milton (*Prose* 3:31–33). Even the change of title from "The Leech-Gatherer" (as it is called in the early correspondence surrounding the poem) to the more generalizing "Resolution and Independence" can be taken as an evaluative act, as is the fact that Wordsworth temporarily sought to give the poem pride of place in *Poems, in Two Volumes* by adding a title page (later removed) to a section he called " 'Resolution and Independence' and other Poems."[4]

If his use of the stone/sea-beast/cloud similes in the 1815 preface places the poem in a high poetic tradition, his later comment to Isabella Fenwick, in which he points out the real-life origins of the poem—"the account of [the old man] is taken from his own mouth . . . . The image of the hare I then observed on a ridge of the fell" (*Poems* 408)—stresses that more commonplace aspect of the poem which had troubled its readers all along. Only, it would seem, when the poem's loftiness had been rendered indisputable could Wordsworth advertise its matter-of-factness.

What we have seen here is the resolution of two systems of writing, the "lofty," which secures the poem's place in what Wordsworth would have seen as the great poetic tradition, and the "true-to-life" or mimetic, which, despite its ancient roots, at the time it was written insured the poem's originality, its apparent break from tradition. The poem could thus be read as at once supremely traditional and radically innovative. Wordsworth's revisions all in fact can be read in terms of his attempt to resolve this debate and to secure this apparently contradictory compliment for his poem.

Evaluation, as I have suggested, begins early in the process of a poem's composition (or, as Wordsworth might himself have put it, even at the time of conception); continues through the various revisions and comments to which the poet subjects the text; and goes on indefatigably through time in the reassessments of innumerable critics right down to the presentation of the poem in the modern classroom. One could say that even negative or at least partially negative evaluations such as those to which "Resolution and Independence" was often subjected have served to keep the poem alive, indeed to keep it in the canon. My own concentration, in this essay, on the difficulties critics have met in justifying the poem's place in the canon itself serves to reassert the poem's canonical status.

To illustrate a relatively late stage in the evaluative history of "Resolution and Independence," let me recapture the ways I myself first presented the poem to undergraduates some thirty or more years ago. This, we now remember, was the age of the New Criticism, a time during which a college teacher felt it incumbent not only to assert the greatness of the works he was presenting to his students, but also to demonstrate this greatness by proving that all the elements one might isolate within the work contributed to making it a perfect organic whole. But this was also an age that, as we know, denigrated romantic writing, with the result that the teacher not only needed to prove the poem a formal success, but was also forced to justify its importance within the literary canon by demonstrating what we used to call the moral vision embodied in the text.

It seems significant, in retrospect, that my defense of "Resolution and Independence," without much conscious intent on my part, fell back on the terms and arguments central to Coleridge's, Bradley's, and in fact the poet's own remarks on the poem. For example, I presented it as a high-risk enterprise in which Wordsworth, I argued, managed to reconcile seemingly trivial language and subject matter with the most lofty poetic and moral concerns. The poem's great success, I further argued, was commensurate with the risks to which the poet had subjected it. Sometimes, certainly, the loftiness seemed a bit too much, as in the impossibly Miltonic language of the line about the "sable orbs of his yet-vivid eyes."[5] I confess that I had paid no attention to what was known of the poem's textual history even at that time, and I simply justified this late addition as an expression of the poem's need, at this point, to balance the commonplace with the highest conceivable style. Even the skimpy critical apparatus in the then-standard De Selincourt edition would, had I consulted it, have relieved me of this need to defend the "sable orbs" by allowing me to substitute the far lower-style line "And there was, while he spake, a fire about his eyes" (*Poetical* 2:238).

But defending this prickly poem also imposed an argumentative burden on someone who, in those days, could score considerably easier teaching triumphs by means of ironic Metaphysical poems or disjunctive modernist ones. I remember making a big point of the fact that Wordsworth waited until near the end of the poem before allowing the leech gatherer to speak directly—by which time, I claimed, he had thoroughly prepared us for this speech, which he carefully kept to a mere three lines. Had I been using the poem's preceding version, in which the old man does not speak directly to the reader at all, I would have argued that the poet, as though afraid of the consequences inherent in his earlier doctrine recommending "a selection of the real language of men" (*Prose* 1:118), carefully employs indirect discourse for his central character throughout the poem without risking the absurdity of having him utter his own banal words. Doubtless I could, and would, have found a way of justifying most anything that Wordsworth had done with the poem. (It does not seem accidental that Lewis Carroll found the perfect means of parodying "Resolution and Independence" by letting *his* old man talk a blue streak [187–90]; in fact I used to juxtapose Carroll's parody with Wordsworth's text to illustrate my point—at the risk of course of having students insist that Carroll had destroyed "Resolution and Independence" once and for all.)

And what if Wordsworth had retained the stanza he discarded in galley proofs— that long physical description about his pale face, his "round & bulky Pack" and his "load of wool or raiment as might seem"? If the final text had retained these lines, I should surely have found a way of accommodating them to my argument: after endowing the old man with near-mythical status in the stone/sea-beast/cloud similes, Wordsworth, I should have argued, felt the need to bring him down to earth in the most commonplace possible way. Or I might have argued that Wordsworth chose a Spenserian mode of description in this stanza in order to give a literary aura to seemingly "unliterary" matter.[6] There is no end to the interpretive inventiveness of which I felt capable when pushed to the wall to defend a poem I loved; indeed, my own evaluation of the poem turned out to be just as independent of what the text was saying as Wordsworth's evaluation of the old man was independent of the latter's narrative.[7]

With a generation's time-span and a long succession of critical paradigms separating me from the person who once sought to justify this poem in the manner I have described, I have come to inquire into how, precisely, we gain the love we feel for particular literary works. It may well be that somewhere during my graduate school days I experienced a particularly powerful effect reading

"Resolution and Independence," an effect that resulted in a strong commitment to the poem that I feel to this very day. It would be convenient if I could record some originary moment in which a commitment of this sort, a conversion experience, as it were, had occurred for me. What, say, if I could tell of meeting some impoverished person, feeling a flood of compassion awaken, and then remembering how a recent reading of the poem had made this compassion possible? Or what if I could simply remember a classroom presentation of the poem that had worked on me rhetorically much as I later sought to work on my own students?

I am unable, however, to reconstruct a moment like this; far more likely, the process bonding me to this poem was cumulative—resulting from the mediation, over a period of years, of rhetorically strong critical voices from Coleridge to Arnold and Bradley down to F.R. Leavis and Lionel Trilling, all of whom, whether they spoke specifically of "Resolution and Independence" or simply of Wordsworth in general, made my response to and justification of the poem a foregone conclusion. Indeed, as I have come to realize retrospectively, it is a poem's critical history and not what was long referred to as "the poem itself," that articulates the poem's value over time. Our respect for the authority of the poem's interpretors serves to define and guarantee our respect for poet and poem.

Yet one must not underestimate the staying power of the bonds one forms with poems, whatever the source of these bonds may be. These bonds have much in common with those one forms with people: they tend to persist for much of one's life even though the intensity with which they are held may vary greatly from one period to another. At times, as with one's ordinary human bonds, they may seem relatively inactive, as though they were merely taken for granted; at other times, however, they may reassert themselves, even to the point of passion. The staying power of these bonds may well help explain the fact that particular poets and poems maintain their status within the official literary canon despite the quite normal changes in taste and critical fashion that take place over time. Indeed, if we wish to reassert the greatness of a poem, we need simply work out a reinterpretion that will fit some reigning critical framework, as I myself did when I sought to accommodate "Resolution and Independence" to the New Criticism.

One may ask why this text, among the many others that have achieved canonical status within the Wordsworth oeuvre, should so often have been singled out as a special testing ground, whether to test the reader's ability to understand Wordsworth, as Bradley and, for that matter, the poet himself put it, or, as the present essay is attempting to do, to examine the process by which we assign values to poetry. Undoubtedly what I have called the high-risk element in this poem invites us to examine our responses to the poem as well as the grounds for these responses. Yet "Resolution and Independence" also seems especially appropriate to discussions of value in general, for this poem is itself overtly concerned with the making of values— for example, with the poet's recognition of high value emanating from the most improbable possible source, an impoverished and simple man, a recognition that manifests itself in the very style of the poem by means of the gap between its sublime and its commonplace language. And we note this concern with values in the process by which the poet tests his own earlier values and, by the end of the poem, rethinks his system of values as a result of the values he claims to find in the leech gatherer. Not only has the poet resolved not to be the victim of his previously fluctuating moods, but he has done so by transferring the work ethic that he has observed in the leech gatherer to the work of poetry: if this man at the lowest level of the economic ladder could perform his work with dignity and even with an air of stability, so too could the poet, who would now presumably convert his self-image from that of an unstable child of nature to that of a working professional.

If teaching this poem, and even at one point writing about it,[8] once worked for me as a way of asserting my own commitment to it, so of course the writing of the poem, and presumably also Wordsworth's own earlier contemplations about what his encounter with the leech gatherer meant to him, also took the form of a commitment to a new way of thinking. But "Resolution and Independence" has also played a special role in asserting Wordsworth's value as a poet: to the extent that his value has traditionally been compromised by accusations that he possessed "two voices," the sublime and the commonplace, which he failed to reconcile, this poem, sporting, as it does, both these voices, can be placed on display by any interpreter who cares to demonstrate that he sometimes *did* manage to reconcile them.[9] Since the conflict between the two voices has been built into the poem's, indeed Wordsworth's, critical history since a relatively early stage, most any value judgment one cares to make, whether positive or negative, is likely to assess the poet's success in resolving this issue.

Moreover, the rhetorical effect that the leech gatherer, however limited his verbal resources, exercised on Wordsworth has much in common with the effect that the poem has characteristically exercised on its readers. To put it another way, let us use the analogy of a performance: the leech gatherer, like Wordsworth's other solitaries, has performed for the poet in much the way that the latter uses his confrontation with the old man to perform for his readers.[10] But the critic or the classroom lecturer who interprets this poem is also staging a performance which, if it works successfully on its audience, not only convinces the latter of the poem's high worth, but also succeeds in propagating, nearly two centuries after Wordsworth's chance encounter with the leech gatherer, the particular values that Wordsworth attributes to him. Yet this is not a simple exchange of values, for the leech gatherer, unbeknownst to himself, has in effect changed the poet's life; similarly, a good critical performance of the poem, based, like all such events, on a continuing tradition of performances before it, can potentially change the lives of its audience—or at least make its members interrupt their everyday routine to reconsider what precisely their values are.

In other words, like a play or an opera, forms whose repeated performance we recognize as necessary to perpetuate them, a poem demands repeated critical performances over time to insure its own continuing life. When we attend a stage performance of some long-famous work, we are ordinarily much more consciously aware of the performer's role in mediating the text than we are with texts written for the study alone: we know that we are experiencing Gielgud's or Burton's Hamlet as well as Shakespeare's, and in recent times we have also sought out the work of particular directors in full knowledge that what we see is as much, say, Peter Brook's as it is Shakespeare's. Something of the same thing happens in the performances we experience of poems and novels, whether we simply read these performances silently in the work of some critic or witness them on the classroom podium. In each instance the performers project something of their own selves at the same time that they claim to be returning us to the literary text itself. Even when contemplating the poem in the private study, we as readers are staging a performance of sorts: directed, as it were, by modes of reading that we have seen demonstrated in the classroom or in written interpretations, and by attitudes that we have picked up in the culture as a whole, we perform for ourselves and, in the process, perpetuate a set of values that we think we see embodied in the poetic text.

But are not the values we ascribe to a poem by definition embodied in the poetic text? the reader may well ask at this point. Certainly a dominant strain in western criticism has claimed such value inherent within the texts that we happen to value. And certainly the academic tradition deriving from I. A. Richards' *Practical Criticism*, with its juxtapositions of "good" and "bad" poems whose intrinsic value students were expected to learn to recognize, has done a good bit to perpetuate this notion within formal literary study. Moreover, as my own experience with "Resolution and Independence" has demonstrated, once readers become convinced of the value of a particular text, they are likely to maintain their attachment to the text and, in the course of time, to defend this initial commitment with whatever arguments are likely to be rhetorically effective at a given moment. When, as with "Resolution and Independence," the text has been much discussed over the years, the length and the prestige of its interpretive history come to determine the strength and staying power of this commitment. The poem achieves, as it were, the status of a sacred text whose never wholly fathomable depths invite a succession of interpretations and whose own ultimate value comes to be accepted as axiomatic.

Yet one can also argue that many of Wordsworth's own pronouncements, both in his criticism and in his poetry, easily encourage a view that the values we ascribe to a poem result from a mediating process initiated by the poet and continued by those convinced of its greatness. One remembers, for example, the statement in the Preface to *Lyrical Ballads* about the "formal engagement . . . contracted" (*Prose* 1:122) between author and reader and, in a passage from the Preface of 1815 that I quoted in the preceding essay, his assertion "that every author, as far as he is great and at the same time *original*, has had the task of *creating* the taste by which he is to be enjoyed" (*Prose* 3:80). Although Wordsworth was himself doubtless convinced that the value of his work was inherent in his texts (note his use of the words *great* and *original*), he also recognized that these texts, without an active mediating process, would, like the Lucy of "She dwelt among th' untrodden ways," have languished "unknown" and with "none to praise/And very few to love" (*Poetical* 2:30). The poet's stress on the role of the reader has also encouraged his commentators to stress the affective quality of his work, sometimes, in fact, to adopt a confessional mode and to ascribe its value to the effect it has exercised upon them. Thus, John Stuart Mill, after testifying to the healing power of *Lyrical Ballads*, baldly transferred value from text to affect by stating, "I long continued to value Wordsworth less according to his intrinsic merits, than by the measure of what he had done for me" (*Autobiography* 90). Within that Wordsworthian critical tradition in which Mill has served as an exemplary voice, whatever "intrinsic merits" remain located in the texts themselves become known to us by means of their performative function, whether to disturb, or heal, or simply to enjoy.

I spoke earlier of interpretations as justifications of whatever value one seeks to find in particular literary works. To the extent that the interpretor establishes a performing presence, the values that are claimed for a text are also made to reflect upon this performer, who, if rhetorically successful, can, like the actor or opera singer, impress his or her own values in consonance with those supposedly within the text. But let us guard against viewing these values as simply the personal expressions uttered by whomever one might be reading or hearing; rather, one might see them instead as representing a widely shared way of thinking that prevails and seems defensible, even natural, at a given time. As I look back to my own classroom performances of "Resolution and Independence" thirty years ago, I recognize that, in the process of accounting for and justifying the greatness of this poem, I was also justifying the then-dominant New Critical view of literature—first, its notions of organic form, which I sought to demonstrate by praising Wordsworth's reconciliation of commonplace and sublime elements, and, second, its moral claims, which I was able to present in terms close to those voiced by Wordsworth himself in his letter to Sara Hutchinson.

But of course "Resolution and Independence," like most any poem, can be used to justify a wide range of critical systems. As it turned out, I never wrote up my classroom presentation of the poem, for the New Critical mode scarcely needed public justification by the mid-1950s. A glance through some characteristic interpretations during the intervening decades will show that the poem has done heavy duty in helping define and defend particular ways of viewing literature. When, for example, we come across the following statement from a book of the 1960s, " 'Resolution and Independence' is the most characteristic of Wordsworth's greater lyrics because of this openness of mind which makes it in mode what it is in subject: a self-confrontation," we recognize that Coleridge and Bradley are echoed not to reiterate their own points, but rather to defend a phenomenological approach to literature in which the poem serves to illustrate what the book's dust jacket calls "the drama of consciousness and maturation in the growth of a poet's mind" (Hartman 272). Or if we move forward to the following statement from a relatively recent book, "The Leech Gatherer, like other sublime objects, both produces and represents a powerful discrepancy, specifically a discrepancy between psychological theme and poetic medium," we note how readily the poem can be made to serve the interests of a deconstructive approach (Steven Knapp 120). Doubtless the present essay, to the extent that it explores the process by which a canon is formed, works to exemplify and justify that recent critical practice called the new history.

In the course of this essay I have suggested what may seem a bewildering array of sources within which we locate value when we discuss a poem such as "Resolution and Independence"—in the figure of the old man himself, in the poet's moral development during the course of the poem, in the efficacy that the poem exercises upon the reader's own moral development, in the personality of the critical performer who mediates the poem, in the school of criticism through which and for which the performer speaks. Yet in the mid- and late twentieth century we are just beginning to recognize another entity that valorizes our efforts and is itself being valorized whenever we take up the poem. I refer here to the institution of literary study, to which we owe the editions in which we read a poem such as "Resolution and Independence"; the books and journals that continue to entertain ever new (if also all too often derivative) interpretations of the poem; the physical means by which the poem is regularly disbursed to a large student population throughout the English-speaking world; and, indeed, that whole larger bureaucracy that regulates such matters as the undergraduate major field, the graduate program in literature, and the rigid career schedule prescribed for those who undertake the professing of literature. If one notes the fortunes of "Resolution and Independence" within this institution (which, as we know, did not even come into being until long after the poem's composition), it is clear that poem and institution have worked in collusion with one another to justify one another's value. Thus, the moral value that the poet sees in the leech gatherer's stance of independence and that makes possible his own moral growth has, like the attitudes we have fished out of innumerable other literary works, supplied a rationale for the moral education that justifies the perpetuation of this institution.

And yet it is also within the framework of this very institution, at least within recent years, that we have come to examine the means by which we assign values to literary works, indeed to the institution itself.[11] A segment of the present essay, for example, was read at a routine institutional function, namely, a Modern Language Association session significantly entitled "The Value of Romanticism." Moreover, much of the research produced within the institution of literary study during the last few years, including the present book, has subjected the values traditionally attributed to individual poems and to literature in general to historical analysis. We have become selfconscious as never before about the historical justifications for the canons that we have inherited and whose rationale, we now recognize, has all too easily been taken for granted. Whether we are discussing matters such as which version of *The Prelude* to teach or print (see Jonathan Wordsworth); or the tenability of a long-accepted notion, for example the primacy of the Great Decade in Wordsworth's career (Siskin 8–9, 182–83, 164–78); or the plausibility of Wordsworth's image of Lake District society (Simpson); or the displacement of the economic and political world in "The Ruined Cottage" and the Simplon Pass passage (Liu, *Wordsworth* 311–58, 3–31), a skepticism toward received knowledge has developed within the institution to a degree unprecedented within living memory. To cite an example relevant to the poem discussed in this essay, Gary Harrison has recently argued that the independence that Wordsworth praises in the leech gatherer should in no way be taken as a cultural universal, but rather as the expression of a particular attitude voiced frequently during the 1790s in debates about the Poor Laws; this attitude, according to Harrison, argues the value of independence among the poor within the economic marketplace and thus helps the poet reconcile himself to his own anxieties about economic survival within the new literary marketplace. If inquiries of this sort are typical of our institution today, "Resolution and Independence" may provide the best test not merely, as Bradley claimed, of how to understand Wordsworth, but also of how to understand some of the ways that values have hitherto been located, universalized, and disseminated within that domain we have demarcated as "literature."

II

GENRE
IN HISTORY

THREE

Theories of Romanticism: From a Theory of Genre to the Genre of Theory

Theories of romanticism have never been in short supply. We are all familiar with the many attempts over the years to demarcate what we term romanticism against some antithetical entity, be it called classicism, Enlightenment, Victorianism, or modernism. Similarly, we have encountered quite varying accounts of the origins of romanticism, sometimes within a temporally adjacent system such as the Kantian philosophy or British empiricism, sometimes within a more distant one such as Neoplatonism. Theories of romanticism have not only focused on matters such as demarcations and origins, but they have also claimed (sometimes also disclaimed) unity among whatever personalities and themes they happen to include, and they have been wont to assess the relative status of romanticism within the history of culture, above all within the history of the theorist's own national culture.

My aim in this essay is not to posit still another theory of romanticism, nor to supply a corrective or revision to some preceding
theory. Nor do I question the power or the usefulness of such
theories (though I hope to account for their power and to suggest
some limits to their usefulness). Rather, I propose to ask questions
that have not often enough been asked about these theories. What
roles, for example, have theories of romanticism played in defining
the history of literature and culture? How do they fulfill particular
cultural needs at particular moments? How do they build upon one
another, even when they seem to be contradicting one another? Do
theories of romanticism possess a uniqueness that distinguishes
them from the theories we create for other periods? If my remarks
are working toward a theory of other theories, they are meant
above all to help illuminate some of the ways in which we make
theoretical statements, both about the past and about what we
take to be matters in general.

I shall start by pointing out certain components to be found
within theories of romanticism that date from widely separated
periods and that were composed for quite divergent rhetorical
occasions. As a model I shall use what may well be the first major
theory of romanticism, Schiller's essay of 1795, *On Naive and Sentimental Poetry*. In this essay, one will remember, Schiller distinguishes sharply between the temperaments or states of mind indicated by his title—the first, the naive, depicted as that condition in
which the subject is unselfconsciously at one with nature; the second, the sentimental, in which the subject has become self-reflec-
tive and alienated from nature. Schiller associates each side of his
dichotomy with a wide variety of phenomena. The naive, for example, is linked historically with the world of ancient Greece (102–
4); philosophically, with an unmediated state (83–84, 104, 154);
ontogenetically, with the innocence of childhood (90, 93, 103); in
literary terms, with artistic genius as manifested in Homer, Shakespeare, and his own, slightly older contemporary, Goethe (96–97,
106–10, 112n, 137–38); linguistically, with a situation in which
signifier is linked to signified by inner necessity (98); in terms of
human action, with a self-sufficient personality type whom Schiller
names the "realist" (177–88). The sentimental type defines itself in
predictably opposing ways: historically, by the complex, sophisticated nature of the modern world (99–103, 109–10); philosophically, by alienation and the need for mediation (104, 111); ontogenetically, by entrance into maturity (85, 153); artistically, by belated,

derivative figures such as Virgil, Ariosto, Milton, and, by implication, Schiller himself (105–8); linguistically, by a consciousness of the separation of signifier from signified (98); in human terms, by that striving, psychologically complex type whom Schiller calls the "idealist" (177–88).

Schiller's schema contains many of the essential traits to be found in subsequent theories of romanticism. For one thing, as a theory it leaves the impression of being all-encompassing, of embracing many realms of human endeavor—the philosophical, the linguistic, the historical, among others. Moreover, in the gap that it posits between the two divergent ways of perceiving and reacting to the world, it suggests a state of crisis, a fall from innocence (146–48) quietly echoing that earlier fall which stands behind the whole Judeo-Christian tradition. Although Schiller's essay purports to speak of a universal condition, it also speaks indirectly as a personal testament, a statement by a particular poet who, finding himself in a time of crisis, seeks to renew his own creative powers.

Similarly, the essay is at once, and contradictorily, a universal typology and a historical narrative. From a historical point of view the transition from the naive to the sentimental state is defined by the shift from that synthesis marking ancient Greek culture (at least as Greek culture had become idealized during the later eighteenth century) to the contradictions characteristic of the modern world. Typologically speaking, there is really no transition at all, no historical narrative, for the naive can manifest itself in such figures as distantly separated in time as Homer, Shakespeare, and Goethe, with such sentimental figures as Virgil and Milton falling temporally in between. Moving through Schiller's essay, the reader is never quite certain whether to view the theory in temporal or essentialist terms. As with later theories of romanticism, the uncertainty readers feel about whether or not they are dealing with a historical narrative, or about whether its focus is personal or universal, easily encourages them to interpret the essay as they see fit.

Again, as with other theories of romanticism, we are aware in this essay of an unspoken historical occasion, namely, the French Revolution. In Schiller's other major philosophical essay, the *On the Aesthetic Education of Man*, written a year before, in 1794, one finds brief but unmistakable allusions to the Reign of Terror (*Aesthetic* 24–29), which, as proof of the ultimate political failure of the Revolution, initiates that movement toward a spiritual revolution which this essay seeks to encourage. In the later essay, despite the absence of such allusions, we imagine, even if we do not precisely hear, the recent political events as a subtext motivating the mental drama that transpires in the course of the argument.

This argument is by no means exhausted by Schiller's contrast of the two states of mind indicated in his title. Like other theories of romanticism, Schiller's essay proposes a means of transcending the dilemma in which the modern, sentimental poet finds himself, and it does so by suggesting a new way of viewing the poetic genres. For Schiller, a genre is no longer to be described in formal terms, as it was throughout the centuries in which the classical tradition dominated literary discourse; rather, a genre represents what Schiller calls an *Empfindungsweise*, literally a mode or manner of perception (*Naive* 102, 125n, 145–47n). Thus the poet's relationship to the world defines the genre in which he is working. Since the type of epic we associate with Homer assumes that the poet is unselfconsciously at one with his world (104–5), this genre is closed to the sentimental poet, who by definition perceives himself alienated from his world.

Poetic genres now take shape according to the stance that the poet takes to the fact of alienation. Thus satire (*Naive* 117–25), especially the Juvenalian variety, becomes a way of expressing the poet's wrath about the distance that the actual world diverges from the ideal he carries in his mind. If he seeks to mourn the gap between real and ideal instead of berating it, he turns to elegy (125–45). Yet for Schiller both satire and elegy remain essentially negative stances. To suggest a more positive stance, Schiller proposes the idyll, or pastoral (145–54), which, unlike the elegy—as well as some earlier forms of pastoral—does not simply express nostalgia for the irretrievably lost condition of naiveté; rather, in a famous line, "nicht mehr nach Arkadien zurück ... [but] nach Elysium [no longer back to Arcadia but forward to Elysium]" (153), Schiller encourages the modern poet to move from nostalgia to affirmation, from a passive to an active stance, in short, from what might have been an acknowledgment of defeat to a claim of triumph.

Certainly anyone familiar with romantic literature, at least as this literature has been mediated to us, will note how archetypal Schiller's schema appears. Even when we allow for the local particularities that characterize individual poets, the movement from naive to sentimental and thence to an active pastoral associated with Elysium bears obvious affinities with, say, Blake's tripartite movement from innocence to experience and then to a higher innocence; or to Wordsworth's shift from childhood vision to the loss of this vision and on to the cultivation of the so-called "philosophic mind" (*Poems* 277); or, to cite an influential recent theory of romanticism that vies in persuasive power with the poems it claims to interpret, Schiller's essay bears an obvious analogy to M. H. Abrams' master narrative of the circuitous journey that ties together a multitude of romantic spiritual journeys (*Natural* 143–324).

Schiller's essay is paradigmatic in other ways as well. Note, for example, the ambivalent attitude that the essay expresses toward the relative value of the two opposing states. To what degree, readers feel encouraged to ask, is the loss of the naive stance really a loss? Comparable ambivalences can be found elsewhere within Schiller's essay. Are we, as I asked earlier, reading a historical narrative or an essentialist statement about the human condition? Can we not hold both these seemingly contradictory perspectives in mind at once? Should we read the essay as a personal statement of its author, or as a description applicable to poets of his time, to poets of all times, to modern man as a whole? The various uncertainties, ambiguities, contradictions that one may locate in an essay such as Schiller's, as well as in other theories of romanticism, are by no means signs of theoretical weakness; rather, they help to account for the power with which it achieves its rhetorical effect, and, just as important, for its power to generate variant theories. Indeed, the more uncertainties, ambiguities, contradictions it contains, the more easily a theory invites variants without losing its identity as a framework within which to think; a theory of romanticism may even engender a new theory that, while claiming to confute the earlier theory, in fact succeeds in valorizing and stabilizing the larger romantic framework within which both the earlier and the later theory participate.

Do theories of romanticism, one might ask at this point, necessarily differ from theories that have been postulated about other periods of literature and culture? Surely one could develop a paper on theories of antiquity, of the Middle Ages, of the Renaissance. What distinguishes the interpretation of romanticism from that of earlier periods is simply that the concept we have of what constitutes a period is itself a product of romanticism. Schiller's essay, for example, propagates a view of ancient Greece that would have been incomprehensible in earlier centuries but that, despite the naiveté we now see in its image of Greek naiveté, supplied the basis for what would become a developing dialogue about Greece in later interpreters such as Hegel, Marx, Nietzsche, and, to some degree, even modern classical scholars. Although thoughtful people during what we call the Renaissance recognized the difference between their world and that of the Middle Ages, the intricately worked out picture we have of what the Renaissance was all about—not to speak of the word we use to designate the period—is itself a product of that historicist mode of thinking which has its roots in romanticism.

Romanticism thus occupies a special and privileged position in our understanding of what constitutes a period. Indeed, certain ideas contained within theories of romanticism have colored the interpretation of earlier periods. For example, when we speak of the rise and decline of a period, often, as I pointed out in the Prologue, with descriptive prefixes such as *pre-*, *high*, and *post-* to designate its various stages; or when we idealize an earlier period at the expense of a later one, as often as not the age in which we ourselves are living— in each instance we are working within that framework of thought we associate with romanticism. Moreover, since a temporal gap exists between earlier periods and the time that they first achieved the status of distinct and namable entities within the history of culture, one cannot point to a continuing discussion of what constitutes their nature; by contrast, the value, nature, and boundaries of romanticism have been debated ever since the phenomenon to which we attach that particular name supposedly occurred.

One might object— and rightly so— that the poets and theorists we today call romantic did not refer to themselves by that name. As René Wellek demonstrated long ago, this term was not used on the continent to describe the period until well into the nineteenth century (136–43), and in England, which adopted the term by continental analogy, critics did not call the early nineteenth-century poets romantic until near the end of the century (149–50).

Properly speaking, Schiller's essay, as well as many other theories of romanticism contemporary with it, should be called a theory of modernity, for, however much it may imply that the stages of development it describes represent a universally recurring phenomenon, its central rhetorical aim is to confront the dilemmas of the modern artist, to whom it offers consolation for his losses and, if I may employ a present-day cliché, moral support to compensate for these losses, or at least to allow him to bypass them.

As a theory of modernity, the essay belongs to a line of thought initiated by Rousseau's *Discourse on Inequality* forty years before. The transition that Rousseau's essay depicts from the state of nature to the degraded condition of modern man parallels and, indeed, anticipates Schiller's movement from naive to sentimental; Rousseau's rhetorical aim is to goad his contemporaries to overcome their condition in much the way that Schiller's is to inspire his fellow poets (as well as himself). Again, as with Schiller, readers of Rousseau have often misread his aim as an attempt to return nostalgically to an earlier, lost condition; indeed, both essays, like most theories of romanticism, present the lost past with an ambiguity of attitude that encourages misreading, and it also serves, as I have indicated, as a source of the rhetorical power exercised by these theories.

According to the reigning academic classificatory systems, Rousseau's treatise belongs to the history of political theory, while Schiller's would properly be placed in the area of literary theory. Yet like all arguments that address themselves to the nature of the modern condition, above all like those that seek to alter this condition, both these essays defy our systems; thus, Rousseau's essay, especially because of the theory of linguistic origins embedded in his description of human communication in the state of nature (*Discourse* 157–62), suggests a literary frame of reference (indeed, it has become a central text for contemporary literary theorists),[1] while Schiller's and other theories of romanticism written in the wake of the Revolution have come to occupy a place in intellectual history because of the political subtexts we read into them.

If theories of romanticism formulated during that time we have labeled romantic could generally be termed theories of modernity, later theories of romanticism have no less tended to concern themselves with the nature and problems of modernity. One could in fact describe the history of theories of romanticism as a history of the changing relationships between romanticism and modernity. Once romanticism had receded in time, and had been named and evaluated by those who sought to use or understand it, it was of course no longer coincident with modernity. Yet to this day one can speak of a problematic relation between romanticism and modernity, a relation, one might add, that has taken quite distinct forms. For many Victorians, romanticism constituted a moment of fullness compared to which the living present seemed a period of decline, and thus romanticism could be used as a measuring stick with which to assess as well as to castigate modernity. For the anti-romantics of the early and mid-twentieth century, romanticism served as a false path, a lapse in literary and cultural history whose burden it remained for the new modernity to overcome. Those who defended romanticism against the anti-romantics during recent decades often argued that modernism was not really the antithesis of romanticism but rather its continuation or completion, though perhaps in disguised form. Whatever the relationship one might predicate between romanticism and modernism, the point of view that critics take to the former has usually been intimately involved with their attitude toward the latter.

This intimate, though also problematic, relationship of romanticism with later movements is exemplified by a particular subgenre of lyric poetry that originated in the 1790s and that has persisted in varying guises until our own time. Although this subgenre has no generally acknowledged name, I borrow the term "greater romantic lyric" that Abrams attached to it in a classic essay ("Structure"). Abrams described its properties and traced its lineage back to some sonnets by the Reverend William Lisle Bowles that happened to inspire the young Coleridge (a more comparative approach doubtless could have spotted its origins in the *Reveries* of Rousseau, in Klopstock, and in some of Goethe's early lyrics). This greater romantic lyric can generally be identified by the presence of a first-person self—variously identified, according to the critical system we employ, as the actual poet, or the speaker, or the lyric "I"—who is placed within a highly particularized scene. This self then engages in reflections that ascribe to itself sufficient temporal experience to give itself a history and, indeed, to constitute itself as an entity in the first place.

From Coleridge's "Frost at Midnight" down to Robert Lowell's confessional poems and its epigones that still appear in little magazines, this genre has maintained an identity as discernible as the identity of the self about which it purports to speak. (Might one speculate that the way we still formulate our conception of a self to ourselves—above all, in such modern thought systems as psychoanalysis and existentialism—was itself anticipated by, to an extent even a creation of, this type of lyric?) Like Schiller's essay and other theories of romanticism, this greater romantic lyric plays upon the various stages in the development of the self; and often, indeed, these stages are similar to those successive states of early bliss, later loss, and eventual recovery with which these theories concerned themselves. (Do we not retain this romantic notion of stages in such taken-for-granted terms as "latency period" and "mirror stage," not to speak of that current popular coinage "mid-life crisis"?) To the extent that it utilizes this older theoretical framework, this type of lyric acknowledges the power of romanticism even when, as in many postromantic examples, it seems to take up arms against the romantic past. Perhaps because of its venerability, perhaps because its poetic principles have been long understood and can no longer perplex the reader, this subgenre has maintained a special prestige—or at least tenure within English departments—against competing forms of poetry that developed outside or in opposition to the romantic tradition.[2]

Because these greater romantic lyrics contain so much of what we have come to see as the essential doctrinal content of romanticism, it scarcely seems accidental that critics often employ these poems—especially such famed early examples as "Tintern Abbey" and Keats's odes—as a means of expounding these doctrines. The usefulness of poetic texts for the uncovering of theoretical principles gives some indication of how fluid the bounds between poetic theory and practice had become within romanticism.[3] For that matter, one does not even need a so-called "greater" lyric to work out these theories. Even a short and simple poem such as "I wandered lonely as a Cloud" can be used—and surely often has been used in classrooms—to develop a theory of romanticism, for, like the greater, that is, the longer and more complex, lyric, it presents a tripartite movement from an initial unselfconscious experience to loss and thence to confidence in the future recovery of the experience; while doing this, it also manages to suggest relationships between memory, consciousness, poets, and self, all of which come to seem constituted, naturalized, and valorized in the course of this seemingly innocuous eighteen-line poem. Similarly, the mere eight lines that make up "A Slumber Did My Spirit Seal" have performed uncommonly heavy duty for those who sought to expound romantic attitudes regarding grief, immortality, sublimity, and the like.

In fact, one can easily put together a theory of romanticism from a virtually random selection of passages by any given poet or group of poets. To play on Goethe's description of his oeuvre as "Bruchstücke einer grossen Konfession [fragments of a great confession]" (*Dichtung* 283), one could say that theories of romanticism are generally stitched together out of fragments of diverse writing, both verse and discursive prose. Since the fragment was, in fact, a privileged artistic form for the romantics, theorists of romanticism can employ both "real" fragments as well as those they themselves extract from larger texts. The theory that any particular interpreter wishes to present will of course differ somewhat according to the fragments he or she chooses. If one concocted Wordsworth's theory of romanticism out of, say, the essay on epitaphs, "A Slumber Did My Spirit Seal," the immortality ode, and some spot of time from *The Prelude*, the resulting theory would stress death, sublimity, temporality, consciousness, imagination, and whatever interrelationships can be set up among these abstractions. Take a different selection, say, "The Ruined Cottage," "Resolution and Independence," *Lyrical Ballads* and its preface of 1800, and a somewhat different theory would emerge, this one stressing social tensions and human interactions.

Or one might juxtapose fragments from the poetry and critical pronouncements of all six of the poets who make up what, in essay 1, I called the "pantheon" of English romanticism. With passages drawn, say, from *Lamia, Childe Harold, Jerusalem*, the immortality ode, the preface to *Prometheus Unbound, Biographia Literaria*, "Ode to the West Wind," a relatively extravagant image of romanticism would emerge—as would an even more extravagant one if the field of inquiry expanded to include continental as well as English romanticism. Yet despite these differences, all of these theories would still bear certain family resemblances to one another, with particular themes receiving varying degrees of prominence—for example, the affirmation of the symbol or of the imagination, the focus on stages of development or on the autonomy of the self, and the role (overt or displaced) of the French Revolution.

In view of the fact that, during the later eighteenth century, literary discourse claimed an independence from, and indeed a superiority to, other discursive forms, it may seem paradoxical that poems and prose prefaces, like those cited in the models for theories listed above, are virtually interchangeable as a means of creating theories of romanticism. Yet once the classical system of literature, with its clear demarcations between various forms of discourse, had broken down, most anything was potentially definable as poetry. As Friedrich Schlegel put it in an Athenäum fragment, "Poetry is whatever has been called poetry at a particular time or in a particular place" (38). Shelley, unwilling to award the highest poetic laurels to Roman poetry, preferred to find the true poetry of ancient Rome in its institutions (494). If most anything is potentially poetic, it seems only natural that theories of romanticism should themselves often aspire to the condition of poetry—witness the high-flown manner of Shelley's *Defence* or the selfconscious literariness of Friedrich Schlegel's fragments, in both of which, as so often within theories of romanticism, the style seeks to imitate the content, indeed, to convince us that one should not constitute style and content as separate categories in the first place. To put it another way, in those rhetorical practices that we label romanticism poetics itself aspires to the condition of poetry. In fact, our own conception of what constitutes the poetics of a particular writer or of a particular age was itself made possible by the foregrounding of poetics that took place among the romantics. Without their precedent we would not likely raise the kinds of questions we raise whenever we describe the nature of medieval or Renaissance poetics, even when we stress the differences between, say, Renaissance and romantic poetics.

In positing their poetics the romantics were not simply theorizing about their own time. They were also making universal claims for literature applicable, as they thought, to all times. Theories of romanticism easily merge with, turn into, or mask as general theories of literature within which the whole literary past is rethought and re-evaluated. Within the space of a few pages Shelley's *Defence* retells the whole history of Western literature (486–500). The celebrated romantic interpretations of earlier literature—Coleridge's analysis of fancy and imagination in Shakespeare, Blake's illuminations of earlier long poems, August Wilhelm Schlegel's narrative about the rise and decline of Greek tragedy (5:48–130)—have not only helped shape our own view of earlier literature, but these interpretations are themselves intended to exercise a generalizing power about literature as a whole. Never before had so much of literary history come within the purview of a group of observers; in fact, never before—not even in that earlier, aesthetically self-conscious age, the sixteenth century in Italy—had such intense and ambitious theorizing about the literary past, the dilemmas of modern writers, and the nature of art as a whole been recorded.

Yet if one observes the settings in which this theorizing took place, one notes small, often isolated groups of people who saw themselves, and were also perceived by others, as marginal to society. Blake did not even enjoy the support of his contemporary poets engaged in a common enterprise. Much theorizing at the time was never recorded, but was accomplished in conversation: what would we not give for a transcript of Wordsworth and Coleridge's literary and philosophical conversations of 1797 and 1798 or of those that took place among the Jena romantics about the same time? Even in those written documents that came down to us, much of the significant theorizing assumed what were meant to appear as informal or unconventional forms—aphorisms, letters, table talk, marginalia, not to speak of the theories embedded indirectly, sometimes even allegorically, within poems. Whether oral or written, romantic theorizing was often directed to those who already belonged to the group and whose assent could easily be assumed; one might add that in theorizing to one another the members of a romantic group sought not so much to inform the others as to stimulate them to further thought, or simply to perform in their presence. Sometimes, as with marginalia, romantic theorizing was directed only to oneself—or to those acquaintances who might later borrow one's books. The journals that provided a home for romantic discourse were often small-group enterprises with the most limited financial resources and with few illusions that, like the *Spectator* or the *Tatler* a century before, they could disseminate their ideas before a large and literate middle-class public.

From a social and institutional point of view we can now see the romantics as ancestors of the various avant-garde groups—each following the other with a rapidity unknown in earlier centuries—who have selfconsciously created and publicized the artistic styles of our own time. Like their modernist descendants, the romantics developed considerable verbal flair in defying the real and imagined establishments who they assumed were opposed to their programs. Like the modernists, they often encapsuled their theories in memorable and also much misunderstood slogans—poetry as the "spontaneous overflow of powerful feelings," poets as the "unacknowledged legislators of the world," or the notion that "all the great writers were romantics in their time."

The prominence of these slogans since romanticism tells us not only about their creators' mode of communicating with the public, but it also suggests the essential simplicity at the heart of most theories of romanticism. Although they sometimes pretend to contain untold complexities, they constantly hover around a limited number of terms and ideas that quickly become familiar, even predictable. Esoteric though they may sometimes sound, they have generally proved easy to learn and to assimilate. Those who have mastered the discourse of romanticism, whether poets, critics, or readers, can apply its characteristic language in an uncommon variety of ways, not simply in their reading and writing, but also in the ways that they conduct their lives. However marginal the romantics took themselves to be, the ability of their discourse to accommodate itself within a variety of situations represents one of the more glamorous success stories in the history of culture.

In speaking of theories of romanticism up to now, I have referred largely to those theories voiced by the romantics themselves. But these very theories have also created later theories *about* romanticism, about its nature, its unity, its ideology, its confines in time and place; to be more specific, one can cite theories attacking or defending romanticism, or theories revising earlier theories about the nature of romanticism. The variety of theories spawned by romanticism, sometimes in fact living parasitically off one another, is itself a sign of the uncommon generative power exercised by the structure of romantic thought and by its rhetoric, as well as by the charismatic force emanating from the personages who represented its ideas before the world.

This generative power is evident in the fact that some of the most influential theories of literature within our own century themselves derive from theories of romanticism. For example, as one reads the opening lines of Lukács's *Theory of the Novel*, "Happy are those ages when the starry sky is the map of all possible paths. ... The world is wide and yet it is like a home, for the fire that burns in the soul is of the same essential nature as the stars" (29), one quickly recognizes that Lukács is deliberately echoing Schiller's description of the naive. Like Schiller before him, Lukács looks backward with a mixture of nostalgia and relief at an earlier, unrecoverable condition that finds its ideal literary embodiment in Homeric epic. For modern, problematic, alienated man, the appropriate genre is the novel, which Lukács subdivided generically into categories such as the novel of "abstract idealism" (exemplified by *Don Quijote* [97–111]) and of the "romanticism of disillusionment" (exemplified, among others, by *L'Éducation sentimentale* [112–31]), just as Schiller divided the genres available to the sentimental poet into satire, elegy, and idyll (*Naive* 117–54) according to the stances that each of these genres takes to the modern dilemma. The experience of temporality that Lukács defines as constitutive of the second of these generic categories was itself a central obsession with the romantics in their attempts to bridge or compensate for the gap that separated them from a lost originary state. The persistence of Schiller's antitheses well over a century after they were formulated—and later mediated by Hegel—testifies to the power of a theory of romanticism to relocate itself and to speak with consolatory effect to a generation disillusioned by the First World War.

Likewise, Northrop Frye's theory of literature transforms a theory of romanticism into terms accessible to a mid-twentieth-century world. Frye's representation of the eras of literary history, moving as they do from myth and romance to irony, carries overtones of the fall from the naive to the sentimental state and, even more specifically, it echoes the historical stages postulated by that early precursor of romantic historicism, Giambattista Vico. As Frye himself admitted (vii), the larger framework out of which his theory of literature is built derives from Blake, or at least as Frye had reconstructed Blake's thought in his own early book on the poet. Harold Bloom's general theory about unceasing generational strife among the great poets displays its link with romanticism even more overtly than does Frye's theory of literature. Based on the romantics' own self-image as the inheritors of a stifling burden of the past—at least as this image was formulated by means of traditional historical method in the work of W. J. Bate—Bloom's theory casts each new poet in a role analogous to that of Schiller's sentimental poet; in the eyes of each successor poet, the precursor himself assumes the role of naive poet even though the latter had earlier taken up the sentimental burden against his own precursor, whom he too had treated as naive. Although Bloom's theory masks as a general theory about how poets relate to one another in an endless chain across time, the romantic poets happen to occupy center stage among his examples. Not only does he present the first and second romantic generations in contention with one another, but, in a tale that Bloom himself narrates romantically with unmistakably Gothic overtones, all the romantics wrestle with their common father Milton, while they in turn emerge as formidable father figures in the eyes of their Victorian and modernist successors.

Just as theories of romanticism still give shape to theories of literature, so have the various retrospective attempts to define and evaluate romanticism themselves retained some essential features of the body of thought upon which they purport to comment. Matthew Arnold, for example, maintains the tripartite scheme of plenitude, loss and recovery. In his "Memorial Verses," occasioned by Wordsworth's death in 1850, he looks back from a dark and dreary present to the fullness and the power represented by the romantics. The poem is centered not only around Wordsworth, but around two other exemplary romantic figures, Goethe and Byron. Each of the three represents a distinct set of values—Goethe, as "physician of the iron age" (*Poetry* 108), the ability to diagnose the ills of the time; Byron, the ability to make us feel passion; Wordsworth, the ability to cure the age's ills with his "healing power" (109). Although Arnold acknowledges that the romantic period was, like his own, an "iron time" (109), at least the earlier age had access to titanic figures such as those eulogized in the poem to bring about its recovery; or, as he wrote of Wordsworth's poetry, it could

> shed
> On spirits that had long been dead,
> Spirits dried up and closely furl'd
> The freshness of the early world.
> (109)

Arnold's generation, by contrast, had no such figures of its own and must perforce count on the redemptive power of the romantics to provide as best they can, if only retrospectively, whatever recovery may become possible for its own time. One might note that despite the pretense that these "memorial verses" constitute simply an occasional poem on a recent public event, Arnold reworks the form and thematic matter of the greater romantic lyric with the poet here presenting himself not as the solitary self customary within this subgenre, but as a collective "we" speaking for his entire generation.

Arnold's most famous poem, "Dover Beach," is a more immediately apparent example of the greater romantic lyric, and as such it invites us to measure its assertions against those of its romantic predecessors. Thus, in "Dover Beach" the only recovery possible within the bleak present age, now that the "Sea of Faith" has withdrawn, lies in personal relationships—"Ah, love, let us be true/ To one another!" (162). Even the lofty past was compromised, for Sophocles, too, hearing the same ebb and flow of the tide that Arnold hears, knew of human misery much as Arnold's generation does. It is significant that Arnold cites a fellow-sufferer such as Sophocles (161) from the Greek past rather than Homer, who, by

romantic convention, would have provided an unproblematically
benign example; yet this brief allusion to a great poet of the past
also exercises its own ability to console, for the weighty cultural
legacy, like the personal relationship invoked near the end of the
poem, provides a bulwark against the clashing of ignorant armies
who symbolize the ills of the modern age.

Within the larger cultural program that Arnold was to work out
in the critical essays composed after his poetic vein gave out, the
great literature of the past from Homer down to Wordsworth and
Byron—with Arnold's contemporary poets, at least the English
ones, notably missing—assumed the burden of cultural recovery.
By means of touchstones that, like biblical verse in an earlier
religious time, could instantly evoke a timeless, saner, more stable
order, literature was to exercise its affective power upon a swiftly
changing society badly in need of bonds to hold it together; indeed,
by offering its system of values to the new masses, that body of
texts which now came to be called literature would hopefully re-
duce the ignorance of the night-clashing armies whom Arnold had
invoked with such awesome fear at the close of his great poem.

Arnold's notion of the transformative and consolatory power of
art itself derives from those early theories of romanticism that
stressed the efficacy of the symbol and that came to see art as
occupying an autonomous realm above and beyond the more practical, everyday modes of communication. This notion remains central within the strident anti-romanticism of the early modernist
poets and critics—except, of course, that they distance themselves
from the romantics. Not that they ignore the potency of romantic
art. Indeed, they fully acknowledge the rhetorical efficacy of romantic poetry, but they declare its effects harmful in the extreme.
T. S. Eliot, for example, described at length the enthusiasm he had
felt for Shelley during adolescence, but he warned of the dangers
that befell those who carried this passion beyond that early stage
of life (*Use* 32–36, 88–98). Leavis similarly linked romanticism
with immaturity, both the immaturity of the genuinely young and
that of grown-ups who, in one way or another, display their refusal
to accept adult responsibility by reading romantic poetry; thus,
Leavis, while acknowledging the power of Shelley's lines about
"Life . . . stain[ing] the white radiance of Eternity," dismisses this
power contemptuously as designed only for "the spell-bound, for
those sharing the simple happiness of intoxication" (232).

Modernist anti-romantic theories of romanticism carefully screen and re-evaluate earlier theories of romanticism to suit their own cultural programs. Thus, they generally insist that the defining feature of romanticism is its anti-rational stance, which they associate with such varied attributes as heterodoxy, immaturity, vagueness, and political liberalism. These anti-romantic theories had their origin in early twentieth-century France, where they were used to support a conservative political program for which Rousseau's purported irrationalism served as scapegoat.[4] Yet this obsession with romantic irrationalism, as strong in the English and American anti-romantics as it was in their French predecessors, has also masked the fact that certain anti-romantic theories maintain a continuity with earlier theories of romanticism. For example, Eliot's view of literary and cultural history, as Frank Kermode pointed out more than thirty years ago (138–61), retains the temporal succession of plenitude, fall, and recovery, except that the fall is pushed backward to the mid-seventeenth century when the so-called dissociation of sensibility took place. Although his view of history is guided by religious and political concerns, Eliot defines the stages of the historical process by what are overtly literary criteria: the great writers before the fall, Dante, the Renaissance dramatists, the metaphysical poets, are praised for their clear and precise images and their use of functional metaphor, while postlapsarian poets lack the capacity to fuse thought and feeling sufficiently to emulate their predecessors' triumphs with language. For Eliot, what happened in the course of the seventeenth century was a most unfortunate fall, "from which," as he put it in his celebrated essay of 1921 on the metaphysical poets, "we have never recovered" (*Selected* 288). Whatever recovery will take place according to Eliot's scheme will come about by means of the early modernist image—clear, clean, precise, unmediated, and without the intrusive rhetoric that would perforce carry along the sentimental baggage characteristic of the preceding poetic age.

In his own major adaptation of the greater romantic lyric, "Gerontion," Eliot hides the self—by romantic convention the central figure inhabiting this type of poem—behind the mask of a dramatic character located at a peculiarly late and hopeless stage in the crisis situation on which the subgenre ordinarily thrives. Past plenitude takes the form of the religious and sexual fulfillment that this character can grasp and communicate in an at best confused and wrong-headed way. No real recovery is suggested within this poem, not even the faith in personal relationships offered within

"Dover Beach." Only in his later religious poetry and in his cultural criticism does Eliot provide the possibility of recovery—and then, as certain German romantics had done more than a century before, by advocating a return to traditional Christianity.

Outside the work of Eliot and his fellow modernists, most of the theorizing about romanticism in our own century has taken place within an academic setting under the constraint of that discipline known variously as philology and literary history. As practiced in America during the first half of the century, this discipline pretended to be value-neutral and to represent the cultural past according to the "as-it-really-was" doctrine of Ranke that I referred to earlier in the Prologue. As such, the historians of romanticism depended pretty much on what the poets and critics of the era took themselves to be doing. Since such major figures as Goethe, Blake, and Coleridge all championed the symbol over allegory, romanticism could be presented, among other ways, as the triumph of a new symbolic mode of writing over an older allegorical mode. Since the romantics argued for the value of the poetic imagination, the primacy of the imagination—despite variations, even some confusion, among the poets as to what this concept really means—could conveniently be offered as a defining characteristic of the age. Yet even if one depends on the images that poets and critics themselves create about the nature of their endeavors, later historians, despite their claims to be value-neutral, characteristically end up picking and choosing those images that best suit their own perceptions of what actually happened, or should have happened, in the past. The images we select for "wie es eigentlich gewesen," as we have come increasingly to recognize in recent years, themselves derive from the particular perspectives within which—by dint of our intellectual training as well as of the larger ideologies in which we unconsciously participate—we happen to view the past.

The range of possible, and sometimes contradictory, perceptions of the past becomes evident if one notes the many inquiries that have sought to establish whether or not English and European romanticism constitutes a unity. At one extreme one can point to the provocative essay that Arthur O. Lovejoy published in 1924 denying the usefulness of romanticism as a single concept. After presenting some conflicting, indeed quite incompatible, attitudes that the so-called romantics took to nature and to classicism, Lovejoy advocated an extreme nominalist position that essentially denied the existence of any single entity one could legitimately name romanticism (228–53). Lovejoy pointed out these varying attitudes in order to promote his own intellectual program, namely, the history of ideas, a mode of historical analysis that was skeptical of the grand period concepts within the Hegelian tradition and that stressed instead the continuity over the ages of what Lovejoy called unit-ideas.

Fully a quarter century after Lovejoy's essay, René Wellek rose to defend the integrity of romanticism as a single movement that cut across England and all of Europe, including the Slavic cultures. The unity that Wellek discerned manifested itself in three closely related concepts, "imagination for the view of poetry," as Wellek put it, "nature for the view of the world," and "symbol and myth for poetic style" (161). Despite some anomalies here and there among the multitude of writers that Wellek considered—for example, he acknowledges Blake's refusal to "share the romantic deification of nature" (182)—Wellek's categories are sufficiently broad and flexible to accommodate most but by no means all of the canonized writers of the time within the romantic orbit. Yet Wellek, like Lovejoy, had his own program to propagate. As one of the founders of comparative literature in America, he could use romanticism to demonstrate the network of interrelationships prevailing among the writers and theorists at a given time within European culture. As defender at once of romanticism and the New Criticism, which his own theoretical pronouncements had helped to make respectable within the university, Wellek's stress on the role of symbol and myth in romanticism could call attention to the continuity between romantic and modernist writing, and it could also work to create a rapprochement between what had become the dominant critical movement in America and a historical period to which this movement, as the defender of modernist concerns, had long been hostile.

Attempts to establish the unity (or disunity) of romanticism have served the most diverse rhetorical purposes, purposes that, in fact, are often incompatible with one another. Theories of romanticism have been used to justify quite distinct political ends, from the conservatism that marked German romantic theory to the liberalism of later French romanticism. Within the politics of criticism, theories of romanticism can be invoked to support a rethinking of literary values, as in the early romantic prefaces and manifestos, and later in Pater and even in the anti-romantic modernists who adapted the romantic redemptive model of literary history to suit their own programs; or, more often than not in postromantic times, theories of romanticism may be used for culturally conservative ends to stabilize the existing canon, as in Wellek's quest for the unity of romanticism; in Abrams' epic attempt (in *Natural*) to justify romantic ways to modern men; or, most recently, in Nemoianu's learned reconstruction and promotion of a European-wide Biedermeier style to represent romanticism's timid last gasp. It is remarkable not only how flexible such theories have been in serving their multiple purposes, but also how, despite the diversity of these purposes, they have built upon a common repertory of motifs, the development of consciousness, both individual and collective, the alternation of periods of crisis and reconciliation, the shifting relationships of romanticism and modernity. Theories of romanticism, moreover, tend to exert extraordinary rhetorical power, for, depicting as they do such matters as the dawning of new ages or the constituting of the self, they engage with the reader's emotions, play upon, indeed, shape one's values, provide satisfactions analogous to those that emanate from religious systems. Like certain religious doctrines (and unlike those earlier theories of poetry that were not overtly religious), theories of romanticism often cause readers to feel that they can help define their own lives, relieve their distress, make them feel reborn.

Can we learn to resist the rhetorical seductions of theories of romanticism? Can we distance ourselves from their characteristic assertions and dialectical turns? Doubtless such distancing will prove difficult, if only because literary study as institutionalized within the modern university itself shares in the romantic legacy. For example, to the extent that literary study still justifies its existence today by the moral efficacy and timelessness it attributes to literary as against "everyday" discourse, it echoes and builds upon an Arnoldian view that is itself derived from romanticism. Indeed, if we seek to escape the spells exercised by theories of romanticism, we must first come to understand precisely how these theories, together with the literary works they exemplify and are themselves exemplified by, have, as I argue in the preceding essays, been mediated for us, codified, institutionalized in actual historical situations.

Such, at least, is the task that the *new* historical study of literature—what, in the final essay, I refer to as the new history—has undertaken in recent years. If any single feature distinguishes the new from an older literary history, it is a certain attitude of suspicion toward established ways of relating literature to its so-called historical setting. Instead of simply asking, as did the older history, how this setting can help us understand and interpret some literary masterpiece, the new history investigates the historical network by which a work came to be canonized as a masterpiece in the first place. Moreover, instead of separating the work from its setting, it recognizes that the setting as we know it is itself made up of verbal texts that are not necessarily different in kind from the literary text. Instead of taking programmatic theoretical statements of writers at face value, the new history treats these statements—as indeed this essay has itself attempted to do—as objects for historical examination. If the older history had faith that it could render the past "wie es eigentlich gewesen," the new history assumes the problematic nature of historical investigation from the outset. Doubtless the deconstructive activities of the last two decades— for example, Derrida's now-classic analysis of such terms as *voice*, *presence*, and *writing* in Rousseau (141–268) or de Man's demonstration that the romantics' vaunted symbol masks an allegorical mode of writing ("Rhetoric" 173–91)—helped shape the attitude of suspicion among those now committed to a new type of historical investigation. Doubtless also the revival of Marxist thought, above all the concept of ideology, has encouraged us to seek social motivations and explanations for theoretical pronouncements that were long taken to mean no more than what they seemed to be saying on the surface. The new history within literary study, as I demonstrate in essay 9, shares its characteristic attitudes with new perspectives that have emerged at much the same time within other disciplines, notably in the interpretive social sciences and in history itself.[5]

Rather than argue whether or not one can posit a unity within romanticism, we can build on Jerome McGann's suggestion that we should distinguish between, on the one hand, *romanticism*, a term that invites us to seek essences and to suppress ideological meanings, and, on the other, *the romantic period*, a historical category that allows us to include writers such as Austen and Crabbe, who cannot be accommodated easily within existing theories of romanticism (*Beauty* 9). Moreover, we can also ask how that body of ideas we have labeled romantic became institutionalized in differing ways within different national cultures. It is significant, for example, that the anti-romantic attitudes prevalent in France and the English-speaking countries had no equivalent in Germany, for which the whole age of Goethe served as the foundation stone grounding the new German nation. Since the English and the French could point to the Renaissance and the seventeenth century, respectively, to define and valorize their cultures, romanticism for them could more easily be dispensed with than in Germany. In addition, the strong nationalist strain within that final phase of the age of Goethe which the Germans label *Romantik* would have precluded a rejection of this phase within a new and economically backward state that sorely needed a nationalist ideology to justify and promote its very existence.[6] One might note that even in the period after World War II, when literary scholarship in both Germany and the English-speaking countries concentrated on ahistorical, supposedly "close" readings of texts, the age of Goethe remained the privileged period for German scholars,[7] while English and American scholars neglected romanticism in favor of other periods that lent themselves more conveniently to their method and to their cultural concerns.

I make these observations about the early development of literary study in order to suggest that the emerging approach to literary history may well modify our image not only of romanticism but above all of what literature as well as the study of literature is all about. The new history views literature as a social and an institutional activity. It shows how what we call literature employs modes of discourse used in those areas that we do not ordinarily associate with literature, and it also investigates the ways and the reasons why we grant literary discourse a special place apart from these other modes. It observes the interrelationships among which literature is produced, transmitted, and canonized. It asks who is addressing what message to whom and through which channels of communications even when, as in John Stuart Mill's unashamedly romantic theory of the lyric, the poet is speaking to himself and is at most merely overheard (*Essays* 12).

Not that the new history ignores all the concerns voiced by theories of romanticism. The French Revolution remains at least as important to the new historical approach to romanticism as it was before, though the Revolution need no longer serve unselfconsciously as a theological fall or a crisis of consciousness but, as I suggest by examining the sources and reception of *Danton's Death* in essay 5, as a unique shaping event—in fact, as a collection of texts, whether or not we choose to call them literature—whose relationship to individual poets, their language, and their modes of plotting can be noted and subjected to analysis.[8] The new history, moreover, continues to view romantic images and plots as secularizations of earlier Christian forms, but it also examines the means by which the process of secularization enabled these images and plots to communicate with readers and to leave their mark on nineteenth-century culture.[9]

Note that I speak of the new history, not of the new historicism that, as I indicate in the final essay, has become the favored name to describe the historical work performed by literary scholars during the 1980s in the United States. The term *history* is sufficiently loose and broad to accommodate a variety of meanings and practices; after all, it refers at once to what is written about the past and to the past that is written about; moreover, it encompasses a whole range of methods from chronicle history to that positivistic mode which believed it could grasp the past as it really was. Whereas history has no history, historicism is loaded with historical baggage, for it evokes the great revolution in historical thought anticipated by Vico, brought to fruition by a succession of thinkers during the half century between Herder and Hegel,[10] and institutionalized within German literary study early in the present century in that academic method called *Geistesgeschichte*.

Whereas history can focus on most any human endeavor from the plight of the poor to the politics and postures of the great, historicism, in its academic if not so much in its early, late eighteenth-century phase, has generally opted for the high road—high ceremony, high art, high politics. Whereas history can, if it chooses, concentrate on the discontinuous, on the individual case, on particular social practices, historicism is committed to grander things—to those larger narratives about the rise and fall of eras and about the crises, collisions, and dialectical movements that raise human actions to the level of drama. Historicism is, in fact, a product and an accomplice of those theories of romanticism with which I have been concerned throughout this essay;[11] to the extent that we attach ourselves to a historicist mode of thought we attach ourselves as well to those very theories of romanticism from which the more recent historical investigations of literature have sought to achieve some distance. And those who cannot do without an "ism" to frame their endeavors would surely fare better with the term *posthistoricist*, which, as I suggested in the Prologue, might serve to establish one's distance from historicism.

All this is not to say that the new history ignores theory. It has, in fact, been common to compliment the more sophisticated historical studies of recent years with the phrase that they practice "history informed by theory"—which is merely to say that certain contemporary literary theories have helped these studies formulate the questions they address. In this essay I have tried to demonstrate the historicity of what I call theories of romanticism, whether these theories mask as general theories of literature or serve simply as tools to understand and evaluate a demarcated portion of the past. But the new history may also have something new to tell us about theory, namely, that theories like the ones I have been describing, as well as the ones we are currently practising, are themselves historical artifacts, in fact that history and theory mutually imply and nourish one another even when we think we are practising one to the exclusion of the other.

FOUR

~⁓∽⁓∾

The History in Opera:
La clemenza di Tito,
Khovanshchina, Moses und Aron

W ho would go to the opera these days to experience history? To the extent that we think of history as a means of approaching some publicly available past, opera, with its heavy musical coating and the attention it calls to the virtuosity of its performers, would seem to raise considerable barriers between us and whatever past we see marked in the scenery and costumes onstage. Quite the contrary with historical drama, which, as I argued in the Prologue, functioned with other forms such as the historical novel and historical painting in the nineteenth century to render the past in all its immediacy. The present essay will argue not only that opera in many instances can be viewed as historical drama, but that the concerns we associate with history are deeply embedded in opera. Just as the preceding essay argued that those theories of romanticism claiming their own timelessness were themselves rooted in history, so the present essay seeks to establish the historicity of a genre that, despite its tendency to seek out historical plots, has long relied on music's claims to universality to suppress the historical particulars attendant upon its creation and its consumption.

As generic categories, certainly, opera and historical drama are neither parallel to nor commensurate with one another. We can define opera, after all, by its formal properties, its use of music, for example, to represent human speech. Historical drama, by contrast, tends to define itself by its subject matter, for instance, its use of such materials from public history as conspiracies or the rise and fall of rulers; as a form, historical drama remains a subcategory within spoken drama, and by no means one that, like tragedy or comedy, has been easy to classify, for it can coexist with either of these dramatic forms, indeed sometimes partake of both at once.

Yet opera and historical drama, however different the criteria by which we define them, have exhibited a natural affinity to one another ever since the composition of the first operas on historical themes early in the seventeenth century.[1] Except for comic operas, Italian opera until well into the nineteenth century drew its plots chiefly from historical, or purportedly historical, narratives. Even when opera composers turned to private domestic life, as Verdi did in *La traviata*, they found it necessary to retain the costumes and décor of earlier periods to keep a temporal distance between the audience and the events onstage. History, or at least the semblance of history, has proved a particularly convenient way of establishing that distance between a real and a represented world that opera has always cultivated.

If opera has shown a continuing penchant for representing history, historical drama has often displayed features that we can characterize as operatic in nature. The strongly ceremonial elements in many historical plays— for example, the pageantry marking shows of royal power or the rituals accompanying a character's path to martyrdom— often seem to cry out for musical realization. To audiences acclimated to the full sonorities of operatic style, a historical drama may well seem like an opera manqué Moreover, within historical plays a feature such as a crowd of citizens venting its anger or praising its leaders rarely lends itself to satisfactory treatment—at least not since the Greeks, who after all had their own, now lost, musical forms to accompany choral speeches. While Shakespeare in *Coriolanus*, or Goethe in *Egmont*, presented stage directors with challenges they have often struggled in vain to meet, the massive choral forces we find in many nineteenth-century operas allow crowds to function dramatically in much the way that individual characters do.²

Despite the fact that music often offers history plays a means of transcending the limits of words alone, the operatic versions of many famous historical dramas and novels have all too often struck their auditors as less substantive in serious historical content than their originals. For example, the *auto da fé* scene that Verdi's librettists added to Schiller's *Don Carlos* in turning the play into a French grand opera, though it extended the play's ceremonial dimensions, is a reminder that opera is less historically reflective than spoken drama. Moreover, the reflectiveness about history that we praise today in works such as Scott's *Old Mortality* and *The Bride of Lammermoor* is notably missing in those celebrated operas, Bellini's *I puritani* and Donizetti's *Lucia di Lammermoor*, that are based on these novels. Among major historical works that have been turned into great operas, perhaps only Musorgsky's *Boris Godunov* elicits praise for its historical seriousness commensurate with that accorded the Pushkin play from which it is derived.

This essay will demonstrate that opera over the centuries has cultivated its own ways of articulating history—and in a manner quite distinct from that of non-musical theater. I propose to look at three operas widely dispersed in time—Mozart's *La clemenza di Tito*, composed in 1791; Musorgsky's *Khovanshchina*, begun in 1872 and left unfinished at the composer's death in 1881; and Arnold Schoenberg's *Moses und Aron*, the first two acts of which were set to music between 1930 and 1932, with the final act left uncomposed, except for some musical sketches, when Schoenberg died in 1951. A study of simply the librettos to these works would give only a partial, sometimes even a misleading indication of how operas function as historical drama. To understand these operas as historical drama, I shall treat them as works deeply embedded in their own historical worlds—works that, like the literary texts I discuss in the other essays of this book, themselves embody, often unconsciously, notions about history we now see as peculiar to and representative of their time.

To start with, let me suggest four distinct layers of history within which historical operas participate. First, one can cite that earlier historical period which the opera purportedly tells us about. The three operas I am discussing draw their materials from three of the major areas that historical operas have traditionally been "about": *La clemenza di Tito* derives from classical history, *Khovanshchina* from the composer's national history, *Moses und Aron* from biblical history. A second historical level encompasses events and attitudes of the composer's own time that, from our present point of view, seem relevant to an understanding of each work. *La clemenza di Tito*, for example, was commissioned to celebrate the coronation of the Holy Roman Emperor Leopold II in his office as king of Bohemia; *Khovanshchina* voices not only the nationalist impulses common within Musorgsky's generation, but above all the sympathies toward the common people and the desire for social change shared by the Russian intelligentsia during the 1860s and '70s; *Moses und Aron* was composed soon after Schoenberg's return to Judaism and at a time that the composer, while witnessing the rise of Nazism and reflecting upon the course of recent Jewish—and in particular Zionist—history, asked himself some fundamental questions about the nature of political leadership.

A third historical level, closely related to the second, consists of those larger ideas about historical change and the uses of history that we, with our own hindsight, can discern underlying each opera. Thus, *La clemenza di Tito* embodies the Enlightenment view that human nature is everywhere and at all times the same, that an incident supposedly from Roman history can serve as an exemplum to enlighten a modern ruler on the virtues of pardoning rather than punishing those who threaten his life. *Khovanshchina*, by contrast, embodies that nineteenth-century view of history as process whereby an older order encumbered by traditional cultural forms gives way to a new order, in this instance the radically new dispensation of Peter the Great. *Moses und Aron*, in a way characteristic of many early modernist writings, treats a crisis drawn from earlier history as at once real and archetypal, and it does not shy away from placing its insights in an explicitly religious and metaphysical framework.

A fourth level of historical meaning is evident in the significations that have accumulated—like those for the Wordsworth poem whose critical history I sketched out in essay 2—for these works since the composer's time through the interpretive efforts of stage directors, performers, and critics. When *La clemenza di Tito* began to be revived during our time it received a variety of interpretations, for, having been virtually forgotten for a century and a half, it lacked a continuing interpretive history against which new approaches were forced to contend. Thus, William Francisco's 1971 production in modern dress could assert the applicability of the

opera to the politics of the Nixon administration, while Jean-Pierre
Ponnelle's television production, filmed in actual Roman ruins and
with the characters clad in Roman costumes, in effect asserted the
temporal discontinuity between the ancient Roman setting and the
cult of ruins that flourished at the time the opera was composed. A
relatively realistic production of *Khovanshchina*, like that designed
by Nicola Benois and used in a number of opera houses, works to
confirm the late nineteenth-century view of history originally propagated by the opera; a less realistic, more stylized production such
as those in London and Geneva during the early 1980s would—to
judge by photographs of the stage sets[3]—distance the audience
from this view, perhaps even make the audience question it. Similarly, a director's choice of a realistic or a stylized approach to
Moses und Aron would readjust the particular balance of real and
archetypal that Schoenberg attempted to achieve.[4]

However different the approaches to history one can locate in
each of these works, all three show certain striking similarities to
one another. All of them, for instance, are structured around conspiracies; as in most historical plays, as I point out elsewhere
(*Historical* 30–38), political plotting becomes a means to organize
dramatic plotting. Thus *La clemenza di Tito* is built around a frustrated attempt against the Emperor Titus by his friend Sextus,
who, in the fashion of neoclassical historical plays, is motivated to
commit the deed through his attachment to a woman, in this instance the fierce Vitellia, herself motivated at once by private and
political concerns; the imperial act of clemency that gives the
opera its title works both to resolve the conspiracy and to make a
didactic statement about the conduct proper to an absolute ruler.

Although Musorgsky eschews the tight classical plotting of Mozart's opera, *Khovanshchina* is built around the struggles that took
place during the 1680s among at least three competing political
factions who either conspire against one another or accuse one
another of conspiring; most of the action consists of plotting and
counterplotting until, by the end, all factions go to their defeat in
the face of the new order represented by Peter the Great. Among all
three operas, *Moses und Aron* contains the most simplified conspiratorial plot—namely, that between Aron and the populace to institute idol-worship against the austere strictures pronounced by Moses
as spokesman for a jealous Hebrew God.

If operas based on history employ conspiratorial plots in much
the same way as non-musical historical plays, music encourages

them to realize another feature common to historical plays—namely, the ceremonial and ritual element latent within their subjects. Indeed, opera can exploit this element in ways that dramatic speech alone could never do. As a recent study of the *La clemenza di Tito* overture points out, "Trumpets and drums, fanfares, and majestic dotted rhythms betoken the imperial ambience in *Titus*," and, as this study goes on to show, the original audience would have associated the elaborate contrapuntal development in the overture with the House of Hapsburg, which, as heir to the Holy Roman Empire, would, by implication, have established its connection with the grandeur of ancient Rome (Heartz, "Overture" 32, 49).[5] In the course of the opera Mozart interrupts the succession of arias and small ensemble groups with a march and several choral numbers that work at once to represent and celebrate imperial power.

The huge historical panorama that Musorgsky created in *Khovanshchina* allowed him to introduce a variety of ceremonial scenes, for example the oriental exoticism of the opera's most familiar music, the dance of the Persian maidens, or the choruses sung in an archaic mode at the end of the opera by the Old Believers as they prepare for their martyrdom. Music, in fact, often allows opera to suggest a certain religious dimension that most historical plays generally touch on lightly, if at all. Thus, the martyrdom of the Old Believers before the triumph of Peter the Great's new order achieves a power and a pathos impossible within non-musical drama by means of the ancient, chant-like forms in which they voice their plight. Among the most gripping musical and dramatic scenes in Musorgsky's opera is the prophecy aria, in which the Old Believer Marfa, the opera's major female character, predicts the downfall of one of the opposing factions; as in much historical drama, prophecy provides a naturalistic means of providing the work with a supernatural dimension.[6]

The strongly ceremonial character of *Moses und Aron* manifests itself right from the start, for biblical precedent allows Schoenberg to introduce the supernatural through the voice of God emanating from the Burning Bush.[7] By mixing a chorus intoning in *Sprechstimme* together with a traditional chorus of singers, Schoenberg creates a mysterious divine voice that sounds like nothing anybody has ever heard before in opera or spoken drama. If divinity seems to speaks more authentically in musical form than it would as straight dramatic speech, the "negative" ceremony of the Golden Calf scene achieves an orgiastic fury attainable only by the strange rhythms and the unconventional combination of instruments Schoenberg uses to accompany the wild doings onstage.

The three works I have chosen to demonstrate the means by which opera becomes historical drama serve as compelling examples for several reasons. For one thing, unlike *Don Carlos* and *Boris Godunov*, none derives from a famous play with which one is forced to compare it and to argue for the virtues of one medium in respect to the other—or to debate which is more "faithful" to history. *La clemenza di Tito* is based on a text that the preeminent eighteenth-century librettist, Pietro Metastasio, had composed nearly sixty years before and that innumerable composers had set in the meantime;[8] the Metastasio text had, in turn, been based on a few lines from Suetonius. The libretto of *Khovanshchina*, by the composer himself with the help of his advisor Vladimir Stasov, derives from memoirs and scholarly accounts. For *Moses und Aron* Schoenberg took a few brief passages from the Old Testament but omitted most of the biblical material about the two brothers.

Moreover, all three of these operas are relatively recent rediscoveries and thus, unlike works with long and continuing interpretive traditions, have given their directors a degree of immunity from the complaints of audiences who want their war-horses done according to time-honored custom. To be sure, *La clemenza di Tito* was once one of Mozart's most popular operas and for the first quarter of a century after its composition shared this popularity only with *Don Giovanni* and *Die Zauberflöte*.[9] Largely because the *opera seria* genre came to seem archaic, *Tito* went out of favor early in the nineteenth century, and it remained virtually forgotten until its recent revivals beginning in the 1960s. Although *Khovanshchina*, doubtless because of its relevance to Soviet political concerns, has remained part of the Russian repertory throughout most of this century, it has excited interest in Europe and North America only since the 1960s (see Duault et al. 173–89).

The staging of *Moses und Aron* was delayed during the last two decades of Schoenberg's life while he sought—unsuccessfully as it turned out—to compose the text he had prepared for the last act. Even so, despite a concert production in Hamburg in 1954 and a first staging in Zurich in 1957, the opera did not excite much attention outside avant-garde circles until the London, Paris and Berlin productions during the 1960s and '70s demonstrated that what had long been thought a forbidding work could communicate with the larger public. Even though none of these three operas has

as yet created a secure place for itself in the international repertory, each has had distinguished and much-publicized productions
in a number of major opera houses.

Although *Moses und Aron* retains the status of a fragmentary
work, despite frequent assertions that the first two acts constitute
a rounded whole, neither of the other two operas was actually
completed by its composer. The hurry to which Mozart was subjected in fulfilling his commission for the coronation ceremonies
caused him to leave the composition of the recitatives to a student,
traditionally thought to be Süssmayr.[10] The textual status of *Khovanshchina*, like that of all Musorgsky's operas, remains problematic. In this instance, except for the orchestration of two brief
passages, only a piano score of the opera was left behind after the
composer's death. Musorgsky's friend Rimsky-Korsakov, whose
musical aesthetic we now recognize as alien to that of the composer, orchestrated and radically cut the opera, and it is Rimsky's
version that is still the most frequently performed today despite
the fact that Shostakovich's version not only restores the cuts but,
unlike Rimsky's, attempts to preserve the composer's bold harmonies. To complicate matters further, Musorgsky failed to bring the
second act to conclusion, and he also left the opera's final scene in
unconnected fragments—with the result that each arranger has
had to decide on the closure appropriate to two uncompleted acts.
Rimsky near the end of the opera reintroduces an earlier theme
associated with Peter the Great and thus presents a view of history,
whether or not consonant with the composer's view, that stresses
the triumph of the new order, while Shostakovich provides alternative endings.[11] If Schoenberg had been able to complete his last
act, audiences might have been left with a somewhat different
interpretation of biblical history, for the spiritual triumph that
Moses voices over Aron in the words of the uncomposed third act
contrasts strikingly with the sense of defeat that Moses admits at
the end of the second act, at the very point where performances
must perforce break off.

If I have stressed Schoenberg's ability to manipulate historical
meanings, different though the resolutions may seem at the end of
his second and third acts, this is also a consequence of the relative
freedom that a modernist composer enjoys. Quite in contrast to
Mozart, who composed *Tito* in response to a commission whose
political purposes he could not control, Schoenberg, who made his
living teaching music, did not have to take commercial matters

into consideration. Even if he had finished *Moses und Aron* in 1932, he could have hoped at best for occasional productions applauded by a few champions of avant-garde music and derided by most of the opera-going public.

The degree of autonomy that Musorgsky enjoyed in determining the historical statements emerging from his opera was surely closer to that of Schoenberg than of Mozart. As author of his own libretto, he could shape the historical events from the chronicles to suit the notions that he and his populist friends embraced. Although it was long believed that the substantial revisions to which he subjected *Boris Godunov* derived from a fear of censorship and a need to conform to the conventions imposed by the imperial theater, the Maryinsky, recent scholarship has affirmed the artistic independence and rigorously experimental attitude that characterizes both versions of the opera (see Taruskin "Musorgsky"). When the vocal score of *Khovanshchina* was submitted to the Maryinsky, the unconventionality of *Boris* remained so strongly imprinted in the officials' minds that they rejected the new opera; even after Rimsky's orchestration had been completed, *Khovanshchina* was performed not by the Maryinsky but by an amateur group, and it did not become a part of the Russian repertory until well into our own century (see Berlin, *"Khovanshchina"* 40). Since the Russian theaters had little tolerance for experimentation and since Musorgsky depended on his job in a government office for his livelihood, he was, in effect, free to treat his theme in as uncompromising a way as he had in *Boris Godunov* (at least in its first version)—even though this meant, as it would later for Schoenberg, that his chances for immediate public performance were meager.

The autonomy that an opera composer can exercise in matching character with voice has often been a register of the freedom he has enjoyed. The relative lack of artistic freedom within the musical world inhabited by Mozart is evident from the fact that the tenor voice that the composer originally intended for the frustrated assassin Sextus gave way to a castrato, the voice that was called for in the contract that Mozart's impresario, Domenico Guardasoni, had earlier signed with the Bohemian authorities sponsoring the coronation ceremonies.[12] It would never have occurred to Mozart to compose an opera that had little chance of performance—or of remuneration, for that matter. By contrast, Musorgsky and Schoenberg did not work under contract nor with any immediate plans for performance. Musorgsky could let his musical imagination create the massive choral forces that dominate the opera regardless of whether these would soon be realized on the stage. Since Schoenberg did not need to consider the biases of audiences, critics, or donors—but only those of his peers and disciples—he could refuse to set his character Moses for any voice that did not suit his aesthetic program; thus, with telling dramatic effect, he could allow Moses to express himself in the conspicuously non-operatic *Sprechstimme* with which he had experimented in *Pierrot Lunaire* two decades before (see Stadlen).

The difficulties that all three of these works experienced before they could be understood and absorbed by the opera-going public may well have to do with the fact that each of them combines what at the time of composition seemed an advanced musical style with a larger dramatic structure that was distinctly old-style. Although some of the arias of *La clemenza di Tito*, notably Sextus's "Parto, parto" and Vitellia's rondo "Non più di fiori," sustain a musical interest commensurate with the major arias of the three great comic operas immediately preceding the composition of *Tito*, the *opera seria* form, which went back to the start of the eighteenth century, did not allow those complex dramatic ensembles associated with *opera buffa:* indeed, it is on these ensembles that Mozart's stature as a great musical dramatist rests today. To be sure, the librettist Caterino Mazzolà, who was assigned to work with Mozart on *Tito*, revised Metastasio's clearly old-fashioned dramatic structure through the substitution of several duets and trios, even a quintet, for the long succession of individual arias that marked the *seria* form.[13] Yet even these revisions were insufficient, after the first quarter of the nineteenth century, to keep the opera from seeming too archaic to hold its place in the repertory with the other late Mozart operas. Wagner's dismissal of *La clemenza di Tito* as "stiff and dry" is a comment at once on the relative backwardness of its dramatic organization and, by implication, on the world of the *ancien régime*, for which Metastasio was a famed spokesman and whose prolongation the opera, through the occasion for which it was commissioned, sought to celebrate.[14] Not that Mozart was even appreciated by the objects of his compliments: at the first performance the empress, who was of Spanish Bourbon extraction and who had lived most of her life in Tuscany, was reported to have labeled the opera a "porcheria tedesca" ("German garbage" [Teuber 2:267]), a comment perhaps suggesting that a local Austrian boy could not possibly beat the Italians at their own game.

This negative attitude was not, however, shared by the whole audience, for a contemporary account describes the first-act finale as "lovely enough to lure the gods down to earth."[15]

The notions of musical progress that Wagner propagated and that stood behind his rejection of *La clemenza di Tito* have also worked to the detriment of Musorgsky's reputation. Although Musorgsky composed *Khovanshchina* at a time that Wagner's conception of music-drama as a continuous musical flow was fast becoming doctrine in progressive musical circles throughout the rest of Europe, he fiercely resisted the Wagnerian model and constructed his opera according to the more traditional structure that divided a work into a series of discrete numbers. Despite this traditional structure, *Khovanshchina* is innovative in some fundamental ways—for instance in Musorgsky's attempts here (though less so than in his earlier work) to accommodate the voice line to Russian speech intonations rather than to seek melodic beauty regardless of the words being sung.[16]

Doubtless Musorgsky's most daring musical experimentation lay in his harmonies, which, as it turns out, still remain little known to the public, which has heard his two major operas, as well as his orchestral songs, mainly in the instrumentation of Rimsky-Korsakov; as part of his heroic effort to preserve his friend's name, Rimsky worked assiduously to conventionalize what he viewed as Musorgsky's untutored musical style. Since stylistic progress has been defined largely through the example of Wagner and his followers—an example that Musorgsky strongly resisted—music historians are only now beginning to recognize that Musorgsky's own style has its own uniqueness and integrity (see Dahlhaus).

Although Schoenberg's use of the twelve-tone system to sustain an extended operatic work would count as progressive according to the prevailing post-Wagnerian model of music history, in its dramatic organization and its employment of large-scale visual and sonic effects *Moses und Aron* remains firmly within the tradition of the Wagnerian *Gesamtkunstwerk*. Despite the overwhelming image that Schoenberg presented to the world as an innovator, one might recall that the aesthetic behind the *Gesamtkunstwerk* goes back eighty years before the composition of *Moses und Aron* to Wagner's tract *Opera and Drama*, directly after which Wagner put his theories into practice by composing the *Ring*.[17] Certainly the economics of performing a grand-scale *Gesamtkunstwerk*, even if it does not deter the production of the Wagnerian music-dramas,

which audiences have now quite assimilated, must make any impresario think twice about mounting a work with as difficult a
musical texture as *Moses und Aron.*

As I have tried to demonstrate thus far, our understanding of
how an opera embodies history must go considerably beyond a
study of its words and music alone. *La clemenza di Tito* serves as a
particularly striking example, not only because the historical occasion for which the opera was composed helps us understand why it
differs as greatly as it does from Mozart's other later operas, but
also because the text that Mozart set resonates with meanings
associated with earlier historical occasions widely separated in
time. Metastasio, who served as official poet—*poeta cesareo*—at
the imperial court in Vienna, originally wrote the libretto (first set
by the composer Antonio Caldara) to celebrate the name-day of
Charles VI in 1734. In the compliments that the text metes out to
rulers who practice clemency, Metastasio, like other court-ap-
pointed poets during the age of absolute monarchy, succeeded at
once in pleasing his employer and making a didactic statement
that anybody could call morally impeccable.

It is significant that Voltaire, while arguing the superiority of
Italian to French recitative in 1748, picked the two most memorable moments from Metastasio's libretto—Titus's confrontation with
the guilt-ridden Sextus and the subsequent monologue in which
the Emperor deliberates whether to grant him clemency—as worthy of Corneille, Racine, and the Greek tragedians at their best.
Voltaire's singling out of these passages is far more than an aesthetic judgment—though even without any musical setting these
lines read quite movingly—but it is also a political recommendation, as Voltaire makes quite clear in pointing out that Titus's
monologue "should serve as an eternal lesson for kings."[18] The
real-life emperor for whom Metastasio had written his libretto was
in fact known for humane qualities similar to those of Titus, though
it is also thought that Metastasio's compliments were intended to
soothe him for losses he had recently suffered on the battlefield (see
Wandruszka 187–88). Certainly Voltaire would not have viewed a
Baroque-style ruler such as Charles VI as an embodiment of Enlightenment ideas. Moreover, the ruler for whom Mozart composed
his opera undid some of the famous reforms of his late brother,
Joseph II,[19] who has provided the model of the enlightened despot
that every school-child learns.

Nor would anybody have used the term *enlightened* in its eighteenth-century sense to characterize Cardinal Richelieu, who, nearly a century before Metastasio's text, was the original recipient of the political message intended by the lines that Voltaire praised. As Voltaire well knew, Metastasio's libretto derives much of its plot and above all its treatment of clemency from Corneille's great play *Cinna*, which, although ostensibly about the Emperor Augustus's clemency toward the conspirator Cinna, would have been viewed by its audiences in the early 1640s as a political statement directed to Cardinal Richelieu in his efforts to stabilize the French monarchy against conspiratorial threats.[20] Metastasio's libretto, one might add, also manages to incorporate elements from two of Racine's tragedies, *Andromaque* and *Bérénice*, of which the latter, like the libretto, presents a benign portrait of the Emperor Titus (see Moberly 288–89, 295–97). I mention these many intertextual connections in order to stress how strongly Mozart's opera, composed as it was a hundred fifty years after Corneille's play, creates the illusion of an ahistorical, timeless world in which rulers from widely different periods are interchangeable with one another and in which absolute rule is made to seem noble if it is sufficiently tempered by magnanimity—also in which artists earn their places in the hierarchy, or at least their livelihoods, through the moral sentiments that they praise in and recommend to their employers.

From our post-Hegelian vantage-point, the timelessness that radiates from *La clemenza di Tito* is radically undercut by the historical realities that lurk beneath the noble images it offers of how rulers rule. Indeed, it would be tempting to note that the hundred-fifty-year span of the dramatic theme initiated by Corneille is co-existent with what history books call the age of absolute monarchy on the Continent. If Cardinal Richelieu stands at the beginning of a historical development, the reigning monarchs of Mozart's time stand quite conspicuously at its end. Note, for example, the political events that we can now view as backdrops to the opera. Three months before its first performance, Marie-Antoinette, sister of the monarch whom Mozart was honoring, lost her final opportunity to escape from France through her capture at Varennes, though she was not to be executed for another two years. Certainly the Emperor Leopold's sister by 1791 was in no position to disburse clemency or even the cake she had supposedly once recommended to a rebellious populace. Moreover, in late August, while Mozart was composing the opera, Leopold, together with the king of Prussia, issued the Declaration of Pillnitz: this turned out to be an ambiguous document, for although it intended to leave open the question of whether Austria would attack the French revolutionary government, it actually rallied the revolutionists to the point that, in the following year, they began the war that was to change the political structure of Europe for all time. Leopold himself died a natural death before the war started and only half a year after the operatic performance that had honored him; Mozart survived this performance by only three months, though not before completing *Die Zauberflöte*, a work that we now praise as an embodiment of Enlightenment humanitarianism.

In view of our own, quite selfconscious way of interpreting history, it is tempting to ask if Mozart could have been aware of the historical ironies surrounding the composition of *La clemenza di Tito* and the earlier uses of its text. I for one doubt that he concerned himself much with these matters, though he awed his contemporaries to the point that one observer at the coronation ceremonies declared he would prefer being Mozart to the new Emperor himself.[21] Although we have romanticized Mozart with the label *genius,* a term that his own example helped define for the romantic generation, it is difficult to assign him the prescience by which he could have understood the historical meanings of *La clemenza di Tito* in the way we are likely to construe them. Surely Mozart was too much a functionary of the social and economic system of the ancien régime to have reflected unduly about the political resonances of his operas as, say, Verdi and Musorgsky were to do during the next century. Certainly the revival of *La clemenza di Tito* in Prague to celebrate the accession of the Emperor Franz Josef during the revolutionary tensions of the year 1848 displayed a typically nineteenth-century reflectiveness, indeed pugnaciousness, about how art can make its political points.[22] The historical ironies to which Mozart doubtless remained oblivious at the opera's performance in 1791 are of course discernible only to those whose view of the past was shaped by that historical consciousness which first developed during the nineteenth century. From our present vantage point, it seems particularly striking—and also ironical—that a theme originating at the beginnings of absolute monarchy in France should be invoked once again in the revolutionary year 1848 to celebrate the coronation of an emperor who, as it turned out, was to continue ruling (though with considerably less than absolute power) until a year before the Russian Revolution.

The historical consciousness largely missing in *La clemenza di Tito* is of course central to *Khovanshchina*. This consciousness is, in fact, built into the musical style, not only, as I indicated earlier, in Musorgsky's attempt to imitate everyday Russian speech, but above all in his ability to differentiate musically between political factions and characters representing different moments in the historical process. For example, the brisk rhythm of the theme associated with the forces of Peter the Great provides a musical embodiment of the militant new order that will bring an end both to the factionalism of the past and to the traditional religious values represented by the Old Believers.[23] Contrasting with this theme are the wild choruses in act III sung by the Streltsy, the unruly and boisterous Moscow urban guard that Ivan Khovansky attempts to bring under his control and that must ultimately make way for the new order. But Musorgsky differentiates from both of these as well in his depiction of the Old Believers. Shortly before they burn to death in a mass suicide at the end of the opera, they chant in an archaic style which, though not based on the actual liturgy of the time, a Russian listener would associate with the old religion (Morosan 126–27). In a letter Musorgsky voiced his conviction that this chorus would create an impression "of old times and truth" (Leyda and Bertensson 277). To provide this impression Musorgsky researched both liturgical and folk music (Morosan 99–101, 103, 110–13, 123–27). The actual folksong that he inserts for his heroine, the Old Believer Marfa, in act III was quite familiar during Musorgsky's time and would probably have suggested a simple, timeless realm to contrast with the rapidly shifting worlds that clash with one another during the course of the opera.

Like a historical novelist such as Walter Scott, Musorgsky treats the outgoing order with a special pathos that is linked to a recognition of its inevitable defeat. It seems no accident that the parts of the opera most moving to listeners are those sung by the Old Believers as a group and by Marfa in particular.[24] Music, of course, can communicate this pathos with an immediacy impossible within narrative prose or even in spoken drama, though the latter form in the nineteenth century often introduced folk songs such as Marfa's to achieve this immediacy. Above all, the varying musical forms in which the warring factions in *Khovanshchina* express themselves enable Musorgsky to represent historical process in a way uniquely different from—and far more economical than—that of the historical novelists and philosophers of history of his century.

If I have implied that *Khovanshchina* propounds a view of history as process, I should add that by emphasizing the centrality of the populace rather than that of rulers and heroic individuals, it represents a peculiarly late nineteenth-century view of this process. In preparing the libretto for *Boris Godunov* Musorgsky had given the populace an even larger role than it had occupied in Pushkin's drama, which is itself regarded as a turning point in the formation of Russian historical consciousness.[25] In *Khovanshchina*, he went even further—to the point that no royalty even appears onstage in the later opera.[26] We know Peter the Great only obliquely through his soldiers, while the regent appears only by means of a letter recited by her minister and lover Galitsin. The most powerful individual roles in the opera, except for Marfa, who voices the plight of the Old Believers, are not rulers but political figures such as Ivan Khovansky and Dosifei, whom we witness actively controlling and attempting to lead their forces.

Through the opportunity it gives for the display of large choral forces, opera can characterize and even glorify the populace to a degree impossible in any other aesthetic form. But Musorgsky's attempt to center his opera around the masses represents far more than the exploitation of an artistic opportunity, as it did for the many nineteenth-century composers who used large choruses to sensationalize history. Rather, his concentration on the masses was an expression of political convictions dominant among the Russian intelligentsia during the 1860s and '70s—convictions that resulted, moreover, in a radical reinterpretation of the Russian past for which *Khovanshchina* provides a major example. The fact that the composer subtitled the opera "a folk music-drama" and did much of his own research into primary documents such as memoirs, letters and sermons, not to speak of the early music he sought out, is a testament to the power exerted by these convictions. The period that Musorgsky researched was of particular interest to historians of Musorgsky's time, for the composer's generation viewed the years just before the ascendancy of Peter the Great as the end of an authentically Russian culture that Peter was to transform irrevocably into an appendage to Western European culture.[27]

The early years during which Musorgsky worked at the opera were also the time that the populist movement reached its height for the younger members of the intelligentsia; during 1873–74 many educated young people went to backward villages to raise peasant consciousness and at the same time to savor the spirit of ancient Russian customs.[28] If *Khovanshchina* had been available to them, they might well have thought they could hear the song of the earth in the folksongs and choral outpourings. *"The finest traits in man's nature* and in *the mass of humanity,"* Musorgsky wrote as he began work on the opera, "tirelessly digging through these little-known regions and conquering them—that is the true mission of the artist" (Leyda and Bertensson 199). But the populist national-ism of *Khovanshchina* was something more than a local Russian phenomenon, for, as Isaiah Berlin puts it in his essay on this opera, the work shares "some of the ideas of William Morris, Ruskin, and Tolstoy: it was part of the opposition to commercialism on the one hand and timeless, contemplative aestheticism on the other." Ber-lin goes on to place *Khovanshchina* within an intellectual ambiance that "looks at history and anthropology for the unique, the individ-ual, the quintessential—the authentic core of a people, a move-ment, a period, a historic outlook" ("*Khovanshchina*" 34). What in one sense seems a wholly local enterprise is, as Berlin reminds us, part of an international movement—similar to the nineteenth-century mentality I discussed in the Prologue—that sought to grant universal significance to local particularities.

The panoramic scope that Musorgsky gave his national music-drama is distinctly missing in *Moses und Aron*. Although the forces that Schoenberg employs are overwhelming in their massiveness, Schoenberg's populace of Hebrews wandering through the Sinai desert is treated with none of the compassion Musorgsky grants his various factions. The crowd in Schoenberg functions as the willing participant in Aron's plot to exercise charismatic leadership over the masses. The central dramatic conflict within the opera is not between leader and followers but between the two brothers, Moses and Aron, who represent contrasting attitudes both to the nature of God's word and to the means by which this word should be trans-mitted. Whereas Moses is inarticulate and unable to communicate God's word adequately to the people, Aron communicates with them all too easily—to the point that he can manipulate them like children through playing on their desire to worship tangible im-ages such as the Golden Calf. Schoenberg uses two sharply diver-gent forms of expression to distinguish the two brothers. By com-municating in *Sprechstimme* within an otherwise operatic context, Moses in effect communicates his difficulty in reaching out to oth-ers. Boldly contrasting with Moses's way of speaking is the sinuous, even mellifluous tenor line of Aron, who expresses his trickiness in what is virtually a parody of traditional operatic discourse. At many points Schoenberg, by allowing the two brothers to speak simultaneously in their contrasting vocal forms, demonstrates how the range of expressive forms possible in opera allows him to characterize his figures with a directness impossible within non-musical drama (see Pamela White 152–53, 214–15, 224–25).

It may seem ironical that the *Sprechstimme* Schoenberg employs for the speeches of Moses and for the divine voice emanating from the Burning Bush should so powerfully express and represent what we are intended to view as inarticulate or inexpressible. Yet Schoenberg, like other modernist artists of his generation, is explicitly concerned with the nature of representation. Whereas a nineteenth-century composer such as Musorgsky could conceive himself representing historical events and processes in all their concreteness, Schoenberg in this opera provides not so much a representation of history as a representation of a problem. To put it another way, his thematic concern with the representability of God and with the inarticulateness of Moses becomes a way of foregrounding his formal concern with representation as an aesthetic problem.[29]

Despite the fact that *Moses und Aron* adopts the external form of Wagnerian music-drama, Schoenberg has shied away from the often chaotic variety of events that fill a nineteenth-century historical opera such as *Khovanshchina* or *Die Meistersinger,* and he has concentrated instead on working out the implications of the conflict between his two characters. To do so he has designed his drama with a mathematical precision analogous to that which he employed in creating the opera's musical structure out of a single twelve-tone row. A nineteenth-century composer surely would have drawn a greater variety of material than Schoenberg did from the biblical source, in which the conflict between Moses and Aron alternates with episodes that depict their collaboration. The rigor with which Schoenberg reduced and manipulated the narrative elements of his source (see Steck) did not allow for a rich and broad historical panorama. It is significant, for instance, that Schoenberg originally planned the work as an oratorio which, to judge from the libretto of this early version (never, as it turned out, set to music), would have been dramatically even more austere than the opera (see Pamela White 21, 92–112). The music of the Golden Calf scene, which Schoenberg considered the most "operatic" part of *Moses und Aron,*[30] does not, moreover, attempt to represent a recognizably Near Eastern world as do the many Orientalistic purple patches to be found in late nineteenth-century operas. One need only recall the Near Eastern intervals and rhythms of Musorgsky's Persian dance and compare these with those strange sounds from the Golden Calf scene, which by themselves would not tell an audience what historical milieu they are meant to evoke. Musorgsky calls upon his audience's associations with what they take to be Near Eastern music, just as he elsewhere claims to represent Russian speech patterns musically; as a result he creates the illusion that *Khovanshchina* allows a "real" world to unfold before us. By contrast, Schoenberg, like other modernist artists, questions the very basis by which we attribute reality to his representations.

Although Schoenberg radically narrows the field of action that had characterized historical operas during the preceding century, the fraternal conflict around which *Moses und Aron* is centered invites its audience to propose an extraordinarily wide range of meanings. As its origins in oratorio form suggest, *Moses und Aron* can be viewed foremost as a statement of religious faith—above all, faith in the monotheistic God who reveals himself to Moses and whose nature Aron perversely chooses to misread. In a letter written to Alban Berg during the composition of the opera Schoenberg admits the autobiographical nature of the work.[31] As a religious testament *Moses und Aron* is deeply embedded in history—first the personal history of its composer, who in the 1920s returned to Judaism after an early conversion to Christianity.[32]

As a narrative concerned with the return of the Jews to Palestine after long exile, the opera refers by implication to public history, above all to certain political and ideological controversies that Schoenberg had observed within the Zionist movement. Shortly before starting *Moses und Aron*, Schoenberg had, in fact, written a play, *Der biblische Weg* (The Biblical Way [1926–27]), which speculates on what might have happened if Theodor Herzl, the founder of the Zionist movement, had succeeded in implementing the so-called Uganda project. This project, espoused by Herzl, but rejected by the Zionist Congress in 1903 in favor of holding out until Palestine should become available, would have created an autonomous Jewish state in East Africa. Although Schoenberg's Herzl-like hero, named Max Aruns in the play, succeeds in founding his East African colony, he is later martyred as a result of a conspiracy instigated by Zionists who are opposed to any settlement except in Palestine itself. Just before Max Aruns undergoes martyrdom, a prophetic figure tells the hero that, as his name implies, he has unsuccessfully sought to combine two opposing types of leader— on the one hand the visionary Moses, on the other the pragmatic and cunning Aaron.[33] In moving from this play to the opera, Schoenberg took two decisive steps: first, he shifted from a contemporary to an ancient biblical setting, and, second, he separated the two leadership types that had been uncomfortably fused within Max Aruns and returned to the biblical archetypes themselves.

Behind the particularities of Jewish experience in *Moses und Aron* one can locate a larger, if also quite implicit, area of significance—namely, the coming to power of the Nazis. Schoenberg, one might remember, was living in Berlin at the time. The political atmosphere surrounding the composition of the opera was that of the last years of the Weimar Republic, a time during which Hitler was demonstrating how powerfully rhetoric could work to command the devotion of a restless, dissatisfied populace.[34] In view of the fascination felt at the time with the role of an individual leader in effecting change or creating stability within a culture, it is scarcely surprising to find a music-drama obsessed with a crisis in leadership, above all with the vulnerability of the masses to a charismatic leader such as Aron.

Beyond the religious and political levels one can also read *Moses und Aron* as an allegory of the avant-garde artist who, like Schoenberg himself in the guise of Moses, is too uncompromising and austere a figure to appeal readily to the public. In describing his conception of Moses to a correspondent, Schoenberg compared his figure to that of Michelangelo, adding, "He is not at all human" (*Briefe* 188). Moses's unbending refusal to allow idol-worship, like Schoenberg's break with the tonal system, thus becomes an act of visionary leadership against which the masses react with hostility and ingratitude, little recognizing the necessity of this act for the benefit of future generations. By contrast, Aron, like those artists who have continued to pursue the tonal system in music and traditional modes of representation in fiction and painting, pursues leadership with a slickness of manner that sacrifices later recognition in favor of immediate popularity. As an allegory about the fate of the artist *Moses und Aron* stands as a peculiarly modern type of historical drama, for in our own century the political actions within the aesthetic realm have achieved the status of public history analogous to those that take place in that area we have traditionally termed political.

What holds together these seemingly diverse areas of significance—the religious, the political, and the aesthetic—is Schoenberg's concern for how a leader can translate his visions effectively
within the practical world. "A Four-Point Program for Jewry," a
document that Schoenberg wrote in English in 1938 but that was
not published until 1979, explicitly links the poetical and the aesthetic realms to indicate what the composer considers the proper
conduct of a leader. For example, he criticizes Herzl for refusing to
play a dictatorial role and instead allowing the Zionist Congress to
overrule him on the Uganda issue. By contrast, he points to his
own conduct as leader of an avant-garde musical group, the Society for Private Musical Performances: "I was a kind of dictator,
1920, in a musical society erected by myself in my ideas." When a
dissident faction within the society sought to oppose his principles,
Schoenberg tells us with pride that he clamped down ruthlessly: "I
did something which under other circumstances could be called
illegal: I dissolved the whole society, built a new one, accepted only
such members who were in perfect agreement with my artistic
principles and excluded the entire opposition" (55). If the political
power that Schoenberg exercised within the aesthetic realm seems
a small matter in comparison with the exercise of power over
masses of people, one might note that in this same document
Schoenberg briefly refers to certain ambitions that he himself en-
tertained to exercising leadership over a large Jewish movement
(51). A few months after Hitler's accession to power in 1933 he had
in fact written a letter in German to several Jewish musicians
expressing first his fear for the survival of the Jews and then the
ambitions he harbored to rectify the situation: "Therefore, I wish
to create a movement to bring the Jews together once more as a
people and to unite them as a state within an enclosed territory"
(*Brief über* 495). Schoenberg's political aspirations, though they
never became translated into real-life actions, were scarcely a whim
of the moment, for some fifteen years later he drafted a document
(still unpublished) in English announcing the formation of a Jewish
government in exile, of which, in words that betray a confidence in
his right to lead similar to that of his character Moses, he declares
himself president: "Here I am, Arn[old] Sch[oenberg], the president of the Government in Exile of the Jewish Nation on a ship
which we have received through the generosity of Pr[esident]
Tr[uman], the Am[erican] Government and the Am[erican] People."[35]

After reading this document, one begins to wonder how many authors of historical dramas have themselves, at least in their private moments, sought to assume the public roles they had created for their famous characters. And one also suspects that the dictatorial powers that Schoenberg had managed to wield successfully over a small group of avant-garde musicians would likely have had disastrous consequences if exercised in the larger world, and that, like his character Max Aruns, the composer might have headed toward a martyr's death. In view of Schoenberg's own evident will to power, one can view *Moses und Aron* as a battleground between the more lofty aspects of power represented by Moses and those meaner aspects represented by Aron. By separating these two aspects of power and placing them within an explicitly religious context, the opera succeeds in idealizing the role of the leader and providing a transcendental authorization for the power he attempts to exercise. The defeat that Moses encounters as a result of Aron's machinations and of the people's fickleness comes to seem a victory, for the providential perspective through which we are asked to view the work makes us recognize the ultimate vindication of Moses's unbending stance on monotheism and representation. The autobiographical and the "religious-philosophical" meanings of the opera that Schoenberg suggests at separate points in his correspondence are thus brought together by means of the composer's attempt to find a divine sanction for the calling he felt to exercise leadership.

In the course of this essay I have tried to show that depictions of history in opera are themselves very much implicated in what we take to be history itself. Schoenberg's obsession with power and leadership within both the musical community and the larger world; Musorgsky's coupling of his generation's populist sentiments with his own version of nineteenth-century historicism in his picture of seventeenth-century political conflicts; Mozart's celebration of the next-to-last Holy Roman Emperor by means of a text celebrating an earlier emperor and itself echoing a text that praises a founder of·absolute monarchy in France—and all these texts purportedly about the first and the tenth ancient Roman emperors: such entanglements are typical of the engagements between opera and the public realm throughout the history of the form.

Similar entanglements mark those other art forms that seek to represent history—history plays, historical novels, historical paintings, and also, as we have come to recognize in recent years,

those historical narratives that disclaim fictiveness in favor of telling it as it really was. What separates historical operas from these
other historical forms is the essential lack of seriousness that has
traditionally been attributed to opera in comparison with the other
genres that make claims upon history. We tend to think of opera as
"sensuous" rather than intellectual, as a mode of entertainment
rather than of enlightenment. (These very dichomoties are themselves products of that older aesthetic whose underlying assumptions I sought to articulate in the preceding essays of this book.)
Even though historical narratives that claim to be telling the truth
have been taken more seriously than the more overtly fictive forms,
at particular times—for example, in the historical novel and in
historical painting during the early nineteenth century—these fictive forms achieved a high degree of prestige for their ability to
represent aspects of the past that elude the more truth-directed
modes of historical narration. Opera has rarely been accorded such
prestige;[36] indeed, the phrase "historical opera" itself sounds awk-
ward—partly because of the lack of seriousness generally ascribed
to opera, partly also because for a long stretch of operatic history
all non-comic operas pretended to draw their materials from history.

Throughout this essay I have tried to show that the seriousness
of an opera's engagement with history can be understood not simply by examining the work itself, but by asking precisely how it
speaks out as history. The history we see (and hear!) in opera exists
at once inside and outside the work—above all, in that interplay
between what we ordinarily call a work of art and its context. The
history we experience in Mozart's coronation opera derives, on one
level, from its celebration of an idealized ruler's power to reconcile
dissident factions and, on another level, from our awareness of the
gap that separates Mozart's idealization from a rapidly changing
world that would soon develop new images—for example, those of
Fidelio little more than a decade later—to make sense of its political life. The history voiced in *Khovanshchina* is the clash of forces
that speak in diverse musical styles to represent diverse stages
within the historical process. The history that emanates from *Moses
und Aron* reveals the composer's despair at the difficulties of political leadership in the modern world; after having represented these
difficulties in the two irreconcilable sides of his dramatic hero Max
Aruns, Schoenberg in the opera divided his hero into two figures
who speak in distinct vocal styles that themselves define distinct

types of leadership. The ceremonial elements that opera can exploit, together with its use of musical styles to define conflicting attitudes, allow the form to create images of history uniquely different from those we find in other forms of historical representation. Like historical drama and the historical novel, opera thrives on the conflicts of history—yet the very sensuousness that prevents it from being taken as seriously as these other genres also allows it to represent these conflicts with an intensity and a transformative power impossible to achieve without musical means. Through its peculiar mode of representation, opera tests and expands our notion of what properly belongs to that domain we call history.

FIVE

The Literature in History: Danton's Death in the Texts of Revolutions

Everybody familiar with the commentary on *Danton's Death* will remember seeing the following quotation from one of Büchner's letters in virtually every serious consideration of the play:

> I studied the history of the Revolution. I felt myself crushed under the frightful fatalism of history. I find in human nature a horrifying sameness, in the human condition an inescapable force, granted to all and to no one. The individual merely foam on the waves, greatness a mere accident, the mastery of genius a puppet play, a ridiculous struggle against an iron law: to recognize it is our highest achievement, to control it is impossible.
>
> [Ich studirte die Geschichte der Revolution. Ich fühlte mich wie zernichtet unter dem gräßlichen Fatalismus der Ge-

schichte. Ich finde in der Menschennatur eine entsetzliche
Gleichheit, in den menschlichen Verhältnissen eine unab-
wendbare Gewalt, Allen und Keinem verliehen. Der Einzelne
nur Schaum auf der Welle, die Größe ein bloßer Zufall, die
Herrschaft des Genies ein Puppenspiel, ein lächerliches Rin-
gen gegen ein ehernes Gesetz, es zu erkennen das Höchste, es
zu beherrschen unmöglich.] (*Sämtliche* 2:425–26)

Even if one were unaware of the play's extensive and controversial interpretive history, one would recognize the documentary
importance of a statement such as this one, which appeared in a
letter that Büchner wrote to his fiancée some nine or ten months
before the composition of the play. Here, after all, one finds the
author expressing his *own* attitude toward the French Revolution
without the problems one encounters interpreting a drama in which
a succession of attitudes, many of them seemingly impossible to
reconcile, are voiced toward the same historical event. With whom,
for instance, does Büchner expect us to sympathize in his play?
With Robespierre and Saint-Just, to whom he extends so little
sympathy, yet who, one might at first think, should be heroes to an
activist radical such as Büchner? With Danton and his friends,
whose world-weary resignation and refusal to continue the Revolution scarcely seem compatible with the writer's recent political
actions—or even with his later radical pronouncements? With the
crowd on the streets, for whose economic plight he shows understanding but whose violent sentiments and manipulability hardly
entitle them to heroic status?

These questions have proved hard enough for the play's commentators to deal with over the years, and it is no accident that
those who have written on *Danton's Death* have reached eagerly for
the letter to give them whatever concrete evidence they needed to
prove what side Büchner was really taking in the play. Yet even if
one ignores the considerable time span between the letter and the
play, or the fact that *between* letter and play Büchner co-authored
his radical manifesto *Der hessische Landbote* and helped lead what
turned out to be an aborted uprising of the poor against the Hessian state—even if one ignores these matters, one encounters interpretive difficulties as soon as one tries to accommodate the
letter to what one takes to be the meaning of the play. With its
fatalistic conception of the individual, above all his helplessness in
the face of historical events, it seems most obviously in harmony

with only a single, though also quite prominent strand in the play—namely, the plight of the title character and his friends as they face the guillotine.

Certainly for those readers who have opted for a conservative or an apolitical view of Büchner and his play the so-called "fatalism" letter has proved a most convenient piece of evidence. When Karl Viëtor, in an essay of 1934, quoted the letter, he used it to separate Büchner decisively from his radical contemporaries: "He [Büchner] thus saw the Revolution quite otherwise from what he had expected and from the way it was presented by his contemporaries who constituted Young Germany" (182). With Büchner's own attitude toward political action defined according to the passivity expressed in the letter, it becomes easy for an interpreter such as Viëtor to claim an anti-activist, indeed a thoroughly apolitical meaning for the play itself: "This drama," Viëtor writes, "has no activist message; it does not glorify the French Revolution or indeed any revolution whatsoever" (174). Behind these statements we note an aesthetic that rigorously separates the realm of art from that of politics: "What we have here is neither propaganda nor polemic; rather it is literature [Dichtung], pure literature" (175–76).

Viëtor's once-influential study of *Danton's Death* stands near the beginning of what one might call the passivist interpretation of the play, an interpretation that ascribes a message to the play as a whole by linking the fatalism letter to the eloquent emotional outpourings of Danton and his friends in the play's prison scenes. This interpretation has known a number of variants depending upon what thought systems were in fashion at a particular time. Thus, Robert Mühlher's essay of 1951, significantly entitled "Georg Büchner und die Mythologie des Nihilismus" (97–145), uses the fatalism letter to place not only the play but Büchner's work as a whole within an anti-rationalist, anti-democratic tradition for which he invokes such names as Novalis, Schopenhauer, Bergson, and his own contemporary Karl Jaspers. When Mühlher claims that "Büchner's new, deeper, pessimistic insight into the 'frightful fatalism of history' removes him forever from the liberal and democratic camp" (100), one notes how convenient the letter has proven for those who seek to claim Büchner for their own conservative positions. Even the chapter I wrote on *Danton's Death* in 1963 in my own book on Büchner, though it argued for a multi-perspectival approach to the play, used the fatalism letter to demonstrate Büchner's anticipation of the absurd view of life encountered in Kafka and other modernist writers.

It is scarcely surprising that the fatalism letter has proved a formidable challenge to critics of the left, especially if they are intent on locating an activist element in *Danton's Death*. Thus, writing for the centenary of Büchner's death in 1937, Georg Lukács, in a head-on confrontation with Viëtor's interpretation of the play, finds two distinct ways to justify the work's revolutionary content. First, though he admits that the letter and the play voice a real philosophical crisis, he attributes this crisis to an earlier, pre-Marxist stage of the historical process: thus, both letter and play reveal the inability of an older, essentially eighteenth-century form of materialism to understand history. Second, to separate Büchner from the "heroic pessimism" that Viëtor had attributed both to the author and his title character, Lukács points to some verbal differences between the sentiments of the letter and those expressed by Danton in the play: whereas Danton echoes only the passive sentiments within the letter, he nowhere displays Büchner's own activist ambition to understand the fatalism of history that Lukács locates in the letter's line "to recognize it is our highest achievement" (*Deutsche* 79–80).

Lukács's efforts to defend Büchner as a thinker of the left pale beside those, a full generation later, of Thomas Michael Mayer, who brings a vast array of philological tools, including considerable archival research, to reassess the meaning of the letter as well as the political import of the play. For example, Mayer cites thinkers from the Enlightenment to Büchner's own time to demonstrate that the term *fatalism* had not yet, when the letter was written, been distinguished from the later, quite separate notion of determinism, that, among other things, it referred to those newer historians who saw history as created by larger forces rather than by individuals ("Büchner und Weidig" 86–91).[1] Moreover, Mayer points out the word *fatalité* in a speech of 1832 by the radical thinker Auguste Blanqui, who linked the tragedy of the revolution to the victory of the middle rather than the impoverished class (91–92). Indeed, Mayer's researches yield a new image of Büchner's political affiliations, for by linking him with the followers of Babeuf, especially Buonarroti and Blanqui (68–72), he is able to portray Büchner as a precommunist economic egalitarian and thus to make sense out of Büchner's evident disdain within the play toward the party of Robespierre, who, as portrayed in the play, showed little concern for economic change (108–19).[2]

I have discussed these various attempts to reconcile Büchner's letter to his play not to attempt still another reconciliatory gesture, but rather to ask some questions about the attitude we characteristically take to the process of interpreting individual literary works. To approach these questions in the most drastic possible way, I shall attempt, in the course of this essay, to break down the generic and evaluative distinctions we customarily make between a literary work and its sources, on the one hand, and, on the other, between the work and its subsequent interpretive history. As a result, I also hope to raise some questions about the status, first, of what we call literary texts, and, second, about the relations of such texts to those we label historical, including those texts we call the "events" of history.

Ever since the institutionalization of literary scholarship a century ago, a certain distinction, as I shall develop in more detail in essay 9, has prevailed between the literary work and what has often been labeled its surrounding context. The work itself has enjoyed a privileged status; indeed, literary scholarship has justified its existence over the years through the expertise it has claimed in preserving, elucidating and transmitting the various texts that make up the canon. The attitudes toward art that prevailed in the Western world during the foundation years of literary scholarship— attitudes I tried to describe in the Prologue and the first three essays of this book—have left an ongoing legacy: the great texts to which scholars devote their custodial efforts can be assumed to possess a certain coherence, and they are often in fact defended by organic metaphors derived from the idealist poetics of the early nineteenth century. This coherence has sometimes been defined in terms of what we are to see as the text's meaning: if, that is, we can assign some sort of meaning to the text, then we can also assume that it has a certain coherence. Moreover, the privileged status that the canonical texts have been given often manifests itself with what we are meant to experience as a magical aura, an aura that is supposedly lacking in texts of a not specifically literary sort. Thus, according to the institutional conventions of literary scholarship, the so-called context surrounding the great literary text, the documents attached to the author's biography, the earlier texts (some themselves canonical) that have influenced the great text under consideration, the intellectual and social milieu that the author somehow absorbed, must perforce occupy a secondary status. By a perverse irony, however, these secondary materials, as one might note from such words as *influential* and *absorbed* in the preceding

sentence, were often deemed to exercise a "causal" effect upon the
primary texts they were meant to elucidate. Yet this secondary
status of the contextual materials functions as a necessary part of
the institutional arrangements within our field: it guarantees the
superior status of the great work under consideration at the same
time that it demonstrates the work's coherence. Text and context
come to have a kind of symbiotic relationship to one another, each
of them, in effect, needing the other to justify the particular attention we pay to it.

Let us return to the relationship between Büchner's fatalism
letter and the play that it claims to elucidate. Among the items we
use in classifying a literary work's context, a letter by the author
on the same subject as the work is considered, at least by accepted
institutional rules, to provide special evidence for assessing the
work's meaning. Only the author's direct comment on the work
(and Büchner has several such comments on *Danton's Death* written after the completion of the play) would ordinarily seem of
greater relevance. From an institutional point of view it scarcely
matters if the contextual evidence is able to elicit quite contradictory results—as the fatalism letter does—when it is applied to the
work by different scholars, and in this particular instance by scholars with quite distinct political agendas. What matters most is that
the letter seems to provide solid evidence of the author's attitude
toward his subject and that, as a result, the letter can help demonstrate the coherence and the meaning, not to speak of the importance, of the work under consideration.

But what if the coherence that we attribute to the work can be
demonstrated only at such a cost that the demonstration leaves its
readers uneasy about the results? At least one study of Büchner
claims several forms of incoherence in *Danton's Death*—for example, the play's inability to reconcile the political Danton with
the romantic, *Weltschmerz*-minded Danton, as well as its lack of
what the critic calls "real dramatic development" (Peacock 194)—
and simply concludes from this that Büchner must have been suf-
fering from "poetic-dramatic immaturity" (191). One could well
imagine this negative judgment taken only a step further to produce a deconstructive reading of the play in the recent American
mode. Such a reading would exploit the irreconcilable elements
that have plagued the play's interpreters to conclude not, like the
above condemnation, that the play reveals its author as immature,
but rather that, regardless of Büchner's intent or of the social and

intellectual milieu out of which *Danton's Death* speaks, its interpretive difficulties become paradigmatic of the tensions and indeterminacies inherent within language itself at all times, in all places.

Must we be tied to a concept of art that demands the demonstration, within a particular work, of total coherence, or of a readily definable meaning, or, if we fail to find such coherence or meaning, to use this failure to condemn the work or to celebrate it as representative of some cultural universal? Let me suggest that the difficulties within the interpretive history of *Danton's Death* may have at least something to do with the genre within which Büchner chose to work, namely, the history play, and, in this instance, a loosely organized form of the genre that Büchner took to be Shakespearean. This genre encouraged him to allow a multiplicity of voices to speak without the need of an overriding voice to guide the audience's responses at every point. The more classically organized forms of historical drama—for example, the plays of Corneille or of the later Schiller—go considerably further than *Danton's Death* in providing guidelines to help the audience determine what they supposedly mean, for they are usually explicit about the particular values the audience is expected to admire, even if their heroes carry these values to excess.

The peculiar difficulties that readers have encountered in assessing the diverse voices within the play are particularly evident when we set *Danton's Death* next to another work on the revolution in a wholly different genre. I refer to Carlyle's *The French Revolution*, subtitled simply *A History*, though in this instance a historical prose narrative with specifically epic ambitions, indeed with many of the rhetorical conventions that we traditionally associate with the long epic poem. Büchner's little more than month-long labor on his play took place, I might add, at precisely the time that Carlyle was in the middle of his several-year-long labor.

Yet two works could scarcely seem more different than *The French Revolution* and *Danton's Death:* the first an overdetermined narrative whose overbearing, prophetic authorial voice is busily imposing order from above upon the chaos it purports to depict; the second, an underdetermined set of dialogues that, given its genre, eschews a firm guiding framework. One need only note Carlyle's portrayal of Danton during the September massacres: "See Danton enter;—the black brows clouded, the colossus-figure tramping heavy; grim energy looking from all features of the rugged man! Strong is that grim Son of France and Son of Earth; a

Reality and not a Formula he too; and surely now if ever, being hurled *low* enough, it is on the Earth and on Realities that he rests" (490). However we choose to assess Büchner's assessment of Danton's role in history, nowhere in the play can we expect the narrative control that Carlyle, in his selfconsciously Miltonic mode, grimly exercises throughout.

Moreover, whereas Carlyle imposes a spiritual meaning upon the often ugly details that he recounts (his condemned figures, whatever their political affiliations, whether king or Jacobin, go to their deaths as Christlike martyrs), Büchner makes little attempt to spiritualize matter, indeed gives the illusion that the historical details he allows to be enacted can and must speak for themselves. The ideological disagreements I have cited among Büchner's commentators would be inconceivable among Carlyle's. When Treitschke, in his history of nineteenth-century Germany, compared these two works, he praised Carlyle for "passionately expressing his moral disgust" at the Terror while expressing his own disgust at Büchner (whose artistic talent he otherwise acknowledged) for "glorifying the Revolution" (4:434); although the German historian doubtless understood the political import in the text of his fellow-conservative, his all-too-pat assessment of Büchner's point of view derives more from his knowledge of the German writer's political activities than from the text of his play.[3]

Let us, for the sake of this argument, think of *Danton's Death* not so much as an enshrined work that stands out as different in kind from other works, but as one among a succession of texts both before and after it, texts that echo, rewrite, absorb one another in a continuing verbal interplay. Thus, the multiple voices within this play become a kind of replay of earlier voices and an anticipation of later voices representing a wide array of historical contexts. Throughout the play, for example, we remain aware of type-scenes common to earlier historical dramas. Robespierre's speech wooing the common people (*Sämtliche* 1:15–16) restages such familiar scenes as Brutus and Antony vying for the assent of the populace in *Julius Caesar* or Menenius quelling the people at the beginning of *Coriolanus*. The street scenes in which the people express their woes echo scenes in both these plays as well in Goethe's *Egmont* and Grabbe's *Napoleon*. In its dramatic structure the confrontation between Danton and Robespierre (*Sämtliche* 1:26–27) has less in common with the brief scene depicted in Büchner's immediate historical sources than with the classic confrontation scenes between leaders in a succession of historical plays from *Antony and Cleopatra* to *Maria Stuart*. The echoes we hear from earlier dramas go well beyond those specifically associated with history plays: the suicide of Danton's wife Julie (*Sämtliche* 1:72–73)—the most conspicuously unhistorical moment in the play, for Danton's widow, actually named Louise, remarried and outlived even Büchner—evokes the love-death by poison of her namesake in *Romeo and Juliet*. Moreover, the Shakespearean dramatic structure that Büchner sought to recapture is one that has been thoroughly mediated by the loosely structured German Shakespearean imitations of the Sturm und Drang period—with the result that *Danton's Death* evokes at once the plays of the 1770s and the actual Shakespearean plays that stand behind them.

The earlier dramas that speak to us through *Danton's Death* constitute only one set of voices that we can identify. The historical narratives and documents of the French Revolution that Büchner absorbed within his play create still another set—to the point that in many sections of the play, above all in the political debates, we are never quite sure as we read whether the words originated from Büchner's pen or from his immediate sources. Few literary works of the past two centuries have elicited such detailed source study as has *Danton's Death*. And few—until the advent, in the 1960s, of documentary drama, itself a form shaped by the example of Büchner's play—are so thoroughly suffused with the materials the author read as is this play. At least a sixth of *Danton's Death* consists of literal transfer from or close paraphrase of other texts; it is a critical commonplace, in fact, to refer to the montage technique that Büchner employed in mixing together his source materials within his text.

In view of the present argument, it seems particularly striking to find that the historical materials absorbed within *Danton's Death* themselves derive from quite distinct temporal and even ideological contexts. In the way that materials drawn from different historical moments are juxtaposed, the play resembles certain European cities in which buildings representing diverse architectural styles from many periods stand unselfconsciously next to one another. To illustrate this diversity of materials, I shall move gradually backward in time from the writing of the play. The most recent materials that Büchner employed are several statements on the Revolution from Heine's recent writings on French politics and art. They include, for example, an apostrophe to Camille Desmoulins and a distinction between the sensualism of the party of Voltaire and the spirituality of Rousseauists, a distinction that Heine employs to castigate Robespierre;[4] in Heine, more than in any other source, Büchner found a means of reconciling hedonism with radical politics.

By far the most extensive sources that Büchner grafted onto his play go back to the decade preceding the July revolution. These consist of three narrative histories, two of them French, a multi-volume version by Adolphe Thiers and a short rendering by his closely allied contemporary François-Auguste Mignet. Both represent a "liberal" view within the context of Restoration politics, and both came from authors who were to play a role in instituting the July monarchy.[5] Büchner, a fervent republican during his student years in the France of Louis-Philippe, could not have identified with their politics nor with the crude sensationalism of his third extended source, Karl Strahlheim's *Die Geschichte unserer Zeit*— yet these voices from the 1820s supplied him with most of the concrete historical details he needed, including long passages from Robespierre's speeches quoted in Strahlheim.[6] Certainly the "fatalistic" view of history in their narrative made its way into *Danton's Death* (as well as into the fatalism letter itself), though Büchner would have been quite aware that the same Thiers who so richly fed his own account of the Revolution was, in his role as interior minister to Louis-Philippe, responsible for putting down a workers' uprising in Paris a month after the writing of the letter and several months before Büchner's own uprising in Hesse. (This was of course the same Thiers who, long after Büchner's death, outdid his earlier acts of repression by destroying the Paris Commune in 1871.)

But Büchner also went back to certain eyewitness accounts of the Revolution dating from the very period about which Büchner was writing. These include, among others, the memoirs of Joachim Vilate, a mysterious figure close to the Dantonists, and Camille Desmoulins's correspondence as well as his periodical *Le vieux Cordelier*,[7] perhaps also a quote from Babeuf (Mayer, "Büchner und Weidig" 110–11). Although the echoes from these early documents are few in number—far less than from the narrative histories of the 1820s—they must have given Büchner the assurance that the language he was evoking was rooted in the very events he sought to render, that, to echo the title of the Prologue to this book, he and his subsequent readers were really "experiencing history."

Yet the historical echoes that scholars have uncovered go back even further in time than the events Büchner depicted, for they include at least two writers of the Enlightenment, Diderot and Holbach. From Diderot (probably transmitted by means of Goethe's translation) Büchner drew a formulation of realist aesthetics voiced not only in the play (*Sämtliche* 1:11), but also in the discussion on art in *Lenz* and in his own letters (Mayer, "Buchner und Weidig" 76–82). In Holbach Büchner found a voice for the materialist sentiments uttered in the play by Thomas Payne and Saint-Just (Dedner 367–74). It is as though Büchner felt the need to return to the intellectual origins of the Revolution as a means of displaying the play's realist credentials.

Yet the image I have just given of distinct temporal layers embedded within *Danton's Death* may well sound too systematic to fit one's notions of how Büchner used the texts associated with the Revolution within his play. After all, these quotations appear in no particular order, and it is sometimes unclear whether Büchner is quoting from an early document or from a much later recounting based on this document. Perhaps I should put the question another way and ask not simply how the text of *Danton's Death* absorbed the texts of the Revolution, but how Büchner himself would have perceived the revolutionary past. Any answer one comes up with would show a jumble of perceptions, many of them irreconcilable with one another in any ordinary way—which may also help us account for that analogous jumble of diverse, seemingly irreconcilable voices we hear in the play.

At the time that *Danton's Death* was composed, Büchner stood forty-one years removed from the events he was depicting—exactly the time span that separates us from the beginnings of the Cold War and, to cite a particular event in this war, the Berlin airlift of 1948. If one measures Büchner's distance in time from the beginning of the Revolution, an equivalent calculation would take us to the middle of World War II, for example, to the battle of Stalingrad. I mention these modern events only because they could not possibly exercise an effect on any twenty-one-year-old today that the various stages of the French Revolution exercised on Büchner and, indeed, on many others of his generation.

For the French Revolution in the early nineteenth century still maintained the status of an inaugural event, a new birth analogous to the birth of Christ, though an event that also, in view of its later stages, suggested that the newly created world was flawed, indeed that, perhaps soon after its birth, it was even coming to its end. No event of our own time has exercised as powerful an effect on the general populace, not even the first nuclear bomb, though the Holocaust has doubtless had a similar end-of-the-world effect on Jews, even on contemporary Jews of Büchner's age who did not personally experience it at the time it occurred. (One could well imagine a twenty-one-year-old Jew today reading some books on the Holocaust and then writing a letter very much like Büchner's fatalism letter.)

Moreover, for a young person with Büchner's radical commitments, choosing the French Revolution as the subject of his first play was like choosing an event from one's own national history. For a more nationalist, conservative-minded writer of the early nineteenth century, an analogous act would have been the writing of a Hohenstaufen drama or, to cite an event that Büchner had once celebrated in a school-exercise (*Sämtliche* 2:7–16), a play about the martyrdom of four hundred Pforzheim soldiers during the Thirty Years War. Just as Shakespeare in his English histories had at once celebrated his nation's triumphs and faced up to its failures, so Büchner could display a significant segment of the Revolution in both its greatness and its horror at once. If the negative aspects of Büchner's portrayal have seemed more prominent than the positive ones in recent times, one must also remember that Shakespeare's histories leave far more powerful evidences of failure than triumph in their readers' memories.

The perceptions of the Revolution that Büchner had stored in his mind must themselves have constituted a jumble, for they came from sources every bit as diverse as the particular sources he echoed in the words of his play. We know, for example, that during his adolescent years he heard his father read from Karl Strahlheim's *Geschichte unserer Zeit* aloud to the family in the evening (Büchner, *Werke* 567). Strahlheim (actually a pseudonym for Johann Konrad Friederich) had served in Napoleon's army, just as Büchner's father himself had. As history, his colorfully written and lengthy work, which appeared serially during the 1820s, was directed to a popular audience and would likely have stimulated the imagination of the young Büchner however much the latter may have come to disagree with Strahlheim's often sensationalized treatment of particular events during the Terror.

But Büchner had also absorbed the standard German nationalistic texts of his time. His school essay on the massacre of the Pforzheim troops borrows as liberally from Fichte's *Reden an die deutsche Nation* as *Danton's Death* borrows from its multiple sources (Mayer, "Eine kurze Chronik" 363). Yet although this text, composed when he was sixteen, celebrates a heroic German event, it also briefly celebrates an analogous event from the French Revolution, namely the refusal of a shipload of French sailors to surrender during Dumouriez's invasion of the Low Countries in 1793 (*Sämtliche* 2:8–9).

As a result of his participation, during his student years in Strasbourg, in the "Societé des droits de l'homme et du citoyen," Büchner must have felt that the Revolution could once again renew itself after its long interregnum. Everything that had passed before—the Robespierre dictatorship, the Directory, the Napoleonic regime, the Restoration, the July monarchy—could be swept aside as the Revolution assumed its new course, this time with an emphasis on the economic equality that had eluded its original leaders. Yet the repressive forces that had aborted the uprising he himself had led—forces that resulted in his own arrest and in his writing his play while hiding from the police—must have caused him to reassess his hopes just as the hopes of his play's characters had been shattered as the Revolution moved through its various stages.

The movement from hope to disillusionment was accompanied by another type of movement, namely, the shifts in perception that Büchner must have experienced as he moved back and forth between two quite distinct political cultures. The first of these was his native Hesse, a backwater still characterized by the repressions characteristic of Restoration Europe. The second was Strasbourg, site of his university studies and of secret groups that could endow ideas drawn from the French Revolution with a new life. As Büchner moved between Hesse and Strasbourg from 1831 to 1834, he must have felt a temporal dislocation resulting from the ways that each of these cultures viewed the world and postulated the possibilities of change. Indeed, his own attempt to establish a secret society on the French model in Giessen and then to help prepare a local revolt, together with the catastrophic failure of this attempt immediately preceding the composition of his play, can perhaps explain the dramatic juxtaposition of divergent voices that have proved so difficult for many of his commentators to reconcile.

The profusion of earlier texts and personal perceptions that nourished *Danton's Death* is matched in variety by a profusion of later texts and interpretations that Büchner's play itself helped to

generate. Just as few works of the past two centuries have been fed
by earlier texts as thoroughly as this play, few have experienced as
wide-ranging and sustained a reception as *Danton's Death*. Its impact upon a long succession of literary movements from the Natu-
ralists through the followers of Brecht has become a commonplace
of literary history. The play's various interpretations on the stage
over the years themselves could help sketch out a history of the
German theater since the beginning of this century. An extensive
body of commentary, not only on *Danton's Death* but on Büchner's
reception in general, developed well before the study of reception
became fashionable within literary study two decades ago.[8]

My concern here is not to rehearse once more the well-known
facts about the play's impact, but to stress its ability to speak out
on revolution—at once the French and later revolutions—in often
unexpected ways over a wide time-span. Let me cite four occasions
on which *Danton's Death* has been put to political use. The first is a
review of Büchner's *Nachgelassene Schriften* that was written in
1851 by Büchner's close friend Wilhelm Schulz but that remained
little noticed by the scholarly community until its republication in
1985. Although Schulz did not meet Büchner until after the completion of *Danton's Death*, he and his wife Caroline were his closest
contacts during the writer's period in Zurich; indeed, our intimate
knowledge of Büchner's final days comes from Caroline Schulz's
well-known chronicle of his illness.

Wilhelm Schulz's review of his friend's writings was intended
above all as a political statement to encourage a renewal of revolutionary hope after the disillusionments of 1848. "May [Büchner's
writings] soon be in everybody's hands—to incite wrath in aristo-
crats and pleasure in democrats!" he writes at the end, leaving no
doubt about the firmness of Büchner's revolutionary sentiments
(82). Schulz quotes several passages from *Danton's Death*, among
them a speech by the Third Citizen (*Sämtliche* 1:15) from which
Schulz italicizes the final five words of the line "wir hängen sechzig
Jahre lang am Strick und zappeln; aber wir werden uns losschnei-
den [we've been hanging on the rope for sixty years and wriggling,
but we shall *cut ourselves loose*]" to transfer the revolutionary
advocacy of an ordinary citizen to an advocacy that Schulz seeks
to hear voiced by the oppressed soldiers of his own time (76).

Drawing upon his personal knowledge of the writer, Schulz quotes
Büchner as complaining of the "damnable good nature" of those
who worry about sparing individuals when the fate and the hopes

of whole peoples and later generations are at stake (78). Schulz even cites the fatalism letter—the very document that was to be used a century later by conservative-minded scholars to demonstrate the apolitical nature of *Danton's Death*—to show that Büchner's despair at the fate of the individual during the Revolution ("the individual merely foam on the waves") must be separated from his far more positive hope for the masses (78). But Schulz does not intend this essay simply for political purposes, in fact does not separate this endeavor from his attempt to enhance his friend's literary reputation. At the start of his essay he defines the qualities peculiar to Büchner's writing, and among these he speaks of something close to what I have earlier called his multi-voicedness: Büchner is notable, according to Schulz, for allowing "each mouth and each thing [to speak] its *own* language" (57, emphasis Schulz's).

My second example of the political efficacy of *Danton's Death* is set a full generation later in a quite distant place. In 1886, before the play had made a major impact on German writers, it was published in its original language both in serialized and book form in the United States under the auspices of German socialists. This was the year of the Haymarket riots in Chicago and a time that revolutionary hopes were being kindled among American workers. As it was for Schulz, the play was intended by its German-American advocates to serve a distinctly revolutionary purpose. An article in the journal *Socialist* viewed the play as history rather than literature, in fact calling it "the best history of the first French Revolution" (see Heiss 256). Although this first revolution, according to the article, had failed, the "coming revolution" (256) should profit from its mistakes, many of which would surely become evident to the prospective readers of *Danton's Death*. A central difference between these two revolutions, the article went on, lay in the fact that the new revolution would be able to count on a better-educated working class than the first, which had been cursed by "so degenerate a mob . . . over which Danton and his group established their leadership" (256). The object-lessons that workers in America would gain from a reading of Büchner's play presumably would help steer the coming revolution into a more successful course than its failed predecessor.

Unlike these two nineteenth-century examples of the play's generative potential, the two modern examples try for something less than a renewal of revolution. The first of these is a student production of *Danton's Death* that took place at the University of California, Berkeley, early in 1971. This was, in fact, the only production of the play I have actually been able to attend. And yet the play, once I saw it, was scarcely recognizable. The director, William I. Oliver, had edited the text considerably and had added a goodly amount of dialogue on his own. A number of new characters were included in the list of *dramatis personae,* including the executioner Samson, who in Büchner's text is simply mentioned by name. The more introspective speeches in the play, if they appeared at all, were nearly drowned out by the hubbub of the crowd.

After nearly two decades, the chief impression I retain of this production is the chaos of crowds busily and loudly moving about the stage, often threatening, sometimes also committing violence. Although the play kept its original setting, the chief referent to which the action pointed was the chaotic and sometimes violent political atmosphere of the Berkeley campus during the preceding six years, the arrests during the Free Speech Movement of 1964, the demonstrations against the attempted closing of People's Park in 1969, continuing tear gas attacks by the police on Telegraph Avenue. Beyond these, one remained aware of the Viet Nam War, which had been raging for so long that many in the audience were probably having difficulty maintaining their rage against it. The production thus became an expression of revolutionary exhaustion in which the meaningless movements of the crowd onstage some-how could be connected with the audience's experience of a political movement that was still persisting yet had lost much of its meaning. Indeed, as one reads accounts of famous past productions of *Danton's Death*—for example, the crowd-centered Max Rein-hardt interpretations of 1916 and 1929, each with an emphasis appropriate to its time, or the "depoliticized" Gustav Gründgens version of 1939 that cautiously minimized the crowd's role[9]—one recognizes how readily this play absorbs and transmits the political tensions prevailing at a given moment.

My final example of the play's continuing generative power is Rudi Dutschke's posthumously published essay devoted jointly to Büchner and to his friend, the writer Peter-Paul Zahl, who was still in prison on terrorist charges at the time Dutschke composed this, his final piece of writing, in 1979. Dutschke's obvious purpose in linking Büchner and Zahl was to help free his friend (77–78). From my own point of view, the central interest in this essay lies in Dutschke's particular interpretation of the play. Dutschke stresses the citizens' various complaints about the oppressiveness of work and connects these with the hedonistic sentiments voiced by Danton, a complex of attitudes with which this erstwhile disciple of Herbert Marcuse clearly identifies (50–52). By a strange irony of history the unlikely combination of sensualism and radicalism by which Heine had left his mark on *Danton's Death* now repeats itself in the influence of the author of *Eros and Civilization* on the most celebrated German student activist of the 1960s.

In the comments that he inscribed in his copy of *Danton's Death*, Dutschke wrote the name *Büchner* next to some of Danton's more world-weary pronouncements (Pinkert 113–14). Not only does he identify the play's hero with its author, but Dutschke, near death at this point from wounds inflicted in an assassination attempt on him many years before, links himself to both; indeed, it is known that he spoke constantly of Büchner (whom he saw as a fellow persecuted student activist) during his final months and took a particular interest in the circumstances surrounding Büchner's death (Pinkert 133–34), circumstances that themselves had shaped the play *Büchners Tod* by Dutschke's Chilean friend Gaston Salvatore, who had staged what he took to be the dying Büchner's hallucinations, among them the persecutions suffered by those comrades who, unlike Büchner, had been imprisoned after the failed Hessian uprising. To complete the story, one might add that Peter-Paul Zahl, reading Dutschke's essay after his death, complained of "a certain lack of radicality" (Pinkert 82).

I have tried thus far to stress the difficulties we encounter when we make too strict a demarcation between a text such as *Danton's Death* and what literary study has conventionally called its context. From an institutional point of view, it ordinarily seems normal and desirable to treat a literary text as an artifact about whose intent and significance the scholarly community (if not necessarily the ordinary reader or the director who prepares it for the stage) can seek to achieve a measure of agreement. Although everybody in the community knows, at some level of consciousness, that this aim is never actually achieved, the very existence of this common aim serves as a stabilizing force to bind the community together at any given time.

The status of a literary text is not altogether different from that of a historical event such as the French Revolution. Literary scholars sometimes entertain the illusion that historians have the advantage of dealing with some "solid" reality different in kind from the unstable verbal fictions that make up the texts on which they

work. Certainly Büchner, to judge from those passages in his letters
that express his desire to keep his play true to the history of the
Revolution (*Sämtliche* 2:435, 438, 443–44), assumed a stability inherent in the events of the past even if the individual, as the fatalism letter makes clear, often has to struggle to make sense of these
events. When Büchner tells us, for instance, that the writer's task
is to render "history as it really happened [die Geschichte, wie sie
sich wirklich begeben]," we recognize him as a contemporary of
Ranke, and when he speaks of the dramatic poet as "nothing more
than a writer of history" (*Sämtliche* 2:443), our own historical sense
quickly identifies him with an up-and-coming literary realism. From
our present-day vantage point, what separates *Danton's Death* from
other historical narratives of the Revolution is its refusal, perhaps
even its inability, to impose a coherence (despite the efforts of the
play's interpretors) on events that historians (and even most dramatists) have traditionally felt the need to treat from a single and
easily recountable point of view.

If, in Büchner's time, both literature and history gravitated toward
what once seemed a stable model of historical reality, in our own
time, as essay 9 will develop in more detail, the model for both
endeavors has assumed a shape that can perhaps best be described
as "textual." Thus, some of the most interesting work that historians have been doing on the Revolution in recent years approaches
these much-written-about events in ways similar to those that we
use to treat a text such as *Danton's Death*. I do not here refer to the
long-standing interpretive conflicts that have marked the historiography of the Revolution since its beginnings. The political battle I
cited earlier between Viëtor and Lukács over *Danton's Death* can
be matched by a multitude of conflicting views that have struggled
against one another for two centuries—between Edmund Burke
and Thomas Paine in the first years of the Revolution, between de
Tocqueville and Michelet in the mid-nineteenth century, between
François Furet and the Marxist school in our own day.

I refer rather to the attempts of some recent historians to analyze what a literary scholar would call the textuality of the Revolution. Note, for instance, the following sentence in Furet's critique
of the historiography of the Revolution: "So the Revolution was
not so much an action as a language, and it was in relation to this
language, the locus of the consensus, that the ideological machine
established differences among men" (178). This sentence is not
simply a polemic against Marxist historians, though it is clearly

that as well: it is also an attempt to call attention to the formal attributes that Furet saw giving shape to revolutionary actions. When, in another spot, he declares, "There were no revolutionary circumstances; there was a Revolution that fed on circumstances" (62), he suggests the primacy of plotting much as a literary critic might demonstrate the formative power of plot over character or individual events in a fictional text.

Once we stress the textuality of history, the historian's emphasis and method shift from matters such as causes and effects to explorations of the language, symbols, and narrative structures that, to most earlier historians, would have seemed irrelevant to the job of retelling the narratives that long constituted the historian's chief business. For example, in her study of the various festivals that were staged during the Revolution, Mona Ozouf, like an anthropologist observing tribal rites or a critic showing how a group of symbols organizes and articulates a poem, demonstrates the centrality of these festivals—traditionally treated as peripheral to events such as wars, assassinations, and executions—to an understanding of how the Revolution conceived of and presented itself.[10] In studying the rhetoric and symbolism of the Revolution another recent historian, Lynn Hunt, applies Northrop Frye's definitions of comedy, romance, and tragedy to analyze the generic plots enacted during diverse stages of the Revolution (34–39).[11]

A literary scholar, Marie-Hélène Huet, has studied the selfconsciously theatrical elements in the trial and execution of Louis XVI and in the assassination of Marat together with a series of actual plays about the latter event that were performed soon after it occurred. Another literary scholar, Ann Rigney, has recently traced a single episode, the flight to Varennes, through ten historical narratives from Mignet and Thiers to the early twentieth century: she notes, for example, the repetition, with significant variations, of certain *topoi* (for example, the Queen's near-meeting with Lafayette as she left the palace) from text to text, or the fact that what one would think to be an "original" historical source, the minutes of the Varennes municipal council, had itself apparently been rewritten for ideological reasons in the version available to historians.

A "literary" reading of the Revolution is by no means unique to our own time: everybody remembers how Marx himself, in "The Eighteenth Brumaire," describes the heroes of the Revolution "performing . . . in Roman costume and with Roman phrases" (301) and the "heroes" of 1848 "parodying" their predecessors (300). Historians, not the least of them Georg Büchner himself in *Danton's Death*, have long emphasized the selfconsciousness with which the figures of the Revolution exploited the parallels they saw between their world and ancient Rome.[12] The prevalence of classical analogy in the speeches and memoirs that have come down to us from the Revolution points to a selfconscious theatricality that breaks down our ordinary notions of the barriers separating the disciplines of history and literary study.

A similar selfconsciousness is itself foregrounded within Büchner's play, not simply by the persistent classical analogies, but also by the characters'—particularly the Dantonists'—emphasis on the role playing in which all around them are engaged, as for example in the discussions, during the last prison scene, on precisely what poses to put on in the face of death (*Sämtliche* 1:70–71). One might note that the real-life Danton, at least as textualized by Michelet, supposedly expressed his impatience about some extraneous talk concerning a new play during the trial of Louis XVI with the comment, "A matter of comedy! What's at stake is the tragedy you owe the nations" (2:174). When I suggested earlier that *Danton's Death* reenacts type-scenes typical of earlier historical drama, I might just as well have added that these type-scenes—for example, confrontations between political opponents, street squabbles among the common people, speeches of defiance against one's judges—can be found embedded in the documents of the Revolution, doubtless indeed in the behavior patterns of the persons who actually enacted the events of the time. Once we recognize the theatrical element in historical events themselves, we also recognize that literature was (if I may borrow a cliché ever-present in contemporary critical discourse) always already there in the history that literature purports to portray.

III

INSTITUTIONS

SIX

The Normality of Canon Change

This essay expands upon a talk I delivered at a number of campuses beginning in 1985. The talk elicited a good bit of discussion at each place I gave it—sometimes up to an hour and a half—and I rewrote it several times to incorporate ideas that came up during these discussions. I abruptly stopped offering it when, during a discussion at the University of Georgia in January 1988, some members of the audience asked me to apply my thoughts to what, according to the news media, was going on at my own university. I recognized that my earlier speculations had now been overtaken by real events— events I attempt to describe, account for, and place in historical perspective in the essay that follows the present one.

I propose to look at three instances of canon change from widely separated times and places.

The first may well be a familiar scene—a meeting of an English department graduate committee that has been called to update the master's degree reading list for the first time in two decades. The committee, like any self-respecting university body these days, contains two student members and a group of faculty carefully selected to represent both the earlier and later periods of English and American literature as well as the interests of women and ethnical minorities. The students have succeeded in persuading the faculty representatives not to increase the amount of reading on the list no matter what changes are ultimately legislated; in addition, the faculty in the earlier fields have persuaded the committee as a whole not to decrease the reading within any single literary period.

In the course of its long and sometimes heated deliberations the

131

committee finds that the need to abide by these rules at the same time that it institutes those changes deemed necessary by certain committee members often resembles the activities of a skilled chess player. Few changes, it turns out, are made in the earlier periods. The nineteenth-century representative, who also speaks for a feminist perspective, suggests that some passages from the *Book of Margery Kempe* might well replace the selections from *Piers Plowman*, but the medievalist musters a sufficient number of historical arguments to retain the present title—for example, the generic incompatibilites between these two works—that she lets the issue drop. Changing titles in the eighteenth century proves a good bit easier. Burney's *Evelina* easily displaces another epistolary novel, *Humphry Clinker*, and in the area of non-fictional prose selected parts of Wollstonecraft's *Vindication of the Rights of Women* displace the equivalent number of pages from the *Spectator*, even though, as someone points out, these texts come from widely divergent moments in the century.

Changes in the nineteenth century are made with a minimum of argument—not simply because the committee representative is a feminist critic, but because the earlier reading list was already quite strong on women novelists such as Austen, the Brontës, and Eliot. A goodly amount of Dorothy Wordsworth's *Journals* makes its way onto the new list, especially since the recent discovery of her brother's short *Two-Part Prelude* enables the committee to do away with some lengthy portions of the 1850 *Prelude* that the old list had included. *Frankenstein* proves easy to accommodate, if only because, it is argued, it shares an interest in the Prometheus theme with the author's husband's *Prometheus Unbound* and is far more accessible to the modern student than the latter work; indeed, even with the displacement of this lengthy dramatic poem, enough of the male poet's remaining work is left on the list to assure an equitable distribution of the Shelleys' community property.

The major changes, as everybody on the committee foresaw, take place in the twentieth-century section of the list. Whereas the old list included only a single item by a black writer, namely Wright's *Native Son*, the new list will make room for works by Zora Neale Hurston and Toni Morrison, who satisfy both the women's and black constituencies on the committee. After considerable argument, the committee removes Beerbohm's *Zuleika Dobson*, which, everybody finally agrees, should actually have been removed during the last revision in 1966, and, in order to make room for Morrison, it does away with Henry Miller's *Tropic of Cancer*, which, having just emerged from censorship before this last revision, seemed more important at the time than it does to the present committee, none of whose members deems it in the least canonical. Although the committee contains no native Americans, the black representative takes it upon himself to argue for the inclusion of N. Scott Momaday's *The Way to Rainy Mountain*, which then replaces a selection of poetry by Ransom, Tate and Robert Penn Warren. At one point a committee member asks if there might be room for writers from places such as Canada, the West Indies, Australia and South Africa, but since nobody on the committee has strong feelings on this issue the matter is dropped.

Everybody feels relieved that all disputes seem more or less settled when a student member suddenly asks if some room might be found for Walter Benjamin's essay, "The Work of Art in the Age of Mechanical Reproduction." She goes to some length to defend the effect that this essay has exercised on her and some of her fellow students when a faculty member in one of the earlier fields interrupts to remind her that the literary canon the reading list is designed to reflect has traditionally been limited to what he calls primary works, indeed that the essay she is describing must surely be a piece of secondary literature. Whatever he may call it, she insists, this essay exercises a verbal power that she has been unable to locate in many long-established texts on the list. He asks her for a brief summary, which he interrupts with the statement that the work she advocates does not even belong to literary criticism but rather to art criticism—to which she counters that the passages on the list from Ruskin's *Modern Painters* are every bit as much art criticism as Benjamin's essay. But Ruskin, he replies, was on the list long before anybody on the present committee had even started teaching, and even if you choose to call it art criticism, it has been sanctified for over a century as a canonical example of English prose style. When the Benjamin advocate is asked to defend her entry for its style, she admits that she has never read it in the original German. "It's in German?" someone asks. "Then what business has it on an English Department reading list?" after which the Benjamin matter, like the commonwealth matter earlier, is quietly dropped. The new reading list is voted in, and the meeting adjourns without further incident, though an older committee member is thought to have muttered "This could never have happened in the old days" as the others filed out.

Whether or not this aging professor actually spoke the words reported of him, let me interject that the canon changes legislated at this meeting could surely have occurred—though for different reasons—in the professor's youth, that indeed such changes have been taking place over the centuries in various cultures ever since people began to consider what works of the past they cared to preserve. I introduce this section entitled "Institutions" with this imagined anecdote in order to demonstrate that the issues with which the section is concerned are neither sociologically abstract nor historically remote, but that they are central to the professional lives of humanistic scholars in the modern university: the generational conflict between older scholars holding on as best they can to an earlier, hard-won status and younger colleagues seeking a still unsecured place for themselves; the process by which newly emerging groups seek to achieve status by transferring the aura emanating from long-standing canonical texts to neglected texts identified with their gender and with their ethnic origins; the rule-bound swapping of texts that reproduces the swapping of favors and testing of power familiar throughout American political life.

Consider now an example from a cultural and institutional situation quite different from the contemporary one that I just improvised. As Peter Uwe Hohendahl has demonstrated in detail in his recent book, *Building a National Literature: The Case of Germany 1830–1870*, the German literary canon as we still know it today was shaped and stabilized during the mid-nineteenth century (140–200), in fact precisely during the forty-year period indicated in the title of his study. At the beginning of this period Goethe did not yet hold the towering status that he enjoyed at the end, by which time he had become linked with Homer, Dante, and Shakespeare within the international pantheon. Indeed, in 1830 and for some time thereafter Schiller was the more popular of the two German writers.

Moreover, several major writers of the late eighteenth and early nineteenth century—for example, Klopstock, Wieland, and Jean Paul—might easily, given the right cultural conditions, have occupied central places in the canon during its process of formation. As it turned out, none of these figures fit the cultural needs of the moment, which demanded the creation of a German national identity defined by writers who could radiate a classical status comparable to that of the Elizabethan writers in England or the French writers of the age of Louis XIV. Wieland, for instance, was deemed too cosmopolitan, indeed too specifically French-oriented a writer to play the role demanded under mid-nineteenth-century cultural conditions, while Jean Paul, respected though he was by an international public, was too digressive, too passive-seeming, indeed too eccentric a writer for this particular role.

The establishment of the German canon, as Hohendahl shows, can be charted by means of a series of widely read literary histories, beginning with that of Gervinus in 1835, as well as by certain influential studies of individual writers and groups of writers by critics such as Dilthey and Haym. Among the arguments that critics used to create Goethe's classical status was to stress his close literary friendship with Schiller and thus to link him with the more popular writer. From there on Goethe and Schiller could be treated as twin stars within the literary firmament, with a special place created for Lessing, who was assigned the role of their precursor, indeed of founding father of the modern German literary tradition. Although Klopstock, Wieland, and Jean Paul remained within the canon, they were made to serve distinctly subsidiary roles.

The forty-year period that Hohendahl analyzes is marked by an important political watershed, the Revolution of 1848, whose failure left profound effects on the process of canonization. Before 1848, for example, the German romantic school was treated as a decadent afterglow to the classical development that had culminated in Goethe and Schiller; the disparagement of the romantics during this period can be attributed both to their anti-classical, eccentric-seeming formal methods and to their political conservatism. Once the revolution had failed and the conservative Prussian state was completing its unification of the country, German romanticism came to be seen as a positive development, indeed as the final stage of a dialectic that had begun with Lessing and proceeded through Storm and Stress and thence through the classicism of Goethe and Schiller. Thus, the nationalist bias of the romantics could be interpreted as the natural culmination of Goethe's classicism, whose nationalist impulses would have seemed unduly weak by the standards of the 1860s.

Lessing's role, moreover, needed reinterpretation after 1848 if he was to keep his status as founding father, and as a result his ties to the European Enlightenment became de-emphasized, while those qualities that looked forward to a later stage of literary development—for example, his disparagement of the French classical system and his interest in Spinoza—became central to the new image created for him. It scarcely seems a coincidence that the German canon stabilized at precisely the time that the unified German state came into existence, nor does it seem accidental, according to Hohendahl, that the canon was institutionalized by means of a new academic discipline, *Germanistik* (201–47), or what became known in this country as Germanic philology. The stability of this discipline—and, in effect, the stability of the newly established canon—was secured by the creation of university chairs for the practice and dissemination of this new academic field. Moreover, the discipline's essentially conservative orientation—reflecting, as it did, the conservative attitudes of its sponsors—was reinforced by the positivistic methodology that came to govern Germanic philology during the last decades of the nineteenth century. This methodology, which we all know as a result of its transfer to literary study in America about the turn of the century, sought to emulate the alleged objectivity of the natural sciences, or at least that conception of the natural sciences which had reigned during the later nineteenth century. According to this model the task of the literary scholar was to serve as little more than a custodian of the great texts of the past, and what this custodian dared state was subject to strict limits. Since the scholar's commentary sought to achieve what was dubbed scientific objectivity, it was pretty much limited to the publicly verifiable facts about a literary work, its editorial problems, its sources in earlier works, and its author's stated intentions about what was supposedly its meaning. Value judgments about the relative worth of the text were scarcely the business of the serious scholar—indeed, value judgments were deemed rather indecorous. Would a geologist, after all, dare pronounce upon the worth of a particular mountain, or an astronomer about the worth of a newly discovered planet? It is no wonder that the canon making that had proceeded with great rapidity in mid-nineteenth-century Germany essentially came to a halt with the establishment of a custodial system that inhibited the questioning of a text's value in relation to other texts past or present.

My final example of canon change comes from a more remote time, so remote, in fact, that we know nothing about the particular individuals who brought about this change, nor can we do more than speculate as to what circumstances motivated it. I refer to the formation of a canon of Greek tragedy, a formation that, as John Winkler argues in a forthcoming book, came about sometime between the third century B.C. and the second century A.D., when a school edition of twenty-four Greek tragedies was produced. The Hellenistic selectors of this edition chose seven tragedies each by Aeschylus and Sophocles and ten by Euripides. Though we have no solid information about these selectors, we know one thing for sure: they possessed a strong bias in favor of a specific kind of play, one that ends in catastrophe; moreover, they displayed a distinct bias against those plays that contained a goodly amount of melo-dramatic action. The plays that these selectors chose for their stu-dents, whose tastes they were obviously attempting to influence, are precisely the plays that have given us our own image of Greek tragedy, sometimes, in fact, our image of those attributes that we have labeled "the tragic."

Throughout antiquity the corpus of Greek tragedy remained quite large, and it included a variety of plays quite different from those chosen for the selectors' school edition. We know a good bit about these other plays from plot summaries made during the Hellenistic period, from references in critics from Aristotle onward, and from the fact that a group of nine additional plays by Euripides—mostly quite different from those in the selectors' group—survived by means of an historical accident, namely the fact that the titles under which they were presumably listed represented a small, continuous segment of the alphabet. What is significant from the point of view of the present essay is that Greek tragedy included many plays with happy endings and with sufficient melodramatic action that they scarcely fit that decorous image of Greek tragedy which has prevailed since the Renaissance. Although we can never know for sure what stands behind the selectors' classicistic bias, Winkler speculates that they may have been championing their quite limited view of the Greek tragic corpus in order to wean their readers away from what they saw as the vulgar melodramatic actions endemic to popular Hellenistic romance in their time.

I have described three quite distinct instances of canon making, instances so distinct that they would seem to have nothing in common with one another except for the fact that each seems rooted in its own time and place, that each manifests certain biases characteristic of this particular time and place; moreover, each of these instances has exercised powerful effects, for the canons it has established have lasted into later times during which those social conditions and attitudes that we can link with earlier changes no longer seem relevant. Indeed, it is precisely when readers during these later times perceive this loss of relevance that it becomes possible to initiate canon change or, at best, to reinterpret canonical figures in the hope of endowing them with a new and hopefully more timely significance. The shifts in attitude that help bring about a change in or a reinterpretation of the canon can generally, if we look hard enough, be linked to particular agents of political change as well as to those social structures that enable the desired change or reinpretation to become implemented. To cite one of my own earlier examples, the accommodation of German romanticism to the German canon was made possible, perhaps even necessitated by the shift from a predominantly liberal to a conservative political atmosphere among the intelligentsia after the suppression of the revolutionary movement in 1848; moreover, the long-term institutionalization of this canon was made possible during the late nineteenth century by means of the relatively strong role played by the German government in awarding academic chairs and in encouraging the use of methodologies that worked to maintain the canon and to discourage those modes of analysis that might threaten it.

Similarly, the motivation for the type of canon change I described in the contemporary American university could easily be traced back to political attitudes that took shape during the 1960s among American intellectuals. Is it accidental, for instance, that a major campaign for canon change did not actually take place during the 1960s or even the 70s, but awaited the time that those who were undergraduates during the 60s finally achieved positions of academic power? Moreover, the ability of this generation of scholars to implement its attitudes within the university derives from the fact that curricular policy maintains a relatively high degree of independence from the federal government—even from a conservative regime such as the one that dominated political life in America throughout the 1980s—and that faculty governance, at least in the more prestigious universities, takes the form of representative democracy, though some might prefer to call it interest-group democracy. (Campaigning for radical canon change can also be interpreted as a means of political protest when other, more activist forms of protest have come to seem futile.) If we knew more than we do about the Hellenistic selectors who determined the Greek tragic canon for us, doubtless we could discover what social and political factors helped motivate their decisions. Of one thing we can be sure: the literary canons recognized by the ancients were not made on Olympus any more than the various canons proposed for the modern literatures were made in heaven.

Even if we agree that our canons were not made in heaven, it is not always clear precisely who are the agents responsible for particular canon changes. When I gave an earlier version of this essay at the Stanford Humanities Center, one of my most respected colleagues—incidentally, the only literary critic still writing today whose work was assigned to me during my own undergraduate years—objected to my stress on the role of institutions and governments in determining the canon. After all, he reminded me, it is the great poets, both through their own practice and through the critical pronouncements they make to defend their practice, who ultimately determine which earlier poets are to stay in the canon and which poets must no longer be valued to the degree they were in the past.

Certainly this notion of poets determining the canons within which they are to be situated is one to which most of us would assent—at least this would likely be our initial response if we were asked how our canons are made. We would think, for example, of Eliot dethroning Tennyson and Browning in order to make room for himself, or of Wordsworth dethroning Thomas Gray to make room for *Lyrical Ballads;* by the same token we would think of Eliot re-enthroning Donne and Marvell to help legitimate his own poetic endeavors. Moreover, the fact that poets in our culture radiate an aura that we cannot readily ascribe to political pressure groups or to bureaucrats within an educational ministry easily encourages us to grant them prime authority in teaching us what poets to value and why, indeed, we should value them at all.

To a certain degree there's a good bit of truth to my colleague's model of poets as canon makers. Within anglophone culture since at least the time of Dryden, as I explained in more detail in the first essay of this book, one notes the recurring phenomenon of the poet who also plays the role of public critic both in his formal essays and in the values he actively seeks to propagate by means of his poetic practice. A social theorist such as Habermas would point out the roots of this phenomenon in the coffee-house culture of the Enlightenment, in which poet-critics would make value judgments about poetry (as well as politics) in conversation with their friends (45–46)—or, for that matter, in frequently published journals that encouraged the transmission of these judgments among coffee-houses throughout the nation (55–57). It is remarkable, moreover, that this model persisted well beyond the world of coffee-houses, for in the late nineteenth century Matthew Arnold performed his canon making in essays addressed to a now much-enlarged middle-class audience whose spiritual values he sought to shape and enhance by means of the values he taught it to discern in the great works of the past he selected for its reading. Indeed, as I indicated in the first essay, the young Eliot and Pound continued to exercise this role even after a large middle-class public for significant new poetry had ceased to exist and after the audience for their critical pronouncements had become restricted largely to readers of avant-garde little magazines.

Appealing though this model of the poet as canonizer may be, on reflection it provides perhaps too simple an explanation of how and why literary canons change. Even if Eliot had never spoken disparagingly of Tennyson and Browning, the modernist sensibility and aesthetic that pervaded all the arts within early twentieth-century Europe would ultimately have made these great Victorian poets seem less immediate and relevant to readers than they had seemed a generation before. The democratization of poetic language and the advocacy of the imagination that are central to Wordsworth's critical pronouncements we now recognize as expressions of a larger configuration of forces for which the individual poet-critic served as spokesman and advocate. Moreover, the notion of granting the individual poet the power to shape the canon may well be more applicable to the anglophone world than elsewhere. If the three examples of canon change with which I began this essay have any cogency, one must surely attribute the reshaping of canons to factors that will likely vary with different cultural situations. Even if the selectors responsible for most of the extant Greek tragic canon were biased against romance, they surely had no notion that in the course of selecting tragedies suitable for schoolchildren they were in effect insuring the permanent loss of many dramas that Aristotle himself had treasured. One might blame this loss as much on the accidents of historical transmission as on the tastes of the selectors; indeed, accidents of this sort were common enough during the many centuries before the invention of printing more or less insured the preservation of works that would at least be available in a multiplicity of libraries for any future re-arrangements of the canon.

Similarly, it is difficult to assign the formation of the German classical canon during the mid-nineteenth century to the same factors that created canons in earlier times and places. The professional literary historians, publishers, and bureaucrats who installed the canon within the educational system were less concerned with the fame or the fate of individual poets than with the larger communal project of creating a plausible narrative for the development of a German national culture, a development suppos- edly reflected in German literature during the century preceding the establishment of a unified nation. The needs of the narrative, one might say, determined the role and the status of the individual writers within this narrative far more than the verbal artistry or the human concerns that critics attributed to these writers to jus- tify their inclusion in the canon. The overwhelming and singular role assigned to Goethe within this narrative reflected the need for a foundation stone on which all other elements within the story could be built. And although Germany at the time of his canoniza- tion could not claim to more than a century of sustained literary activity of the first rank, the presence of an author such as Goethe, for whom it could claim world status, allowed it to compete with such long-standing national literatures as Italian, Spanish, and English, each of which boasted a similar foundation stone. (The absence of a single author in French with a status comparable to that of Dante, Cervantes, or Shakespeare does not derive from a lack of literary "greatness"—the reputations of a number of writ- ers such as Rabelais, Racine, Voltaire, or Balzac might have been tailored for this role—but is more likely due to the unresolved tensions in French cultural life between the so-called classical and romantic, between the political right and left.)

Within contemporary America the attempt to find a place for women and ethnic writers within the canon, as the essay that follows will illustrate with a recent example, is part of a wider project to rethink the whole nature of what constitutes literature and its uses. Where are the borderlines, we are asking these days, between those texts we have customarily labeled literature and other texts within our culture? What forms of knowledge and social practice can or should we expect the literature we read to instill in us and in those students whose educational development we take it upon ourselves to shape? How is it, in fact, that the way we define and evaluate literature has become inextricably linked to what we perceive as educational needs? Fundamental questions such as these are raised only at those times, such as our own, when many have lost confidence in what was a long-accepted canon of great works. Analogous questions were asked on other major occasions of canon change, by the German romantic critics, for instance, or by the classicizing critical schools that flourished in sixteenth-century Italy and during the succeeding century in France. On those occasions the discussion of the literary canon, together with the evaluation of individual authors and texts, becomes inseparable from the discussion of what precisely constitutes literature, of what are the uses of literature, indeed of what constitutes the values of the particular culture that designates its canon.

However different the reasons we can give for canon changes in different cultural situations, it has generally proved easier to add authors to the canon than to remove them completely. The dislodgment of Milton about which F. R. Leavis exulted half a century ago (42–67) proved to be a far more temporary phenomenon than Leavis could have imagined, though the Milton who returned to the canon has come to us clothed in a variety of new critical garments that nobody, whether pro- or anti-Milton, could have imagined at the time. Although the various texts removed from the reading list at my fictive committee meeting will likely be checked out of the library less often than they were in the past, they will never disappear as completely as did the Greek tragedies not included in the two collections that have come down to us. Some of the texts the department committee removes may even return to the reading list at a later time, and even if they do not, the interpretive history that has accumulated for them over the years assures them a respite from oblivion. By the same token, some of the texts added to the list may not make it the next time round; yet these too will meanwhile accumulate their own history to a degree that they might never have done without the canonization that they were awarded, albeit temporarily. The once highly esteemed team of Beaumont and Fletcher, like those once-celebrated eighteenth-century German writers who went down in rank when they failed to meet mid-nineteenth-century needs, at least remain available in every university library, sometimes even in bookstores. Although I earlier claimed that the German classical canon remained relatively stable for a century after its institutionalization, I might have added that during this century it managed to accommodate three authors from the early nineteenth century—Hölderlin, Kleist, and Büchner—who, for various reasons, had been virtually forgotten (and in Hölderlin's and Büchner's case, only partially published) during the major period of canon formation. Although German literary history succeeded in absorbing all three into its national narrative, it is significant that during this time no author deemed central to the canon was dislodged, even though Schiller's star eventually came to shine a bit less brightly than it had in earlier days.

In stressing the persistence of canon change, I do not mean to ignore the fact that certain canons can lay claim to being closed for vast stretches of time. The Jewish Bible, for instance, achieved its "final" stage about 70 A.D. at the time that the second temple was destroyed. We know of a conference held at Jabneh (Gabel and Wheeler 77–78) to determine precisely which books would be included. (Could the political tensions at this conference, from which we are told no written records remain, have in any way resembled those at my imaginary English department committee? Did the supposedly controversial Song of Songs make it through the sponsorship of some rabbi sympathetic to the lot of dark-skinned women? Did the image of women depicted in the Book of Ruth seem less threatening than that depicted in the Book of Judith?) But even a closed canon such as the Jewish Bible is closed only in the sense that the actual texts (and their order in relation to one another) remain the same. What allows a canon to remain closed is the fact that new interpretations may accumulate over succeeding ages to open up fresh areas of significance, to close others, and, in a form of argument that has often made the adjective *Talmudic* synonymous with *quibbling,* to argue the proper meaning of the most minute points and thus keep the whole enterprise floating over millennia.

But literary canons, though they can never claim finality in the way that overtly sacred canons do, also undergo change by means of changing interpretive procedures. The long-standing six-poet English-romantic pantheon, as I mentioned in essay 1, still occupies a privileged position in the latest edition of *The Norton Anthology of English Literature,* despite the addition of substantial passages by Wollstonecraft and Dorothy Wordsworth. Yet the same contemporary pressures that have expanded the canon of English romanticism have also given a new interpretive life to the traditional six, as one notes in recent studies of the economics of peddling and weaving as embodied in "The Ruined Cottage" (Liu, *Wordsworth* 311–58), of Byron's sexist language (Hofkosh), of Keats's relation to matters such as social class, money, and masturbation (Levinson *Keats's*). Even Homer, that stalwart of Western culture, has come to us in many guises—and this despite the pretense of stability that Hume voiced in his oft-quoted pronouncement, "The same Homer, who pleased at Athens and Rome two thousand years ago, is still admired at Paris and at London" (316). In order to retain his long-standing role as a foundation stone (not simply of Greek, but of what came to be known as Western culture), Homer

was forced to undergo a series of interpretive transformations—
from the allegorized Hellenistic Homer, to the Christianized (or,
more precisely, pre-Christianized) medieval Homer, to the classi-
cized Renaissance Homer and, starting just about the time that
Hume pronounced upon his continuing identity, to the primitive
bard who, with the recently added though disputed role of oral
performer, persists to our day. Similarly, the postmodern and often
outrageous-seeming interpretations of classical operas that I shall
describe in essay 8 are attempts to give a continuing life to works
that threaten to turn into clichés. To play on a phrase from a
discourse quite foreign to those of art and religion, interpretive
change represents a continuation of canon change by other means.

Readers may note that, in the course of this essay, I have avoided
attributing canon change to individual human agents, but have
instead invoked a vaguer, more communal set of agents such as
bureaucracies, educational planning groups, or simply—if one seeks
to avoid naming human agents altogether—political pressures.
Doubtless my refusal to credit individual agents reflects that larger
bias within historical study today that ascribes change to unnamed
forces and to the perceived needs of particular and often nameless
groups. Yet whether we name individual agents or inchoate forces,
the making, unmaking and remaking of canons—as the examples
with which I began this essay were meant to demonstrate—involve
a struggle for power among competing interests. Nietzsche, who (if
I may name an individual causal agent) has served as chief mentor
to contemporary thinkers on the presence, the workings and the
pervasiveness of power relationships, at one point described the
operatic war between the adherents of Gluck and Piccinni during
the 1770s in baldly political terms: "Aesthetic wars are like political wars, and they are won by power, not by reason. We can take
Gluck's superiority for granted not because he was necessarily
right, but because he happened to win" (1:938). Is it possible that
those who, like the now forgotten composer Piccinni, failed to win,
are really very good, even great? As it turns out, we have canonized
Milton, not Abraham Cowley; Donne, not (despite the vigorous
arguments of Yvor Winters [44–52]), Fulke Greville; Virginia Woolf,
not Dorothy Richardson. Whether or not the canon makers were
right can never be known for sure, for we have learned to value the
victors, not the losers. To use a contemporary cliché, we have
"bonded" with these victors over the years as we do with members
of our own families (no wonder a Milton can never be dismissed

once and for all as Leavis hoped). To name a Cowley or a Greville or a Dorothy Richardson among the very great is something like embracing a stranger as a long-lost child. Moreover, the power struggles that must be waged to achieve canonical status for a particular figure require a redistribution of what often turns out to be limited resources: just as the manufacturers of consumer products struggle for supermarket shelf space, so those who seek to expand the canon must compete for limited space in anthologies, limited time in college courses, and, perhaps even more fundamentally, the limited capacity of readers to hold a lengthy list of towering authors in mind at once.

The relative volatility that has characterized the making of canons over the centuries is of course a peculiarity we associate with literature and not necessarily with other forms of art. Indeed, throughout most of Western history one could hardly speak of classical works in these other forms in quite the way one could speak of classical literature. To be sure, certain Greek sculptors remained legendary long after their works were no longer extant, and Roman architecture left its classical mark, though in varying ways, on both Romanesque and Renaissance style. But the systematic attempts at canon making that Ernst Robert Curtius, for instance, has traced in literary discussions from antiquity to the modern period (247–72) did not manifest itself in the visual arts until the late Renaissance when Vasari, in his *Lives* of the various Italian painters during the preceding centuries, created a sustained narrative of technical progress culminating in Michelangelo, who from that time onward could assume the role of a classical figure in the manner of a Virgil or a Dante. The idea of a musical canon with its reigning classical figures came far later, for music throughout most of its history was an expendable art that, except for the sacred works associated with the Catholic liturgy, did not attempt to preserve its texts for future consumption. It was not until the latter half of the eighteenth century that music became self-conscious of its history and sought to preserve at least some relics of its past; indeed, the first secular composer to be awarded canonical status on the order of the great literary classics was Handel.

Yet in one crucial respect the notion of a literary canon differs sharply from that of a canon within music or within the visual arts. Ever since the time of the Greeks, literary canons, unlike those in music and art, have functioned as a central part of a culture's educational system. Music and art have of course also played roles in educating the young. Music, for example, was a member of the medieval quadrivium, where its role, however, was more akin to that of the other members, arithmetic, geometry, and astronomy, than it was to that of literature; like those other members, music was a technique to be mastered rather than, like literature, the study of classical authorities. Moreover, literature has traditionally exercised a unique function, namely that of shaping a student's moral growth. Yet the type of literature that we take to be a proper means of effecting this growth, indeed our very conception of the nature of morality, has differed markedly in different times and places. One could speculate that changes in the literary canon have often been accompanied by changes of perception of what properly constitutes an appropriate moral education. It is scarcely accidental that the three instances of canon change with which I began this essay all displayed an intimate connection between the perceived moral content of literary texts and the moral demands of a particular culture. Whether or not the Hellenistic selectors privately relished the violence within romance, they doubtless sought to protect their young by feeding them carefully selected tragic plots. The mid-nineteenth century shapers of the German canon recognized the usefulness of literature for shaping obedient citizens within the new German state. Although we doubtless lack the temporal distance to speak with an adequate understanding of our own time, I have no doubt that the conferral of canonical status to works by and about people who not too long ago were deemed marginal is a serious attempt to raise the moral consciousness of a culture that many of us are dedicated to change by means of education. Yet the connection I have suggested between canon change and moral growth is by no means limited to the education of the young. The moral values that Matthew Arnold sought to propagate by invoking touchstones from his list of canonical authors were designed not so much for the schoolchildren to whom Arnold was responsible in his role as school inspector as to the newly literate masses for whom these values were to serve as a means of what we have come to call "continuing education."

Throughout this essay I have stressed the prevalence and the persistence of change in the making of literary canons. Yet the language we use to approach those works we have canonized characteristically employs a vocabulary suggesting that some higher force has enshrined these works for all time. Literary critics— whether in their role of teachers, scholars, reviewers, or editors of anthologies and school texts—invoke words such as *immortal, uni-*

versal, classic, timeless, even *transcendant,* to describe the readings they prize and recommend. How can we account for this defiance of temporality on the part of intellectuals who, at some level of awareness, must surely know that they are asserting the timelessness of a text in order to question the timelessness of works that others before them have advocated? The only answer one can offer is that the critic must awaken the reader's love for a work, create what, in essay 1, I called a "binding mechanism" to tie reader to work, before the reader is willing to recognize the work's canonical status. Indeed, my own manner of presenting Wordsworth's "Resolution and Independence" to students many years ago, as I indicated in essay 2, shamelessly used every rhetorical technique at my command to instill an attitude of love for the poem. To create this attitude, critics since at least the time of the Greeks have had to employ a rhetoric that suggests the permanence of the canons they advocate.

In this sense the discourse of criticism is far less like the discourse of scientific or historical inquiry than it is like the discourse of love. Whereas the former discourse recognizes, indeed presumes the idea of temporal change, the latter cultivates a vocabulary of timelessness. Those who argued for the inclusion of some recent ethnic text at the committee meeting I invented for this essay undoubtedly hoped—perhaps believed—that this text would remain canonical as long as the English language remained in use. "You always think it's forever when you take the vows," a thrice-married friend once told me to justify the discrepancy between those notions of time voiced at the altar and those practiced in everyday life. Thus, lovers have traditionally sought to convince the objects of their pursuits that their love knows no temporal bounds, and often, no doubt, these objects have responded to their lovers' rhetoric to the point that they too became convinced of the timelessness of these lovers' love and then return this love in kind. Sometimes, of course, even the most rhetorically skillful lover pursues a beloved who balks at these efforts and replies, "But unfortunately I do not really love you." To which the lover is likely to reply, "But you can learn to love me." So it is with literature, the love of which is an activity learned in and mediated by institutions. With sufficient rhetorical skill we can persuade others to love, revere and enshrine the works we ourselves have decided to treasure, and we can even—as those who revise the canon have normally done at all times—persuade them to question their earlier commitments, indeed to change the objects of their literary affections.

SEVEN

On the Sacrality of Reading Lists: The Western Culture Debate at Stanford University

During the first few months of 1988 the university at which I teach, then in the midst of its centennial celebration, found itself continuously in the national and sometimes even international news. This attention from the media did not, as one might think, derive from recent discoveries in Stanford's science laboratories or even from the record contributions made to the centennial's fund-raising campaign. Rather, the events deemed most newsworthy at Stanford were the deliberations taking place within the Academic Senate as to whether or not to retain a list of fifteen works that, for the preceding eight years, had been required reading in the course in Western culture taken by all undergraduates during their first year.

The list that attracted this attention reads as follows:

Hebrew Bible, Genesis
Homer, major selections from *Iliad* or *Odyssey* or both

At least one Greek tragedy
Plato, *Republic*, major portions of Books I-VII
New Testament, selections including a gospel
Augustine, *Confessions*, I-IX
Dante, *Inferno*
More, *Utopia*
Machiavelli, *The Prince*
Luther, *Christian Liberty*
Galileo, *The Starry Messenger* and *The Assayer*
Voltaire, *Candide*
Marx and Engels, *The Communist Manifesto*
Darwin, selections
Freud, *Outline of Psychoanalysis* and *Civilization
and Its Discontents*

In addition to these required texts, a list of categories including
such works as the *Aeneid*, selections from Thomas Aquinas, Hob-
bes's *Leviathan*, Goethe's *Faust* and *Werther*, and a nineteenth-century novel (the last-named to be chosen by the instructor) was
"strongly recommended."

The reaction to the proposed dropping of the fifteen required
texts (referred to at Stanford as the "core list") was marked by a
degree of media sensationalism uncommon for an event centered
around figures such as Plato and St. Augustine. A full-page report
on Stanford's deliberations in *Newsweek* was headlined "Say Goodnight Socrates: Stanford University and the decline of the West,"
and it was accompanied by a color reproduction of David's *Death
of Socrates* (Gates). The local morning newspaper, the San Francisco *Chronicle*, rarely known for its intellectual concerns, reported
the Senate's ultimate abandonment of the core list with the headline "Stanford Puts an End to Western Civilization" (Workman). A
somewhat hysterical opinion column in Turin's *La Stampa* bore the
headline "I Classici banditi [The Classics Banished]" (Bolelli) while
a much more sober follow-up article by another writer two months
later was headed "Alla ricerca di un Dante nero [In Search of a
Black Dante]" (Cavalli-Sforza).[1] In addition, one might note that
the executive branch of the United States government entered the
controversy in the person of then Secretary of Education William
Bennett, who, in various public speeches, berated Stanford for even
considering giving up its reading list of established classics. Once

the list had been dropped, Bennett debated Stanford's president, Donald Kennedy, in a nationally shown news telecast.

How can one account for all this excitement surrounding a change in a required course? Certainly the immediate motivation for the public's keen interest in what might otherwise have remained a local issue was the nationwide discussion of university curricular issues set off by the publication some months earlier of two best-sellers by humanistic scholars, Allan Bloom's *The Closing of the American Mind* and E. D. Hirsch's *Cultural Literacy*, the latter of which bore the prescriptive subtitle *What Every American Needs to Know*. Each of these books, though in differing ways, argued for the retention of what it claimed to be traditional cultural values, and each as well decried what it saw as a shift toward relativism and contempt for the past. For those like Secretary Bennett, who made no secret of his admiration for these books, Stanford University's abandonment of its reading list offered living proof that the changes dreaded by Hirsch and Bloom were being implemented at one of the country's most prestigious educational institutions.

Beyond this immediate cause, the public's interest in Stanford's discussion was doubtless motivated as well by the conservative turn that marked American political culture during the 1980s. Thus, the rejection of a reading list of established classical texts from literature, philosophy, science, and political theory could be inter-preted—indeed, *was* interpreted—as a sign that the ethnical mi-norities and feminists who had achieved political consciousness since the 1960s had not merely succeeded in taking over the univer-sities, but that their influence on the curriculum threatened the cultural values articulated by Hirsch and Bloom and also the social stability that some felt had been achieved during the past decade.

The larger political implications that people read into Stan-ford's debate derived from the fact that the move to change the course began with a complaint from the Stanford Black Student Union, which, in testimony before the Senate's committee on un-dergraduate studies, called the course "racist" and claimed that the core list failed to reflect the needs of the many black students who had been recruited to Stanford during recent years. This com-plaint was voiced during the spring of 1986, a year before the publication of Bloom's and Hirsch's books. The union noted that the core list included no works by black writers—though some-times a single text such as Frantz Fanon's *The Wretched of the Earth* or Ralph Ellison's *The Invisible Man* would appear on an individual syllabus. The union's charge was quickly followed by complaints from groups representing Hispanic students and feminists, both of whom claimed that the course was biased against their particular interests. The peculiar tone of these complaints can be heard in the following statements by Bill King, then president of the Black Student Union, in testimony before the Academic Senate two years after the initial charge:

> I know Professors . . . [here King names four English professors supporting retention of the core list] are simply preserving that tradition which they consider correct and which guided their life in a positive way. But by focusing these ideas on all of us they are crushing the psyche of those others to whom Locke, Hume, and Plato are not speaking, and they are denying the freshmen and women a chance to broaden their perspective to accept both Hume and Imhotep, Machiavelli and Al Malgili, Rousseau and Mary Wollstonecraft. . . . The Western culture program as it is presently structured around a core list and an outdated philosophy of the West being Greece, Europe, and Euro-America is wrong, and worse, it hurts people mentally and emotionally in ways that are not even recognized.

What, one might ask at this point, was the disputed core list actually supposed to represent? What precisely was its legitimacy? How was this particular list and not some other list of Western classics chosen for the required course in the first place? What rationale has governed this course and similar courses at other institutions? How was it that books long held sacrosanct (however controversial many of them were when first read) could now be accused of "crushing the psyche" and "hurting people mentally and emotionally"?

To answer these questions and thus to provide some historical context for Stanford's much-publicized debate, one needs to sketch out the history of these courses. For one thing, courses of this type are unique to the United States, in which an undergraduate college education is not, as in most other countries, devoted to mastering one or two disciplines, but is designed to provide what is generally called a "liberal arts" background. Thus, besides their concentrated study of a single field, American students ordinarily take a number of introductory courses in a number of fields, some of these being chosen from a large slate, others, like Stanford's Western

Culture, being required of all students. Foreign professors who visit American universities often express amazement at the introductory nature of these courses, which they sometimes even characterize as "superficial"—to which the host usually replies by speculating that in other lands students surely receive this necessary background in secondary school.

The direct ancestor of Stanford's Western Culture is a course in the origins of Western civilization that Columbia University instituted in 1919.[2] This course, which, unlike Stanford's one-year course, has been spread over two years since 1929, was followed by an equally influential course begun in 1931 under Robert Hutchins' presidency at the University of Chicago. Both these courses treated European civilization as a unity and had little, if anything, to say about non-European cultures. Both of them also came to stress the reading of major texts rather than modern commentaries on these texts. One can, in fact, speak of two types of courses that, in the course of time, became fused into the characteristic Western Civilization course of the mid-twentieth century: first, what was essentially a history course, taught by historians, as in Columbia's original Contemporary Civilization and, second, a "Great Books" course developed for Columbia honors students and later providing the central idea for general education at Chicago (Graff 133–36). Although literary and philosophical texts predominated in Western Civilization courses as they added original sources, documents from the history of science, and sometimes also examples from art and music, were soon introduced.

A number of variants of these courses had spread across the United States by mid-century. Stanford initiated its first such course in 1935 under the title Western Civilization. Administered by the department of history (an arrangement used in many other universities), this required first-year course utilized materials developed at Columbia, including, for some years, a source book prepared by the Columbia staff for its own students (*Introduction*). In view of the recent controversy over the core list, it is significant that Stanford's earlier course did not even have a stipulated reading list, but simply relied upon the large number of texts (several times more than the core list of fifteen, though often only snippets of famous works) included in the Columbia anthology. By stressing texts rather than commentary, these courses attempted to make students feel that they were directly experiencing the sources of what they were meant to call their own civilization.

With our present historical hindsight, we can discern certain ideas and motives from an earlier time guiding these courses. It seems of no small interest, for example, to find that Columbia's course derives directly from a special course created in 1918, a year before its founding, to educate recently conscripted American soldiers about to fight in France. This course, called the War Issues course and offered at the time in a number of universities besides Columbia, sought to introduce Americans to the European heritage in whose defense they were soon to risk their lives (Allardyce 706–7). As they assumed their new leadership role in world politics, Americans could come to see themselves as the heirs to a culture going back to its supposed dual fountainheads in ancient Israel and Greece.

But the courses that burgeoned during the 1920s and '30s responded to other concerns as well. Many educators believed—often with what can best be described as a kind of spiritual mission—that if students could read the very words uttered by the great men of the West (albeit usually in translation), they would be better able to cope with the cultural crisis that the most advanced thinkers of the time took to be a fact of contemporary life. How can we make contact with our intellectual past during a period in which technological and social changes were working to obliterate this past? How could the children of America's newly emerging middle class, many of immigrant (or, more precisely, European immigrant) background, be made familiar with the writings that their teachers deemed to be the materials binding our culture together? The sense of crisis that permeated these courses, especially in their early days, can be linked with a particular mood that pervaded Europe and America in the wake of the First World War and that manifested itself in such otherwise diverse writings as Spengler's *Decline of the West* and Eliot's *The Waste Land*. It seems significant, for example, that Eliot composed his poem during the early years of Columbia's course. Like this course in its later form, Eliot's poem was made up of snippets of quotations ranging in time from the Bible and the Greeks down to modernist writers, in Eliot's case Baudelaire and Hermann Hesse (37–55). And like the teachers of these courses, Eliot used these quotations to establish an immediacy of contact between the modern reader and a swiftly vanishing cultural past; the fact that Eliot, unlike these teachers, presented the quotations in their original languages worked to increase the experience of immediacy.

Yet the pessimistic mood that helped motivate these courses and writings of the early twentieth century cannot simply be attributed to the aftermath of the war. One finds this mood as well in much late nineteenth-century thought, above all in the criticism of Matthew Arnold, whose faith in the healing and uplifting power inherent in the greatest poets since Homer helped fuel the sense of mission of those who developed and taught these courses during the succeeding century.[3] It hardly seems accidental that one of the key teachers of the Columbia course for many years was Lionel Trilling, Arnold's disciple and intellectual biographer, whose own writings can be viewed as extensions at once of Arnold's concerns and of the concerns guiding the course itself.

Stanford's Western Civilization course lasted until the campus disturbances of the late 1960s when, like many liberal-arts requirements at Stanford and at other American universities, it fell victim to sentiments voiced by students and faculty members alike that students should feel free to choose their own courses. Yet despite the fact that it had declined in quality during its final years, the course still evokes considerable nostalgia from Stanford alumni, who often cite it as a high point in their educational experience. By the mid-1970s many Stanford faculty members recognized that the courses students chose outside their major disciplines all too often failed to achieve any coherence as a group, and, as a result, the Academic Senate gradually instituted a new set of liberal-arts requirements. One of these new requirements was Western Culture, with the second word intended to distinguish it from the old course, though the repetition of "Western" signaled a continuing commitment to the European intellectual tradition.

In one respect, however, Western Culture differed strikingly from Western Civilization. Instead of being a single course administered by one department, it was designed as a group of related courses with significantly different emphases. Moreover, departments and programs were invited to submit course proposals stressing the concerns of their particular disciplines. Soon after the requirement was instituted in 1980, it boasted some half dozen "tracks" from which incoming Stanford undergraduates selected a single one according to their interests at that point in their development. Thus, the departments of history and philosophy created tracks built around their traditional subject matter. Comparative literature, which I headed at the time, developed an achronological, thematically organized track that adapted perspectives from re-

cent critical theory to create confrontations of intertextually related readings: Dante's *Inferno*, for example, confronted Aristotle's
Ethics in one direction and Eliot's *The Waste Land* in the other,
with love poems by Catullus, Petrarch, St. John of the Cross, Goethe,
and Baudelaire (all presented bilingually) jostling against one another. The track sponsored by the program in Values, Technology,
Science, and Society—a track that has proved especially popular
with students in engineering and the hard sciences—offered texts
stressing the role of technology and science in the history of our
culture; since the contributions of Chinese and Arabs could not be
ignored in this track, the latter was never quite as Western-ori-
ented as the other tracks.

The required list of fifteen texts with which this essay began was
created on pragmatic grounds to respond to the diversity of tracks
that marked the new course. Since each track came from an area
with its own intellectual agenda, a list of texts to be read in all
tracks was necessary, it was agreed, to assure what was at the time
termed a "common experience" for all Stanford students. Doubtless the distant memory of the once-successful single-track Western
Civilization helped motivate this desire for some commonality of
reading. Moreover, it was hoped (in vain, some later admitted),
that students from diverse tracks would discuss and argue about
the *Republic*, the *Inferno*, and other works from the core list at
breakfast or late at night in their dormitory rooms. Those who
selected the list claim that it was never intended to serve as a
canon and that it certainly did not have for them the sacred aura
that its later opponents accused them of attaching to it. Indeed,
they readily admit that any number of other texts (including those
from the "strongly recommended" list) might just as easily have
made it to the core list. Above all, this list was kept deliberately
short in order to leave ample room for each track to add texts
suitable to the orientation of its own discipline.

Soon after it was instituted, Western Culture looked in every
way like an extraordinarily successful course. Student evaluations,
though varying somewhat from track to track, remained exception-
ally high for a required course. Those teaching in the course were,
for the most part, enthusiastic about their work. But problems
emerged here and there even before the criticisms of the Black
Student Union. Nearly all tracks, it turned out, were somewhat
cavalier in their commitment to the core list, if only because it was
difficult to build a coherent narrative at once around the list and

around the interests of a particular discipline: the philosophy track, for example, found it could accommodate St. Augustine into its narrative more satisfactorily with *The City of God* than with the stipulated *Confessions*, while the Values, Technology, Science and Society track never knew quite how to fit St. Augustine in at all. Some faculty members, especially younger ones, refused altogether to teach in the course. For example, social scientists in non-Western area studies felt alienated by the course's exclusively Western orientation. Feminist and minority faculty complained from the beginning that the core list did not leave them enough space to pursue their particular agendas. To be sure, most tracks, in the course of the 1980s, had already evolved somewhat in directions responding to the criticisms later leveled against the course as a whole. Readings by women writers such as Sappho and Christine de Pisan made their way into most tracks. Students in a few tracks were reminded of the Arab influence on medieval philosophy in the West. The slave narratives of Equiano and Frederick Douglass came to share students' bookshelf space with *Candide* and *Civilization and Its Discontents*. Yet the course's ground-rules, including the core list, remained in place, and critics sometimes described the changes taking place in the various tracks as tokenism.

The two-year debate that began with the Black Student Union's complaints resulted, as so often within contemporary academic culture, in a compromise. After a year and a half of deliberations by a task force appointed by Stanford's provost and then after several months of debate in the Academic Senate, the latter body authorized a new course entitled Cultures, Ideas, Values. The succession of nouns making up the title was selected so that the course could be known by its initials, C.I.V., which evokes the old Western Civilization (traditionally called Western Civ), while omitting only the now-controversial adjective.

Yet this new course could also be viewed as a further evolution of the Western Culture course. Most of the older tracks remain in place, though with certain mandatory changes. Since the core list, despite the original intent (or lack of intent) that its selectors claimed, had come to be viewed by some as a sacred canon (at least the course's opponents believed that some took it to be sacred), no single reading list would henceforth be required. Instead, the perceived need for some common experience among students in all tracks will now be met by an annually selected list of several texts, authors, or issues. In order that no trace of sacrality could attach itself to this list, these texts, authors, or issues would be chosen by the teaching staff assigned to the course for a particular year. The first year's list (used in 1988–89) consisted of the Bible, Plato, St. Augustine, Machiavelli, Rousseau, and Marx; one might note that by naming mainly authors that year (the Bible was named by title because of the awkwardness in citing its authorship), tracks could choose those aspects of the author's work that best fit their disciplinary and narrative needs. The staff for the following year (1989–90) named only two authors, Marx and Freud, plus the Bible, and otherwise stipulated simply categories to insure an appropriate coverage of genre and historical period: thus, they called for "a classical Greek philosopher" (nobody disputes that this will mean Plato or Aristotle, perhaps even both); "an early Christian thinker" (St. Augustine, obviously, for most tracks, but St. Benedict, with his time-schedules and his architectural schemes, for Values, Technology, Science, and Society); "a Renaissance dramatist" (whom nobody imagines will be anybody but Shakespeare); "an Enlightenment thinker" (which would allow a track to weight its narrative in a direction suggested either by Voltaire or Rousseau). The refusal to name the last four authors can be taken as part of the whole desacralizing process that the proponents of the new course sought to initiate from the start: by naming only categories (except of course for the Bible, Marx and Freud), the staff signals its disdain for the casting of an author into the role of what, in the preceding essay, I called the foundation stone of a particular culture.

In addition to designating these common categories, the new C.I.V. is required to operate according to certain guidelines that respond to the main criticisms of the earlier course. Each track must "include the study of works by women, minorities, and persons of color," and it must study "at least one of the non-European cultures that have become components of our diverse American society." One might note that the latter guideline can presumably be met through, say, the inclusion of the *Bhagavad-Gita*, some classical Chinese poems, or a Latin American novel. Indeed, the attempt to approach foreign cultures that have left their impact upon modern America is not altogether different from the attempt by the War Issues course to stress America's European heritage— except that now the turn is away from the West to the non-West. If the old course could be accused of ethnocentrism, so of course can the new, though one might call it an ethnocentrism of the left rather than of the right. Moreover, it remains to be seen to what degree the choice of new texts for the course will reflect the make-up of the university's minority population, which, at the time the course was instituted, was approaching forty percent of the undergraduate student body. Will these texts be allocated by some form of proportional representation according to the particular minorities making up the student body? If so, the relative paucity of East Indian students would leave little if any room for the Hindu scriptures. Since the legislation speaks of "cultures that have become components of our diverse American society," does it mandate or encourage texts representing an ethnic group such as the Vietnamese, which, though fast increasing its numbers within the larger population, has not yet sent many students to Stanford? And what would determine the choice of texts from the already well-represented minorities? Will Chinese-American students consider the poetry of the T'ang dynasty as an essential part of their heritage, or will they insist on depictions of the so-called Chinese-American experience as portrayed, say, in the writings of Maxine Hong Kingston? And what about a group such as Japanese-Americans, who have not yet produced a figure with the stature of a Kingston? Does Stanford's now considerable Jewish population, which was quite small throughout the tenure of the old Western Civilization course, count as a minority, and will Jewish students express desires analogous to those voiced before the Academic Senate by Bill King? If so, would the Old Testament, Marx, and Freud provide sufficient representation, or would they demand one of the countless novels of the last half century about Jewish life in America? (The statistics issued on the minority population at Stanford do not include Jews.) Finally, one must ask what precisely determines that which is "non-Western." If the concept of an autonomous "Western" culture has become controversial, then so must its non-Western opposite. To what extent are we making the culture of the underprivileged in America synonymous with non-Western? Like most legislation born of controversy, Stanford's leaves these questions discretely open—with the appropriate accommodations to be made as the course's various tracks (as well as changing student and faculty concerns) develop.

In addition, during each of the course's three terms, at least one text, regardless of its author's personal background, is to be used "explicitly . . . to give substantial attention to the issues of race, gender, and class." Thus, Greek slavery could presumably enter a discussion of Aristotle's *Ethics* or *Politics*, and later forms of slavery could be explored by way of Caliban's role in *The Tempest* (both in Shakespeare and in Aimé Césaire's reworking of the play); gender could be central to analyses of such texts by male writers as the *Antigone* and *Madame Bovary*. Even if the texts are familiar, the interpretations are new—indeed, very much in keeping with the methods of research most actively being pursued in the humanities today. And, as I argued in the preceding essay, major changes in the interpretation of canonical texts are themselves a way of effecting canon change by what I called "other means."

Although C.I.V. is empowered to stress texts from the past "six to eight centuries," all tracks are required to "include treatment of ancient and medieval cultures." Note the plural in the last word, which would allow Islamic or ancient Chinese texts to play key roles in some future track. Despite the encouragement the new policy gives to the adoption of non-Western materials, the course will undoubtedly continue to stress the European texts that dominated its predecessor, if only because most available faculty were themselves trained solely within the so-called Western tradition. During 1988–89, however, an experimental track, directed by two Latin Americanists from different disciplines and by a black classical scholar who also specializes in Caribbean literature, was developed to concentrate on cultural conflict and interchange between Europe and the Americas; since this conflict began only five centuries ago, the ancient and medieval requirement for this track was met by introducing analogies of cultural conflict in texts such as the *Medea* and the *Chanson de Roland*. Moreover, by taking an achronological approach like the earlier comparative literature track, it sought to confront long-canonical texts with others still little known, for example Augustine's *Confessions* with a Navaho autobiography, *Son of Old Man Hat*.

The extensive use of third-world texts in this new track, entitled "Europe and the Americas," prolonged the public controversy surrounding C.I.V. well beyond the resolution of the debate in the Academic Senate in March, 1988. Soon after this track began, the *Wall Street Journal* gained access to its syllabus, which it derided both in an editorial and in an op-ed column. The editorial, for instance, expresses what might be described as a new form of culture shock:

> Dante's "Inferno" is out, for example, but "I . . . Rigoberta Menchu" is in. This epic tracks Ms. Menchu's progress from

poverty to Guatemalan revolutionary and "the effects on her of feminist and socialist ideologies." . . . We await the lecture that interprets Marx (still required) through the work of Groucho and Harpo. ("The Stanford Mind")

The *Journal* editorialist seeks to go for the jugular through such traditional rhetorical techniques as making fun of unfamiliar foreign names ("Ms. Menchu") and playing on a more familiar name, Marx, whose best-known referents were inspired by quite incompatible muses. Soon after this editorial appeared, Allan Bloom himself, writing from Paris, entered the fray with a letter to the *Journal's* editor condemning the whole new enterprise symbolized by C.I.V.:

Stanford students are to be indoctrinated with ephemeral ideologies and taught that there can be no intellectual resistance to one's own time and its passions. . . . This total surrender to the present and abandonment of the quest for standards with which to judge it are the very definition of the closing of the American mind, and I could hope for no more stunning confirmation of my thesis. ("Educational")

Since the nerve that Bloom's book touched in 1987 helped to transform what might have remained a local issue into a national one, the now-celebrated author must have taken special satisfaction in administering what he took to be the *coup de grâce* to Stanford's new course. But he may also have forgotten that the complaints he leveled against "indoctrination with ephemeral ideologies" and "surrender to the present" bear a striking similarity to the complaints to be found against his beloved Rousseau in the British press during the 1790s.

The publicity surrounding Stanford's debate obviously stressed the issue's political dimension, with the more extreme statements accusing the University (or, more precisely, its representative body, the Senate) of caving in to the demands of a small but highly vocal constituency. For those who experienced the debate on the spot the political lines were never quite as clearly defined as many in the media may have thought. For example, a number of left-leaning faculty members, especially some based in history and in the various literature departments, supported the retention of the old core list, while several members of the Classics Department, which presumably had most to lose under the C.I.V. guidelines, supported the new course. Faculty sentiments could more generally be correlated with their methodological commitments within their respective fields than with their voting behavior outside the university.

Yet it would be dishonest to deny a political dimension to the dispute. I prefer to put it another way: attempts to modify or replace canons are always in some sense political, though what we label "political" can itself not easily be separated from what we call "cultural." When these terms are kept apart, the first becomes loaded with negative meanings—Machiavellian machinations, the intimidation exercised by defiant crowds, corruption in the back room. "Cultural," by contrast, suggests generally positive things—folkloristic costumes and dances, the strivings of lowly groups to achieve their own identity, a cultivation of spiritual rather than material goals. Yet how can these terms be treated separately if we seek to understand the formation and function of literary canons? The conservative and nationalistic policies that guided the creation of the German canon, as I described it in the preceding essay, represented at once a political and a cultural program, though, from our present point of view, we are likely to stress the political side of this program, if only because we think we see the nationalist bias in the canon culminating in the ideology of Nazism. Similarly, it has been fashionable in recent years to view the development of English studies during the late nineteenth century as a means of social control (Eagleton 17–30) over a potentially rebellious mass. From a contemporary liberal or radical point of view we are likely to read this development as predominantly political—even a bit sinister—in its motives. Yet a recent study of the institution of the first English-literature professorship in England during the late 1820s portrays a more benign program, namely, the attempt of utilitarian reformers to promote useful reading habits and general cultural advancement among the newly literate masses through exposure to the best writing in their native tongue (Court). By the same token, the institution of the new C.I.V. course must look like a political conspiracy to those who oppose it, while to those more positively inclined, it may well seem like the affirmation of a sense of community among peoples who had been culturally disenfranchised. If one insists on separating the political from the cultural, one is likely to gain at best a partial view of the picture.

A study of the major canon changes of the past would reveal a complex of factors that range considerably beyond either one of those categories I have described as political or cultural. The devel-

opment of the French classical system during the seventeenth century encompasses such diverse though closely related phenomena
as the consolidation of absolute monarchy, the taming of the old
nobility, and the cultivation of new values such as *honnêteté* and
biensèance that straddle the ethical and the aesthetic realms. The
German shift in taste from French to English literary models during the late eighteenth century is at once an expression of a new
bourgeois class consciousness and a revolt against French cultural
hegemony. The development of separate national literary canons
in the course of the nineteenth century can scarcely be separated
from the attempts of every European state to instill national consciousness within its people—and of some of these states to pursue
imperial ambitions. The institution of Western civilization courses
in America in the wake of the First World War responded not only
to the European sense of cultural crisis, but, coming as it did
precisely at the time that the United States first felt itself a world
power, served to portray this power as heir to that whole tradition
we came to call Western. Stanford's recent move toward a more
globally oriented course recognizes at once the increasingly heter-
ogeneous make-up of the country's college-student population and
America's entanglement in a world economy over which it can no
longer exercise the control it once enjoyed. Might one speculate
that the new course also articulates the waning of America's earlier
power?

EIGHT

From Opera to Postmodernity:
Institutions as Frames

Among the performance art forms flourishing today, none would seem more distant from a postmodernist sensibility than opera. One need merely visualize the well-groomed crowd in any of the world's major opera houses as it scurries through the lobby to reach the auditorium before the lights go out precisely at their appointed time. (Lateness is generally punished with a mandatory stay in the lobby throughout the first act, though sometimes with the performance thrown in on closed-circuit tv to remind the stragglers what they might be seeing in the flesh had they been less dilatory.) Those in the darkened auditorium accept a role of silence and passivity (programs these days caution the audience to switch off their digital-watch alarms) as they witness the active goings on just the other side of the proscenium.

This proscenium, which became a part of theater architecture at more or less the time opera was invented nearly four centuries ago,

163

has, especially since the mid-nineteenth century, worked in effect to separate audience from singers, to assure that the stage illusion remain inviolate. It hardly matters if the singers are obese or are unable to act with the verisimilitude that audiences have come to expect in the non-musical theater. Indeed, the programs in the spectators' hands (not to speak of those supertitles projected with increasing frequency these days above the proscenium) seek to guarantee a correspondence between the doings onstage and the text that is being enacted. "When Padre Guardiano answers her call for help, Alvaro curses his fate, but Guardiano and the dying Leonora beg him to find salvation in religion," one reads at the end of a typical program synopsis ("Synopsis"). Whatever these fateful words may mean, we are expected to take their relationship to the stage action on faith.

The correspondence we accept between this action and some given narrative itself corresponds to the unity we are expected to experience between the music and the actual words it is setting. Ever since opera's beginnings, composers and theorists have justified opera as a medium by means of its ability to wed music and text. Although most often they have made words the dominant partner, even those composers who have favored music over words—for example Berlioz or Wagner in his later phase—would not have questioned the underlying unity that had traditionally defined opera. To insure that their audiences experience this unity properly, opera companies go to great lengths to encourage them to come to the performance well prepared. Thus, local opera guilds sponsor demonstration lectures on how to listen to key passages, and company-sponsored shops sell recordings of a particular season's repertory so that operagoers may prepare themselves, libretto in hand and earphones on head, in the privacy of their dens.

The passivity that one notes in opera audiences is encouraged as well in the settings within which performances take place. As an edifice the opera house has characteristically cultivated grandeur both by its size and its trappings. Moreover, many of the world's great opera houses are placed as centrally and conspicuously as cathedrals were in earlier days. The imperial or the royal box (even in countries that have overthrown hereditary government since the time their opera houses were constructed) serves as a visual reminder that opera has traditionally been nurtured and flaunted by those who held power. (In a country such as ours, which has never known royalty, the so-called Diamond Horseshoe of boxes at the old Metropolitan in New York kept the audience aware of the patronizing power exercised by the local financial oligarchy.)

As an art form intimately connected with the reigning establishment, it is no wonder that opera projects an image of something considerably larger than life. As I once put it in another context, opera is the last remaining refuge of the high style (*Opera* 15). As such it establishes a relationship with its consumers much like that of an earlier high-style genre, epic poetry. Like literary epic, opera cultivates heroic and often extravagant actions that nobody would take to be (nor even desire to view as) typical of everyday life. The traditional critical vocabulary that we associate with epic, for example terms such as *awe, admiration,* and *wonder,* more adequately describes the emotions that operagoers expect to experience than does the terminology associated with the more modest literary genres.

The extravagance that marks the style and content of opera, not to speak of the physical characteristics of the opera house, is matched by an economic extravagance demanded of operatic productions, whose costs are passed on to the spectators and benefactors (whether the latter come from the private or the public sector depends on the institutional arrangements for the arts in a particular country). Impresarios have complained of singers' financial demands since the seventeenth century. Even without these demands, total production costs (and also often ticket prices) have generally proved higher for opera than for the other live performing arts at any given time. In view of the extravagance that the form demands (and that is in turn demanded of those seeking entrance into the opera house), it is no wonder that opera finds little room for minimalism or for any of the other currents which might question its essential aesthetic.

Thus far I have suggested what might seem an essentially timeless image of opera as a form whose changes over the years have been less significant than its continuities. Although certain issues have been central to opera since its early days—for example, debates on the relation of music to text—the image I have presented of opera as a deliberately and selfconsciously elevated form of art is one that developed only during the last century. One need only compare this image to, say, the carnivalesque world of the eighteenth-century Italian opera house to note the most striking differences. Instead of the silent contemporary audience sitting in darkness and devoting all its attention to the stage illusion before it, the

Italian audience two centuries ago would have walked in and out
at will and paid at best sporadic attention to the singers onstage.
Since theater lighting was dependent on candles, lights could not
easily be switched on and off; indeed, the darkened auditorium
was not introduced until the time of Wagner, who exploited a new
technology to achieve a highly illusionistic theatrical effect. The
same Italian opera houses that today function as palaces of high
art were, in their early days, similar to social clubs, for the boxes
were owned by families who came to the opera to carouse, to play
cards, and occasionally—if the famed castrato onstage was about
to embark on some bravura passage—to pay brief attention to the
music itself. In view of the noise and the confusion, the sustained
theatrical illusion we have come to know during the last century
was impossible. Whatever awe or admiration the audience experienced was occasioned by the vocal prowess of individual singers
and not, as in more recent times, by the massive combination of
forces—large orchestra, dance, scenery, lighting—that unite with
the singers to produce that larger-than-life effect we have come to
associate with opera.

If the admiration that a singer excited was particularly strong,
the opera could be interrupted with a demand for an encore; by the
same token, a performance that for one reason or another did not
please could be interrupted by a vehement display of hissing that
itself rivaled the stage action in its theatricality. Musical scores
made no pretense to record what would actually take place in real
performance, for singers, somewhat analogous to actors in the com-
media dell'arte, were expected to add their own elaborations to the
vocal lines in the text. Even those members of the audience who
paid more attention to the singing than to the card games could
dispense with the extensive preparation—pre-opera lectures, record listening, program notes—that our contemporary audience
needs or demands. At most, they might have bought a libretto to
follow during the performance (baroque vocal style did not make
for comprehensible diction even in one's own tongue). From a
musical point of view operas presented no special difficulties to
their audiences. The works one heard were all new or nearly new,
much as the films one attends today are. The dramatic and musical
conventions governing new operas were so familiar to everybody
that the audience preparation we demand today would have seemed
both unnecessary and ridiculous.

I have presented two contrasting images of opera, not, as some readers might suspect, to portray an ancestor of postmodern aesthetics in the boisterous and non-illusionistic world of eighteenth-century Italian opera, but to show how a genre— like those I took up in part 2 as well as the canons in the preceding two essays— is rooted in particular institutional frameworks at different historical moments. The earlier form satisfied social and aesthetic needs quite distinct from those we have come to associate with opera during the last century. Moreover, what we call an operatic text—whether in the form of libretto or full score—has little meaning outside the institutional framework in which it is performed. Thus, whenever an eighteenth-century *opera seria* is revived today in the major houses, it would be experienced by its audience far differently than in its own time. Not only are earlier performance practices difficult to reproduce, but the later audience's demand for a sustained theatrical illusion encourages extensive cuts and the addition of massive scenic effects that would have seemed quite foreign to the earlier aesthetic. (It is little wonder that these revivals in the major houses are still relatively rare—and then largely to serve as vehicles for virtuoso singers.)

From an institutional point of view the opera house that has emerged during the past century has much in common with another institution that developed at the same time, namely the art museum.[1] Both the opera house and the museum are heirs to that nineteenth-century historical mentality that, as I described it in the Prologue, sought to reconstitute what was deemed to be every aesthetically significant period of time and then offer it to the public in a readily consumable form. The museum presents as many historical periods as a particular collection and current taste will allow: thus, any visitor to a major collection can expect to find rooms devoted to seventeenth-century Dutch landscape, *quattrocento* Florentine painting, and the French impressionists, not to speak of Egyptian, Greek, and Roman art (though ancient cultures, as well as twentieth-century art, may sometimes be housed in separate collections within the same city). In recent years museums have sought to accommodate artifacts from more distant cultures, for example oceanic and pre-Columbian art, or previously non-canonical areas such as French academic painting of the nineteenth century and American art before abstract expressionism.

Although its historical range is far more circumscribed in time and place than the museum, the modern opera house during any given season seeks a repertory representing what it takes to be the major moments of operatic history; thus, a typical season would mount productions of a so-called "bel canto" opera of the early nineteenth century, a French and a Russian opera of the later nineteenth century, a sprinkling of works to display each of those composers—above all, Mozart, Verdi, Wagner, Puccini, and Strauss—deemed sufficiently towering in stature to have defined the genre for today's audiences. In recent years, managements have made forays into pre-Mozart opera and have re-canonized such once-famed opera composers as Monteverdi, Handel, and Gluck, though no single work during this extended period, which encompasses virtually half the history of the genre, has yet achieved a secure hold in the contemporary repertory; similarly, certain areas new to the art museum, for example oceanic sculpture and Near Eastern textiles, have yet to attract the imagination of most museum visitors.

Both the museum and the opera house depend on extensive educational programs to mediate their offerings to the public. Just as opera mediates by way of recordings, televized broadcasts, and guide-books, as well as the lectures and program-notes that a particular house organizes for its clientele, so the museum educates its public with art-books, docent lectures, curator's notes on the walls, and descriptive catalogues prepared for special shows. Both the opera house and the museum have become the domain for specialists attached to the style of a particular historical period.[2] Opera identifies singers, conductors, and sometimes even stage directors especially suited to and trained for, say, the style of bel canto, Wagnerian music-drama, Italian *verismo*. Similarly, the most prestigious museums boast curators in specialties such French nineteenth-century painting, Egyptian art, and pre-Columbian pottery. Whether or not they receive their funding directly from public sources, both the museum and the opera house are objects of civic and often national pride, and the buildings that house them (as well as the sites at which they are constructed) are expected to demonstrate that they are worthy of this pride. Both, in fact, together with the standard literary anthologies used in classrooms, speak for what passes as the official culture of their time and place.

In view of their role in defining and expressing this official culture, it is scarcely any wonder that both the museum and the opera house maintained a skeptical, sometimes overtly hostile attitude to the more radical movements that took place within art and music during the early part of this century. To the extent that modernism has questioned the validity of earlier canons, it questions the very idea of an operatic repertory or of a museum devoted to preserving the artifacts of earlier periods. It is significant that a Metropolitan Opera impresario, when asked some years ago why he rarely produced new works, replied proudly that an opera house is essentially a museum devoted to the past. Yet the analogy this impresario sought to make no longer seems as convincing as it once did, for the opera house and the museum have come to differ in one essential respect: whereas the former has never made its peace with modernity, the latter, at least since the middle years of this century, has managed to accommodate even those strains of contemporary art that defy the very idea of a museum. To be sure, the art of our century has often had recourse to special museums of modern art to display itself. Yet these modern museums have themselves absorbed the historicist principles as well as the whole institutional framework behind the traditional art museum. For example, just as the latter is organized around specific historical periods that visitors pass through in more or less chronological order, so the typical museum of modern art directs its clientele through the many periods and schools—for example, cubism (analytic and synthetic), futurism, expressionism, surrealism, pop— that have blazed forth (if only briefly) in the course of this century. It is characteristic of modern museums, indeed of many traditional museums as well, that they include examples of the latest postmodern style—be it minimalism, conceptualism, neo-expressionism— not only in special shows but also in special rooms (often placed so that visitors will reach them in the proper chronological place at the end of their itinerary) that quickly transform this new style into a permanent historical category.

One asks why the art museum's capacity in recent years to transform the new into a historical category has not been shared by opera. Whatever answers one may come up with, one must first acknowledge the fact that even modernist operas from the early part of this century do not have the secure place in the repertory that comparable works in the visual arts have in the museum. The "regular" operatic repertory common to houses throughout Europe and North America extends barely 140 years from, say, *Le nozze di Figaro* (1786) to *Turandot* (1926). Among the twentieth-century works that have achieved this status, most of them by Strauss and Puccini, all except Strauss's early *Salome* and *Elektra*, together with Debussy's *Pelléas et Mélisande*, were deemed musically conservative in their own time. By regular repertory I refer to works that opera administrations can count on to draw audiences and that record companies need not hesitate to produce even if rival recordings are already available. Beyond this repertory there exists what could be called a peripheral repertory of modern works that are presented sporadically. Among musically "difficult" works, the two Alban Berg operas, several Janacek operas, Schoenberg's *Moses und Aron*, and Stravinsky's *Rake's Progress* now belong to the peripheral repertory in North America. Yet even this peripheral repertory contains far fewer "advanced" works than it does works that, however "distinguished" one may deem them, are unashamedly conservative in musical and often also in theatrical style: one thinks here of the later Strauss, of Benjamin Britten, of Francis Poulenc's *Dialogues des Carmélites*. (What counts as regular and peripheral repertory often differs according to location: *Wozzeck*, for instance, has achieved regular status in many German houses, and several Britten operas enjoy this status in the United Kingdom.) One can also speak of a peripheral repertory of works that are not only musically conservative, but also conspicuously undistinguished—works such as Douglas Moore's *Ballad of Baby Doe* or the various Gian Carlo Menotti operas that managements exhume in the hope that they can sell their audiences on contemporary opera, which in such instances means simply operas that were composed in long-since-assimilated idioms during the audience's own time.

Even though one can speak of a sizable peripheral repertory of twentieth-century works, one might also note that an uncommonly large number waited many years before they gained entrance into the opera house. Although during much of its first half century *Porgy and Bess* appeared in occasional theatrical productions outside the opera house, only in recent years has it come to seem worthy of the official operatic stage. Even conservative composers such as Britten and Menotti felt forced to produce their own operas at festivals that they themselves created so that these works might gain sufficient familiarity to eventually reach the opera house. Among the more musically advanced scores, some could be heard for years only in concert performances under the sponsorship of societies dedicated to contemporary music; many such scores owe their survival to the fact that some influential conductor could prove them performable.

It is true that opera houses, despite their general unfriendliness to new work, occasionally commission operas for special occasions, usually of a festive sort. Thus, the Metropolitan commissioned Samuel Barber's *Antony and Cleopatra* for the opening of its new quarters in 1966, and San Francisco commissioned Andrew Imbrie's *Angle of Repose* for the city's (and country's) bicentennial ten years later; despite the festiveness (and expense) with which they come into the world, the act of commissioning is often perceived as a kiss of death, and such works rarely if ever enter even the peripheral repertory. New works are of course more common in European, especially German, opera houses than they are in North America, if only because the former can count on government subvention;[3] yet the ten- or twenty-year survival rate of these new work. is not, I suspect, significantly greater than that of the relatively fewer new works performed on this side of the Atlantic. A large proportion of the new works performed here are done outside the major opera centers by smaller companies in, say, Minneapolis or St. Louis that seek to draw in big-city reviewers and to demonstrate that their town hopefully does not belong to a cultural hinterland.[4] Costs of these companies can be kept low by a deliberate reigning in of resources, for example the use of relatively unknown (and thus inexpensive) singers, of a small orchestra, and with little of the spectacle that audiences have traditionally associated with grand opera. Perhaps most important, these companies are usually not saddled with the huge opera houses (much larger than their European equivalents) to which the more established companies are tied, and, as a result, they can perform in smaller theaters— sometimes converted old movie houses—that do not demand either the vocal power of major singers or the attendance figures of a large house.

In view of the obscurity to which most operatic writing in our century has been doomed, it is a wonder how many composers and librettists of the most varying talents and styles have continued to work in the medium. Here the comparison between opera house and art museum may once more be instructive. Whereas even the most popular older operas are financial burdens that depend on extreme munificence (whether from governmental or private sources), modernist visual artifacts, at least since the middle of this century, have been successful financial commodities whose ownership, whether by affluent individuals, corporations, or by the museums to which they are often donated, confers a prestige commensurate with their perceived monetary value. About the only big money to be made in opera goes to a few top singers whose voices rarely show off well in (or are even necessary to) contemporary musical styles; by contrast, since the middle of the century a range of people within the art world—private gallery owners, collectors (who often view themselves as investors), and sometimes even the artists themselves—have been able to profit handsomely from the latest art. Moreover, whereas the opera house must cope with the wrath of subscribers forced to pay for an evening's performance of a new work that they usually dread attending, the museum can display its more provocative new acquisitions in special rooms that its visitors may, if they so desire, skip without feeling they have wasted their time or money.

Considerably more is at stake in the composition and production of an opera than in the making and display of visual artifacts. Whereas the productivity of opera composers has declined from several works a year in the early nineteenth century to not many more per lifetime in our own century, visual artists by and large have continued the productivity that marked their predecessors in earlier centuries. From the consumer's point of view, new operas demand much greater exposure (whether by recordings or by live performers) than visual artifacts before they can be assimilated; visual artifacts, moreover, can be looked at relatively quickly, and once the consumers have assimilated a particular style (or assimilated the work of an artist with a pronouncedly individual style), they can absorb stylistically similar artifacts with relative ease. Even if one were thoroughly at ease with *Moses und Aron* or *The Rake's Progress*, a new opera in an equivalent style by Schoenberg or Stravinsky—even if there were one—would demand considerable exposure and preparation on the listener's part; by contrast, one can visit a museum with, say, a previously unfamiliar Rothko or Pollock and deal with it in relatively short order. It is surely harder for consumers of opera than of visual artifacts to justify (whether to themselves or others) the effort that must be expended in mastering a new work, especially since they can tell themselves (quite correctly) that the opera will likely soon be forgotten. (Audiences before the mid-nineteenth century of course rarely expected the operas they attended to last beyond a single season.) Moreover, whereas opera functions principally as "entertainment" (even if also of a most prestigious sort), the new visual artifact can claim to meet a functional need—for example, filling an otherwise blank domestic or corporate wall or monumentalizing some public space.

The historicizing mission that both the opera house and the art museum have undertaken has resulted, in recent years, in the reassessment and revival of past periods that had long been neglected or had fallen into disrepute. Just as the museum has transferred its French nineteenth-century academic paintings from the basement and found room as well for non-Western artifacts that—comparable to the non-Western texts that became the focal point of the Stanford debate discussed in the preceding essay—had earlier seemed too primitive to warrant precious exhibition space, so the opera house has restored the bel canto repertory (with the result that specialist singers who can negotiate the florid passages undertake rigorous training to meet the new demand) and has moved backward in time before Mozart to produce (if only as part of the peripheral repertory) the occasional Handel or Vivaldi work or, even further backward, to opera's beginnings to restore (with a good bit of guess-work about what its proper instrumentation should be) a Monteverdi or a Cavalli. The great difference between the two institutions is that the art museum, unlike the opera house, has proved able to convince its consumers that the latest style belongs to a historical period that it behooves them to know as intimately as any earlier style, while the opera house invites groans and protests when it asks the equivalent from its audiences.

The difference between the two institutions does not derive simply from the fact that visual artifacts, as I have suggested, breed familiarity more readily than auditory ones. Non-operatic "serious" music during this century has had as difficult a time establishing itself with audiences as opera. What distinguishes opera in this respect from, say, symphonic music is that opera does not seem to fare well in small packages. (The formality and sublimity of style that non-comic opera has traditionally cultivated themselves discourage brevity.) Although symphony orchestras perform new works with a regularity not shared by opera companies, the typical new symphonic work is a twenty-minute piece that an audience is generally willing to tolerate as a means of paying its duty to high culture, but on condition that this piece merely supplement such familiar fare as, say, a Beethoven concerto or a Strauss tone poem. (Composers, in fact, consciously cultivate brevity of style in order to get themselves heard.) Similarly, ballet companies have been able to offer their more experimental products in small packages that can be grouped in a program with more classical pieces; thus, the New York City Ballet can stage Jerome Robbins's distinctly postmodern *Moves: A Ballet in Silence*—a less-than-half-hour work without musical accompaniment and with its dancers practising abstract movements in informal dress—together with, say, a group of Balanchine pieces that, however abstract *their* movements, are danced in costumes and accompanied by reassuringly familiar music. A considerable number of musical experiments in our time have not even taken place in either the symphonic or operatic medium but in diverse (and usually small) combinations of instruments and/or singers that, if they get performed at all, have had to depend on specialized organizations, with equally specialized (and usually small) audiences such as Schoenberg's Gesellschaft für musikalische Privataufführungen in Vienna around 1920 or the Monday evening concerts inspired by Stravinsky and Robert Craft in Los Angeles during the 1950s.

If short operas had not experienced the difficulty they have had in getting heard, many hard-to-digest works would have been able—like short instrumental pieces and ballets—to make themselves familiar to audiences in our time. Yet operas of less than a full evening's length have rarely succeeded in entering the regular repertory. There is of course no shortage of fine one-act operas going back to the early eighteenth century in Italy when short comic operas such as Pergolesi's *La serva padrona* were composed to serve as intermission diversions between the acts of *opere serie*. Yet in our own century a natural place for these works has not been found. Impresarios nowadays can justify making a full evening out of Strauss's *Salome* or *Elektra* since each of these, despite encompassing only a single act, offers close to two hours of music—more, in fact, than such an opera as *La Boheme*, whose brevity is masked by its three intermissions. Despite the odds against less-than-full-length operas, composers of our century have produced them in considerable numbers, often because the experimental modes in which they were working could best be realized in brief, tense works such as Schoenberg's *Erwartung* and *Die glückliche Hand* or Stravinsky's *Oedipus Rex*. Although opera houses have often put together evenings of such works in varying combinations, none has secured much of a place for itself in the repertory—nor have such less rigorously experimental works as Ravel's two one-act operas or the multitude of short operas by composers the likes of Hindemith and Bartok.

As with poetry and the non-musical theater, that modernist impulse toward achieving intensity by means of suggestiveness rather than explicitness manifests itself in works—often of a quite ambitious sort—of considerably more brevity than one finds in earlier centuries. From this point of view such operas as *Erwartung* and Poulenc's *La Voix humaine*—each with only a single character and without chorus or ballet or the scenic resources associated with grand opera—are paradigmatic modernist works. Yet this impulse toward brevity (and austerity) also conflicts with the desire of the opera audience for a sustained illusion, for a prescribed period in which it can submit itself passively to the overpowering auditory and visual forces that emanate from the stage. It is significant that the only short operas that remain part of the regular repertory are Mascagni's *Cavalleria rusticana* and Leoncavallo's *I pagliacci*, which, though by different composers, are in musically similar styles and on a similar theme—namely the consequences of illicit love among the southern Italian poor—that the audience can experience twice over, sometimes even with the same tenor and baritone appearing in each. (Despite many recent attempts to vary this double bill by substituting another short opera [as often as not a member of Puccini's *Trittico*] for either Mascagni's or Leoncavallo's, these two works have proved difficult to separate—as one notes from the fact that in recent years they have been rechristened with a single name, *Cav/Pag*.)

The opera audience's essential passivity and its perceived need for illusion have manifested themselves not only in a bias toward full-length works, but also in the fact that those modernist works that have entered even the peripheral repertory have posed only moderate challenges toward operatic form. As opera developed over the years, and especially during the nineteenth century, it defined itself as an institution through a particular mix and range of personnel—an orchestra of a certain amplitude; a group of singers who, despite differences in period styles, carefully distinguish themselves both from speaking actors and from singers in such popular forms as operetta and folksong; and, despite their relative unimportance in certain operatic period styles, chorus and dancers. To the extent that modernism in the various arts has challenged and questioned the materials and means by which a particular art form has traditionally realized itself, one would expect that modernist operas would call for an orchestra with new types of instruments, or perhaps for no orchestra at all; or with singers who pursue a technique wholly different from that with which opera singers have ordinarily been trained. As it turns out, challenges of this sort, even if occasionally posed, have not entrenched themselves in the way that, say, collage and various types of mixed media have entered the mainstream of the visual arts.

Indeed, those modernist operas that have more or less entered the repertory have each tended to challenge only a single aspect of that institution we call opera. Whatever we may call modernist in *Ariadne auf Naxos* lies less in its use of opera personnel—though Strauss has here reduced the gigantic orchestra of his earlier operas to Mozartian proportions—than in its theatrical idea, namely the use of a play within a play and, even more conspicuously modernist, its selfconscious juxtaposition of tragic and comic conventions; even when Strauss parodies earlier operatic styles, the audience has come to experience these parodies in an unselfconscious way, very much as it hears Mozart's parodies of *opere serie* in his Italian comic operas.

Similarly, from a musical point of view the Brecht/Weill *Mahagonny* and *Porgy and Bess* challenge the institution principally through their use of jazz techniques, which, when they were composed during the 1930s, must have seemed to subvert operatic claims to represent high as against popular art. An audience today would no longer hear this challenge, for in the intervening half century a profusion of new and often louder musical styles has reshaped our conception of what constitutes popular culture. Indeed, now that these two operas have entered at least the peripheral repertory, we come to experience their jazz rhythms in much the same way that we experience such earlier popular forms as the oriental marches in Mozart or the tunes blasted out onstage by a Verdi *banda*. (The political irreverence of *Mahagonny* is scarcely more shocking today than that of *Le nozze di Figaro;* moreover, sung irreverence is ordinarily less explosive than its spoken equivalent.)

For many years, as I pointed out in essay 4, it was assumed that *Moses und Aron* was too forbidding a work to enjoy the success it has turned out to have in those opera houses enterprising enough to stage it. Yet except for its use of serial composition (an attribute it shares with Berg's *Lulu*, which has established itself even more widely than Schoenberg's opera), *Moses und Aron* challenges its audience with only one conspicuously "unoperatic" feature—the assignment of the Moses role (and of some choral passages) not to a conventional singing voice but to that amalgam of song and speech that the composer called *Sprechstimme*. Once an audience reconciles itself to the opera's use of *Sprechstimme* and its lack of tonality, it can discover amply traditional operatic elements in the score—for example, the extravagantly florid singing of Aron, sufficiently massive orchestral and choral forces to overwhelm it in the manner of late nineteenth-century opera, and, in the Dance around the Gold Calf, an orientalist purple patch with the lurid appeal of the Bacchanal in *Samson et Dalila* or the Dance of the Seven Veils in *Salome*.

In view of the resistance that opera, in comparison with other art forms, has shown to change, one may ask how opera has responded to that attitude which we have come to call postmodernism in the various arts. Postmodern opera, if such a style has developed at all, should in fact threaten the very foundation upon which opera as an institution has rested during the last century and more. To the extent that opera has defined itself as a bastion of high art, it would presumably resist the attempt of postmodernists to break down the traditional distinction between "high" and "low" cultural artifacts. To the extent that opera has been committed to the union of word and music, it would resist a postmodernist attempt not only to rupture this union, but also to question any sort of unity that the work might claim. To the extent that it seeks to overwhelm its audience into a passive state, it would not, like much postmodernist art, encourage its audiences to participate actively in its creation, or analysis, or questioning, or even rejection.[5]

Yet despite these resistances, a postmodern intrusion into the opera house has in fact been taking place, and it has manifested itself principally in two forms—first, in new modes of interpreting the operatic canon and, second, in some new approaches to operatic form. The first, and thus far the more pervasive of these intrusions has been the development, primarily during the last twenty years, of what can be called directorial opera, namely the reinterpretation of canonical works in often iconoclastic ways—what, in speaking of literary reinterpretations in essay 6, I called canon change "by other means." I refer here to the controversial restagings of classic operas by directors such as Jean-Pierre Ponnelle, Götz Friedrich, Patrice Chéreau, and Peter Sellars, who seek to rethink and control the visual elements of a performance to a far greater degree than opera directors before them did. (Some, as Ponnelle did, not only direct the stage action, but also design their own scenery and costumes.) However iconoclastic a postmodernist operatic interpretation may be, it allows opera to maintain itself as an institution, for, just as new reading strategies may change our perception of a familiar literary work without altering its text or even questioning its place in the canon, it preserves the traditional canon and ordinarily leaves a work's original music and text intact; indeed, since the reinterpretation normally takes place purely in visual terms, audience members who feel offended by what the director is doing to a beloved opera may simply close their eyes and listen to a quite familiar score emanating from the singers and orchestra.

But of course audiences who have purchased tickets for this, the most expensive of the performing arts, are rarely willing to close their eyes; they are much more likely, in fact, to use the opportunity of an iconoclastic production to express their outrage that what they take to be a sacred work of art has been subjected to a form of sacrilege. Nowadays the vehement expression of outrage that we associate with the reception of modernist experiments in the other arts early in this century is most likely to take place in opera—and, in particular, in postmodern interpretations of canonical operas. This outrage against what is perceived as violating some timeless image of a great work emanates not only from audiences threatening to cancel their subscriptions, but also from performers, for example the famed soprano who cancelled just before the opening of a Ponnelle production of *Cavalleria rusticana* in San Francisco after she was asked to appear pregnant and submit herself to obscene gestures; from opera house staff, sometimes even from the impresario who had hired the director without quite realizing what he was getting into; from the local newspaper critics, who write in the hope that their denunciations will insure more traditional productions in the future; from scholars, for example the theater historian who recently attacked contemporary directorial opera in a book aptly (though also naively) entitled *Misdirection*.[6]

The most common accusation made against director-dominated opera is that directors take a cavalier, sometimes even defiant attitude toward the opera's libretto: not only does the stage action often contradict or ignore the words uttered by the singers, but it also belies the stage directions that the librettist and/or composer wrote into the score. For example, Ponnelle aroused considerable furor with *Der fliegende Holländer*, in which the whole action is turned into a dream of the helmsman, with the latter doubling (and sung by the same tenor) as the rejected lover Erik. Since even the

boldest of directorial opera productions tend to retain the traditional vocal and orchestral score, the imposition of a visual action
at odds with the text creates a rupture that not only undermines
the claims that opera has traditionally made to unify music and
text but also challenges opera's pretensions (at least since Wagner's
time) to create an organic work of art all of whose parts function
harmoniously with one another. (One wonders whether the recent
craze for supertitles represents a conspiracy between opera managements and the public to provide a check against the contemporary directorial imagination; it is significant, for instance, that
Ponnelle objected to supertitles.)

But directorial reinterpetation often goes far beyond simply con-
flating characters and changing stage directions and plots. Contemporary audiences may expect to find such verbal signals as graffiti
painted on flats or Brechtian projections directing them how to
interpret the action they witness on stage. Visual objects associated
with popular culture are displayed as a means of challenging operatic claims to represent a "higher" form of culture. Historical settings stipulated in the score are often discarded in favor of new
settings intended to demythify the opera. (Changes in historical
milieu have been common since at least mid-century in the non-
musical theater, especially in the production of Shakespeare, whom
audiences—perhaps because they are often reminded by directors
that Elizabethans played Romans in Elizabethan guise—are increasingly willing to accept in, say, Victorian or even punk dress.)
Thus, Friedrich's *Aida* used stage sets of sheet metal suggesting a
technological culture as a means of commenting on Verdi's image
of Egypt. Chéreau's *Ring des Nibelungen*, commissioned by Wagner's descendants for the Bayreuth centennial in 1976, relocated its
characters from their mythical ancient realm into the nineteenth-
century world of the composer, with the Rhine maidens transformed into prostitutes and prancing about a hydro-electric dam.
(Despite the family sponsorship, the Chéreau production's power
to outrage was reflected in many critical reviews as well as in the
refusal of Wagner's aged daughter-in-law to meet the director.)

Outside the institutional constraints of the opera house, directorial opera can take even freer forms. Film enables visual effects
different from those possible on the stage, and, perhaps even more
important, film can remain impervious to the complaints of the
opera subscriber. For example, Hans-Jürgen Syberberg's filmed
version of *Parsifal*, though as faithful to the music as any stage

performance, cultivates a variety of alienating effects such as the refusal fully to synchronize vocal sounds with the mouths from which they supposedly emanate to the transformation of the hero visually from male to female (though retaining his accustomed tenor voice) at the point that he resists Kundry's temptation. Similarly, a directorial reinterpretation on a non-operatic stage allows for less traditionally operatic expectations. For instance, Peter Brook's *Carmen*, designed for an intimate theater, departs radically from the musical score, which it reduces to the smallest of proportions: whole singing roles are eradicated, choral and orchestral forces minimalized, arias cut down to what are no more than suggestive fragments of their familiar selves, and, to counter the effect of the proscenium in ordinary opera, the spectators sit in a circle around the singers. It seems no accident that many admirers of the Brook *Carmen* were persons with distinctly postmodern tastes and with a disdain for opera; by the same token, many operagoers willing to close their eyes to the visual violence done by iconoclastic directors in the opera house found to their disappointment that Brook's *Carmen* did not even compensate them with their long-familiar musical score.

Although director-dominated opera has been the chief means by which a postmodernist sensibility has entered the opera house, one can suggest at least the beginning of a second threat to operatic tradition in the composition of new operas within a distinctly postmodernist mode. In view of the argument of this paper, a rigorously postmodern opera would seem a contradiction in terms; indeed, as I shall indicate, those contemporary operas that seek entrance into the opera house are forced to subdue the anti-aesthetic attitude we have come to associate with postmodernism.[7] The possibility of a significant postmodern opera first became evident in the work of Philip Glass, most forcefully perhaps in the first piece he called an opera, *Einstein on the Beach* (1976). By attaching this label to his work, Glass challenged his audience's generic expectations in a way he could not have done by simply labeling *Einstein*, say, a "performance," "mixed media," or some other term without the historical burden inherent in the word "opera." Moreover, the Metropolitan Opera House was the first American site in which *Einstein* was performed, a fact that did not so much confirm the work's status as opera as underline the gap separating it from the other works that audiences experienced in the same setting.

Indeed, these performances did not even emanate from the Met-

ropolitan as an institution (they were not part of the regular sub-
scription series and, like much contemporary music, were subsi-
dized by a foundation) nor could they have, for they did not use
either operatic voices or an opera orchestra. The small instrumental group, in fact, was the Philip Glass Ensemble, which, in the best
modernist fashion, the composer had put together over the years as
a means of getting his own compositions performed. The sounds
coming from this ensemble must have sounded strange in the opera
house, for they were processed by an electronic synthesizer. About
the only traditionally operatic elements in *Einstein* were the chorus
and the dancing—but the choral text consisted of counting numbers to the changing musical rhythms or naming the notes being
vocalized, while the dancing maintained a considerable distance
from the classical ballet style that still dominates operatic productions. In addition, Glass and the director/designer, Robert Wilson
(whose name, significantly, preceded the composer's on the program and whose collaborative role was considerably greater than
that of the traditional opera librettist) challenged the traditional
operatic attempt to unite words and music by making the text
seem irrelevant not only to the music being heard but also to the
whole Einstein theme.[8]

This text, most of which is spoken against a musical background, is in fact notable for the pop-culture elements it shares
with other forms of postmodern writing—for example, appropriations from advertising ("so if you're tired of glasses. Go to New
York a Phonic Center on/Ele/ven West Fourty-Second Street near
Fifth Avenue for sight with no hassle" [*Music* 72]); clichés drawn
from such diverse areas of modern life as male-female relationships
("Finally she spoke. 'Do you love me, John?' she asked. 'You know
I love you, darling.' " [78]) and travel ("One of the most beautiful
streets of Paris is called Les Champs-Elysées, which means the
Elysian Fields" [69]); apparently contextless phrases that resonate
with undetermined meanings ("Mr Bojangles So if you see any of
those baggy pants chuck the hills it was huge" [68]). Although the
music seems to go its own way independent of the text, it too
mimics elements from everyday life, both those of an overtly musical nature such as chorales and those of a "non-musical" sort such
as the rhythms of a train.

Despite the fact that the text and music provide no narrative of
the kind one expects to witness in opera, the spectacle enacted
onstage presents at least the semblance of narrative development,

namely the transition from a nineteenth-century world to the nuclear age. But the work refuses any form of organization that one could call an operatic plot, and what we see of the title character is certainly not the "real" person Einstein, but rather the mythical image he projected onto the world with his incessant violin playing (rendered with the repetitive rhythms central to Glass's style) and with his role as father of nuclear energy. Since Glass's style, like that of his fellow minimalist composers, eschews the narrative development characteristic of the mainstream of Western music, the relative absence of plot in the opera's verbal text constitutes what would seem a double questioning of the traditional notion that an opera, like a symphony or a non-musical play, should transport its audience toward some sort of cathartic experience. Glass has himself defined the tradition in which he is working through his list of those who left an imprint on his work—Brecht, Beckett, Balanchine, Cage, Cunningham, and, to cite a specifically non-Western mentor, Ravi Shankar (*Music* 34–38).

Philip Glass's systematic deviations from operatic norms include, in addition, a challenge to the customarily passive role of the audience, as one can see from the following note on the Metropolitan program: "As *Einstein on the Beach* is performed without intermission, the audience is invited to leave and reenter the auditorium quietly, as necessary" (Wilson et al. 6). By inviting the audience to come and go at will, Glass is suggesting a return to the anti-illusionistic world of eighteenth-century *opera seria* or, to cite an analogy more likely on the composer's mind, to the world of Oriental theater. Yet with the final words of this note ("quietly, as necessary") it is evident that Glass's invitation is something less than hearty, that it amounts to little more than encouraging one's guests to use the bathroom if they happen to feel the need. Indeed, the hypnotic quality of Glass's repetitive musical style, together with the high-tech precision of Wilson's stage spectacle, may well work to keep the audience passively in its place as firmly as more traditional operas manage to do.

Could it be that Glass is not quite so iconoclastic as one might think? Certainly in subsequent years he has been willing to accommodate himself increasingly to operatic tradition, especially since he is now being commissioned to compose for opera houses. For example, in *Satyagraha*, composed for the Netherlands Opera in 1980, Glass writes for real opera singers and a real opera orchestra, though his musical style remains as identifiable as ever, and the text (passages from the *Bhagavad Gita* sung in Sanskrit) maintains a conspicuous distance from the stage spectacle, which consists of scenes from the early political life of Gandhi. Like Einstein in the earlier opera, Gandhi appears principally as a mythical image which is in turn juxtaposed with the public images of three other kindred spirits, Tolstoy, Tagore, and Martin Luther King. It may well be that the compromises Glass made—analogous perhaps to the operatic compromises that Richard Strauss made when he moved from the avant-garde *Elektra* to the easier-to-digest *Rosenkavalier*—enabled *Satyagraha* to achieve what few if any recent operas have done, namely, to play to large and enthusiastic crowds in several American cities.

If there is indeed such a style as "postmodern opera," it may well remain a compromise between the two antithetical terms encompassed by the phrase. To the extent that the term "postmodern" challenges most everything we associate with opera from the performing personnel to the role of consuming audience, any operatic work that rigorously pursues a postmodern program must seek its audience, if it can, outside the opera house. Perhaps only a figure commanding the authority of John Cage can pursue such a program within the opera house. Cage's *Europeras 1 & 2*, commissioned by the Frankfurt Opera and performed in 1987, selfconsciously scours the whole history of opera, which it recapitulates in collage-like, aleatorily organized appropriations of musical and dramatic themes and costumes drawn from a multitude of earlier operas[9]—a process evident in the following lines from Cage's scenario:

> She sells his soul to her father with the aim of improving his impaired finances. Even her loving relatives are shocked. They rescue him. He retires. She agrees. Torn, they, in shame, pardon all conspirators. He agrees to marry her. She kills herself. He is chosen the victor. ("Synopses" 166)

Without the name of John Cage attached to it, an unbendingly avant-garde work such as *Europeras 1 & 2* can generally hope for at best a single performance before a small group that is already committed to its aesthetic (or, more precisely, its anti-aesthetic) program. Take the example of Stephen Dickman's first opera, *Real Magic in New York*, a radically minimalist work that makes *Einstein on the Beach* seem positively operatic, and that, in 1971, received its single performance not in an opera house or even in a theater or concert hall, but in a former warehouse in downtown New York with about fifty persons in the audience. Lack of funding necessitated an unstaged performance, though slides were projected on a screen to indicate stage directions. Richard Foreman's surrealistic libretto, about a man who becomes Christ, consists largely of entrances of the hero's doctors and relatives, with people falling off chairs and clocks coming in through windows. The personnel includes singers and chorus, but no orchestra; percussive effects, emanating from a pre-recorded tape, are supplied by crackling sounds derived from the crumpling of paper. The musical style is neither tonal nor serial, but an *ad hoc* creation of the composer, who assigns each character a particular note with which he or she starts every musical phrase, which is then subjected to considerable dynamic range and rhythmic variation.

Like the vast majority of avant-garde theatrical works of its time (whether musical or non-musical), Dickman's first opera has perforce languished in obscurity. By contrast, visual works of art in, say, the minimalist or conceptualist mode of that period could hope for a continuing life in a collector's home or in a museum. Even poetry and fiction in an equivalent mode maintain a certain availability to the reader, though often only in obscure little magazines and chapbooks. With his current opera-in-progress, *Tibetan Dreams,* Dickman makes sufficient concessions to institutional concerns to hope for more of a performance life than his austere first opera achieved. Even so, a composer such as Dickman has had to rely on outside subsidies—both private fund raising and a grant from the National Endowment for the Arts—to make its completion and its first performances possible. Besides employing such traditionally operatic resources as a chorus and solo singers, *Tibetan Dreams,* unlike its predecessor, employs an orchestra—a considerable luxury in a non-commercial setting. Again, unlike its predecessor, it is designed as a full evening's performance. The theatrical resources it demands can be adjusted to either a small or large house. Its musical style, which, like Glass', shows the influence of non-Western music, is less forbidding than that of *Real Magic in New York;* indeed, it even contains some discernible melodies—though on scales invented by the composer and somewhat foreign to the Western musical ear—that are repeated with sufficient frequency to implant themselves in the audience's mind. At least as important, the new opera even sports a plot (based on a novel) that narrates a spiritual quest much in the tradition of the operatic quests that shape *Die Zauberflöte* and *Parsifal*, though here (with the help of his librettist Gary Glickman) with a contemporary slant that selfconsciously examines the very idea of a quest. As with Glass' operas, the presence of a compelling thematic idea may go a long way to mitigate an audience's difficulties with what it will also perceive as an unfamiliar musical style.

Indeed, Glass and, more recently, John Adams have fleshed out their thematic ideas by means of historical figures who have achieved mythical status for their audiences. Thus, in *Nixon in China*, commissioned by the Houston Grand Opera, which has shown a particular interest in new operas, Adams (in collaboration with his librettist Alice Goodman) presents larger-than-life portraits of recent world leaders against an instrumental background influenced by American big bands of the 1940s. Explaining his refusal to use the classical myths common to many earlier operas, Adams says, "It seemed to me the subconscious of our culture is really more profoundly affected by myths of the great world figures, and in Nixon and in Mao I was able to identify very strong archetypes" (Rothman). But in turning to world-historical figures, Adams is not quite so distant from operatic tradition as he may think: though his heroes are drawn from a more recent past than those of earlier operas, they also belong to a long line of historical figures from Monteverdi's Nero through Handel's Julius Caesar and Mozart's Titus to Berlioz's Benvenuto Cellini, Verdi's Philip II, Musorgsky's Boris Godunov, and, for that matter, Glass's Gandhi. And in its appropriation of a recognizable popular musical style, Adams, like visual artists who draw images from popular culture, stands a chance of tapping his audience's communal memory, even if he may also test their assumption that opera belongs solely to the realm of high culture. One might add that the strong presence of the librettist in Adams' and also in Dickman's and Glass' operatic projects (even if the music often pretends to move independently of the text) attests to the continuing power of the collaborative effort between writer and composer endemic to opera since the time of Monteverdi.

Although I have argued for the relative conservatism of opera in relation to other art forms, one should recognize that the institutional pressures and strategies determining the composition, production, and preservation of operas represent an extreme instance of pressures and strategies characteristic, as well, of these other forms. If postmodernism has found a less problematic reception in

the museum than in the opera house (to return to my earlier analogy between the two institutions), one should also note that the
museum has worked assiduously in recent decades to educate—
one might also say manipulate—its viewers to assent to incoming
experimental styles. The museum's way of mediating between work
of art and viewer is evident, for example, in an exhibition of contemporary British sculpture at the San Francisco Museum of Modern Art in 1987.

Among the works in the show was a collection of objects—for
example, a workman's worn glove and shoe, a rusty paint can, a
rock, an empty beer bottle, the remains of an old barrel—that seem
to be strewn randomly on the floor. As though to ward off too easy
a dismissal of these objects ("That's the sort of mess my five-year-
old might make if he could get his hands on those worthless things!"),
the museum provides at least three framing devices to direct the
viewer's response: first the fact that the display is part of an officially sponsored event within the museum walls, in this instance
within a conspicuously premodern building in elegant Beaux Arts
style; second, the title and medium designated on a nearby wall by
the artist, Tony Cragg; and third, an explanatory statement on
another wall by the show's curator justifying what he takes to be
Cragg's contribution to modern art. (One could cite such additional
framing devices as the show's catalogue, the regularly scheduled
docent talks, and the newspaper reviews.) Just as Philip Glass
entitles the apparently non- or anti-operatic *Einstein on the Beach*
an "opera in four acts" on the Metropolitan program, so Cragg
labels his objects *Axehead* (*mixed materials*)—with the result that a
potentially skeptical viewer discovers that Cragg's objects are not
randomly strewn at all, but assume the shape of an axehead; moreover, even if the materials are "mixed," one's recognition that the
phrase "mixed materials" belongs to a verbal category parallel to,
say, "oil on canvas" works to confirm its status as art. An institution's framing devices, in short, serve to assimilate into the canon
many contemporary works that might otherwise not even strike
their viewers as "art."

And just as John Adams justifies his use of recent historical
figures as myths to which a contemporary audience can easily
respond, so the curator teaches his museum audience how to relate
Cragg's objects (not only in *Axehead* but also in his other contributions to the show) to what he takes to be their own needs and
concerns: "Cragg uses the remnants of our packaged and media-

interpreted world and re-presents them, allowing us to reconsider them as first-order experiences so that we may better understand our relationship to the objects, images, and materials of our world" (Beal). If the title and generic label confer aesthetic status, the curator's statement, with its romantic formula expressing disdain for the modern world, confers social relevance on Cragg's postmodernist work (as though to ward off in advance any accusations that postmodernism might be socially indifferent)—while the building in which it is housed serves as a reminder of the museum's tie to official culture.

Indeed, museum visitors entering the building would note the ornate neo-Renaissance city hall directly across the street. Moreover, the museum's building is externally, at least, virtually a twin of the opera house down the same block. Before opera matinees one ordinarily sees a goodly number of operagoers making their way through the latest postmodern exhibit. To be sure, the closest they are likely to get to a postmodern experience in that particular opera house is the occasional production of a classic work by an iconoclastic director. One might note, however, that visitors to the museum might, in the spring of 1987, have watched the installation of Cragg's *Axehead* before attending an unstaged run-through of *Nixon in China*—emphatically not sponsored by the San Francisco Opera, whose then-impresario supposedly walked out—in a small theater in the museum's building dedicated to the performance of chamber music and, though at relatively rare intervals, of non-canonical operas.

Despite the disparity in the commitment of opera house and museum to what is radically new, the repeated viewing and hearing of works that at first elicit a puzzled and often also outraged response, together with the mediating process organized within both these institutions, can serve to transform this response into something less discomforting, sometimes, in fact, to canonize these works. Rauschenberg's grainy silk-screen enlargements of Kennedy photos, like the Warhol paintings of Marilyn Monroe, have, after a quarter century of viewing, gained a classical aura in the eyes of many viewers—much as the latter now view early Picasso and Braque collages with the same attitude they take to long-canonical paintings. (It has become the burden of scholarship in recent years to recapture the revolutionary ambiance in which each of the great modernist waves broke upon a stunned and hostile public.) Audiences who witnessed repetitions of the Chéreau *Ring* for several seasons subsequent to its premiere complained less loudly than before and not simply because the director modified some of his concepts; indeed, the repeated viewings of this production on educational television even after it was retired from the stage have routinized our response to the point that the once demythified Rhinemaidens have gradually become remythified. After repeated hearings of *Einstein on the Beach* we become so habituated to what we hear that the arbitrariness we were intended to note in the relation of text and music gives way to the perception that the spoken words and the accompanying music really *do* belong together. The framing accomplished by institutions inevitably results in taming—yet it also assures a continuing life to artifacts that, whatever their power to provoke, inspire, offend, would otherwise (though quite in conformity with that postmodern attitude which marks works of art as disposable) disappear from view.

NINE

~~~~

Toward (and After) a New History in Literary Study

Since this essay was written in 1983, near the beginning of the development that it describes, I have not revised it except to bring the documentation up to date. Instead, I have added an afterword that reflects briefly on this development at the end of the decade during which it took place.

F or as long as most of us can remember, being branded a historical scholar did not seem much of a compliment. Those old enough to recall the entrance of the New Criticism into the university are familiar with the plight of teachers who, for better or worse, proudly made the term *historical* central to their professorial identity. These were the people whom we spoke of (often gloatingly) as learned philistines, scholars who, despite the multitude of facts at their command, seemed blind and deaf to the verbal nuances whose proper understanding we deemed the chief task of literary study in America. Of course, even during the New Critical age one could occasionally acknowledge the greatness of certain monuments of historical scholarship, though the way these monuments were received often revealed the biases of their anti-historical readers. For example, the development of the organic principle that M. H. Abrams documented so meticulously in *The Mirror and the Lamp* provided a rationale for that organic view of the literary text prevailing at the time. When Erich Auerbach's *Mimesis* appeared in English in 1953, readers otherwise unfamiliar with Romance stylistics felt an immediate affinity between the author's detailed analyses of great passages and the close readings in which they were themselves engaged— even if they ignored his reconstructions of earlier epochs, above all that perspectivistic view of history which gave away Auerbach's fundamental commitment to the German historicist tradition.[1]

Those who took themselves to be in the critical vanguard thirty years ago, we now recognize, have come to occupy a position much like that of the historical scholars whom they sought to displace. Yet for the most part the new paradigms that established themselves in the critical marketplace during the intervening years were as little concerned with history—whether as background, process, or determining principle—as the New Criticism. Talented critics with historical interests often cared little about bringing criticism and history together in their work: one might note the divided professional life of a W. K. Wimsatt, who published a theoretical rationale for the New Criticism the same year as his catalogue of Pope's portraits, or that of a Maynard Mack, whose exemplary edition of *An Essay on Man* came out shortly before his equally exemplary interpretive essay on *Hamlet*. Historical scholarship all too often was a task an academic critic pursued quietly while counting on his critical accomplishments to exercise whatever intellectual leadership he hoped to achieve. Whereas the avant-garde scholarship that emerged in Germany in the wake of the Frankfurt school has been tenaciously sociological and historical in orientation, the characteristic strengths of American criticism have manifested themselves in ahistorical, sometimes even in anti-historical forms—in explorations of the consciousness unifying a particular author or work, for example, or, to cite a more recent instance, in the dialogue that supposedly transpires between the individual reader and the individual text. Thus, it comes as something of a surprise to find that history is making a powerful comeback in literary study.

But the new history we are beginning to see these days has little in common with the old, and for an interesting historical reason: its practitioners were nurtured in the theoretical climate of the 1970s, a time during which the individual literary work came to lose its organic unity; when literature as an organized body of knowledge abandoned the boundaries that had hitherto enclosed it, to an extent even abandoned its claims to knowledge; and when history began to seem discontinuous, sometimes in fact no more than just another fiction. It is no wonder that the scholarship we now pursue cannot take the forms or speak the language of the older literary history. Note, for example, the sharply divergent roles that the practitioners of the old and the new history see themselves playing. The traditional literary historian viewed himself in a relatively subservient role. He was essentially the guardian of tradition, a glorified custodian whose task was the preservation and transmission of what had long since passed as sanctified. Self-effacement was his characteristic stance as he confronted those great works he felt himself elected to keep intact for the posterity he could confidently assume would be revering them in future centuries.

Whereas self-effacement was a natural enough stance for those who felt themselves part of a single and continuous intellectual tradition, the scholars who came to maturity in the 1960s and after saw their relation to literary history, indeed to history itself, as problematic. Unlike the older historians, they scarcely deemed it either appropriate or responsible to efface themselves. In view of the upheavals to which canons have been subjected in recent years, custodianship of a fixed canon would seem at best a trivial occupation. Indeed, these very upheavals have suggested a project for the new historians—namely, tracing the changes in canons at various moments in the past, seeking out the motivations behind these changes, studying the ideological and institutional framework that creates a particular canon at a particular time. How, for example, did the prevailing canon of English romantic writers come into being? In what ways, as Jerome McGann has asked in his book on the ideology of romanticism, have presumably self-effacing scholars allowed the poets they were studying to dictate the terms by which these poets were to be interpreted and evaluated and, for that matter, to exclude or subordinate those writers who represented competing sets of values?

The detachment and self-effacement that marked scholarly inquiry in the older history finds its counterpart in the suspiciousness and self-conscious playfulness of the new history. The older history could take for granted the integrity and autonomy of the work of art; the scholar's task was to provide a suitable background of sources, details of publication, and biographical materials, as well as an accurate text, to enshrine the work within its appropriate tradition. By contrast, the new history has no illusions about a work's unity, autonomy, or, for that matter, its need for enshrinement. As the Cornell edition of Wordsworth amply illustrates, what we have traditionally considered a literary work of art consists essentially of layers of text, often, in fact, unfinished layers none of which necessarily commands more authority than the others; for example, the volume devoted to the *Prelude* of 1798–99 offers a version that Wordsworth rejected soon after completion and that its editor, Stephen Parrish, has had to reconstruct from several manuscripts. Given the suspicion we have developed in recent years toward authorial authority, even an author's authorized text need have no more authority than we choose to give it.

Not only does the work of art occupy a different status within the old and the new history, but so does history itself. For the older history, history served essentially as the background against which the work could be mounted, situated, stabilized. Thus, history remained a static repository of supposedly solid facts that could help readers gain access to a work whose vocabulary or philosophical themes had come to seem foreign in the course of time. The new history, by contrast, is unable to accept a sharp demarcation between history and its artifacts. Historical writing, as we have come to see in recent years, imitates and expresses the characteristic gestures and practices of the artistic realm as surely as the latter feeds upon what could once confidently be isolated as the historical realm. To put it another way, the interactions we discern between history and art quickly compromise whatever dividing lines we set up between them. If I may cite a distinguished recent anthropological work relevant to literary study, Clifford Geertz analyzes the state organization of nineteenth-century Bali (*Negara*) in terms of the theatrical spectacle through which the political life of Bali expressed and defined itself. Aesthetics and history thus become overlapping concepts that do not easily lend themselves to disentanglement. In a similar attempt to remove traditional barriers separating the understanding of art from that of the "real" world, Jurij Lotman has applied the same semiotic techniques he uses for literary works to the interpretation of events from Russian history, as in his analysis of the theatrical masks that Alexander I employed in dismissing his minister Speranskii during the Napoleonic invasion.

Likewise, chronology plays a distinctly different role in the old and the new history. The old history liked to tell its stories pretty much in the order in which they occurred. For the sake of convenience it demarcated literary history into periods—in England, with its bias toward tradition, often according to monarchical designations such as Restoration and Victorian; in France, with its rationalistic bias, according to the numerical designations of centuries. The old history was centrally concerned with how literary events follow one another in time, how a particular event evolved from an earlier one, how individual authors and works fit what were often pre-established period designations within their respective national literatures. The basic task was to establish origins, evolutionary directions (often with strong teleological overtones) and a chain of causes and effects to link beginnings and ends. Note the following lines chosen at random from E. K. Chambers' *The Mediaeval Stage*, one of the monuments of the older literary history:

> The evolution of the liturgic play described in the last two chapters may be fairly held to have been complete about the middle of the thirteenth century. The condition of any further advance was that the play should cease to be liturgic. The following hundred years are a transition period. . . . Already, when Hilarius could write plays to serve indifferently for use at Matins or at Vespers, the primitive relation of *repraesentatio* to liturgy had been sensibly weakened. By the middle of the fourteenth century it was a mere survival. (2:69)

If later representatives of the older history were less blatant than Chambers in their use of a Darwinian model (note such phrases as "any further advance" and "a mere survival," not to speak of the word *evolution*), they were no less inclined to structure their observations around a pattern that privileged origins and a subsequent chain of causes and effects. A segment of time that could not easily be labeled according to prevailing categories was assimilated to the cause-and-effect chain with a term such as Chambers' "transition period." As a result of this temporal scheme, certain phenomena—for example an author's sources or the fortunes of a literary theme over time—received considerable attention at the expense of other phenomena that remained ignored.[2]

The new history, though perfectly willing to believe that things in the past happened in some sort of chronological order, sees no reason to structure its narratives about literary events in this order—any more than a storyteller, if I may resort to Russian Formalist terminology, feels the need to make the *suzhet* follow the same sequence as the *fabula*. Through its awareness that the seemingly straightforward chronological accounts of scholars such as Chambers were organized within preconceived patterns that implied a particular view of historical progress, the new history organizes its stories in whatever way these can best make their intended point. Thus, within the new historiography the juxtaposition of works or events from diverse periods can often reveal more about temporal sequence than a narrative that is forced to reconstitute this sequence. As I myself found in organizing my recent book on opera, one can sometimes best pinpoint the changing nature of a genre or a convention by moving backward and forward in time; often, too, the juxtaposition of works or events from widely separated periods can better illuminate historical constants and differences, continuities and disruptions, than would a chronological narrative. Nor do the traditional period designations, with their accustomed dates of origin and termination, retain any more authority than the new historian chooses to give them. If the older historians thought they were cultivating a transparent form of narrative as far removed as possible from the narratives they were studying, the new historians recognize that since history does not belong to an intrinsically different order of writing from the order it studies, it can consciously exploit the resources of literary narrative to make significant historical connections that the narrative of the older history rarely allowed.

The old and the new history differ as well in what they take to be original and relevant. Originality within the old history was confined to the unearthing of factual matter surrounding literary work and author—a new dating of a work, for example, or a new source that an author was likely to have read, or the glossing of a word whose meaning had shifted over the years. One of the most desirable ways to be original, according to the old history, was to counter or correct a prevailing view, not so much through asking oneself if an older interpretation was interesting or if it made sense, but through the display of new factual evidence that could presumably render the earlier interpretation useless. One rarely if ever questioned the theoretical model within which one's facts were crammed, for the theoretical statements necessary to refute a model did not themselves ordinarily constitute a sufficiently concrete form of evidence. What counted as evidence in the old history was much the same as what could be introduced into a courtroom; anything else one might have to say about a literary work or situation (bright or stimulating though one's insights might be) did not meet the criterion of relevance to which the traditional historian was tied. Relevance and originality thus became closely linked: the only things it was relevant to say professionally about literature were what could fit the quite narrow concept of originality. We have all heard traditional historians comment on the insights of their less traditional colleagues or students in terms such as these: "This may well be the sort of thing a reader thinks privately, and it may even be brilliant for all I know, but it's hardly the sort of information you write up formally." Although the older literary historians of the last generation were often willing to acknowledge brilliance, if not relevance, to forms of inquiry different from those in which they had been trained, a field such as art history, in which the older historical model maintained its hold far later than in literary study, could be brutally contemptuous of work that seemed lacking in courtroom evidence. Note for instance the following reaction reported by the distinguished art historian Leo Steinberg as typical of his field until quite recently: "But it's only an interpretation; in two years from now someone will come up with another interpretation, and then what have you got?" (xviii).[3]

The new history has vastly extended the domain of what can count as original and relevant, to the point that these terms are themselves scarcely relevant as criteria. It does not of course deny the importance of the factual information whose discovery provided traditional historians with their central form of scholarly activity. Indeed, the new historians constantly make use of the massive data—the learned annotations, the reprints of archival materials, the biographical details—collected by their predecessors. Yet the new historians also recognize a far wider concept of originality and relevance than the latter. Conditioned as they are by the theoretical advances of recent years, they are easily suspicious of any method that, like the older history, claims itself to be natural or in tune with common sense.

For one thing, they know that all methods are implicated in the ideologies within which they first developed. Thus, the older literary history, rooted as it is in a nineteenth-century critical paradigm, centered its area of inquiry in the relation between author and work, or between the author and the environment he inhabited. It is no wonder that source studies played an uncommonly large role in scholarship, for within this paradigm it seemed natu-

ral to view the work as a product of an individual creator's expres-
siveness; if the resulting scholarship often seemed to question the
magic of creativity by locating the work's origin in an author's
reading—for example, in John Livingston Lowes's celebrated study
of Coleridge's verbal echoes—this scholarship no less hovered within
that area of inquiry which the nineteenth-century paradigm had
staked out for itself.

By contrast, the new history has developed out of a contemporary—one might almost say postmodernist—critical paradigm.
Unlike the older history, which often remained unreflective about
the model of historical change it was using, the new history is
aware that models do not exist in nature, that they function as
frameworks within which to observe and interpret phenomena that
seem important but that stand outside the area of inquiry investi-
gated by the older history. The fact that the Marxist model happens
to play a considerable role in the new history is less a sign of its
adherents' political commitments than of their recognition that
Marxism has provided tools to analyze a number of matters with
which they are concerned—for example, the ways that literary
form, or the public image a writer projects, is related to the economics of production or the ideology of a class at a particular time.
For that matter, the new history does not even recognize a single
form of Marxism, but uses a number of contemporary Marxist
variants,[4] as well as the alternative to the Marxist view of historical
change proposed by Michel Foucault.[5] One might also turn the
order of things around and suggest that the general resurgence of
Marxist thought during the last two decades (together with that of
its variants and alternatives) has itself suggested the centrality of
areas of inquiry that earlier critical paradigms could not accommodate.

Again unlike the older history, which expected evidence present-
able in a courtroom, the new history is willing to establish connections between phenomena that, at first or even second glance, would
seem incompatible with one another. Within the Marxist tradition
and in the work of Foucault one has become accustomed to the
juxtaposition of phenomena from quite distinct and ordinarily "unconnected" orders of life. The new history has, among other things,
undertaken the task of connecting the literary order with other
orders, even if such connections violate earlier notions of common
sense and scholarly decorum. For example, as John Bender has
suggested (*Imagining*), the development of narrative in eighteenth-

century England parallels and, indeed, interacts with, the changes that took place at that time in the architecture and organization of prisons. Similarly, Stephen Greenblatt has mutually illuminated Elizabethan literary texts and contemporary accounts of New World exploration (*Renaissance* 184, 193–94)—with the result that both the literary and the historical texts look somewhat different to us than they did before. Originality does not come simply from a new factual discovery—though none of us would hesitate publishing one if we thought it significant—but from looking at phenomena from a new, often even a strange angle of vision. When we speak of relevance within the new history, nobody demands, as early historians often did, that the method we pursue, or the results we come up with, remain valid and interesting for all time. What is relevant is simply what seems significant and worth exploring at the moment we are doing it.

The liberal criterion for what is conceivably relevant within the new history is reflected in the large range of information that its proponents are willing, often in fact eager to bring to bear on literary works and problems. With its narrow definition of relevance, the older history was content to investigate an author's or a work's immediate environment—circumstances of composition or publication, earlier authors and works that served directly as influences, later authors and works that were in turn influenced by the author or work under consideration. A scholar was expected to spend his time tracking down this information in fairly predictable situations, for example, interviewing his author's descendants and asking to search their attics, checking his vital statistics in public records offices, scouring research libraries for sermons he must have heard or heard echoed. If the scholar chose to read works from a national literature with which his author had had no contact, or if he read in, say, contemporary sociology or linguistics, this was all well and good, but it counted strictly as leisure-time reading.

Since even the most unexpected perspectives may become relevant within the new history, its proponents do not shy away from anything that might yield interesting results. Certainly they are as likely as the older historians to track down what they can in archives and libraries; unlike their antihistorical predecessors, whose work-days were spent pondering a single, much-reprinted text or simply pondering to themselves, they are dirtying their hands with the dust of books nobody has touched in years or exercising their wits against those legally empowered to guard the secrets of the past. But they are just as likely to seek out ideas in disciplines that, on the surface, would seem to have no bearing on the literary matters they are supposedly pursuing. Anthropology, above all the work of Clifford Geertz and Victor Turner, is especially prominent among the "foreign" disciplines in which they are reading. It scarcely matters that within their own field these two anthropologists count as doyens of diverse and not altogether friendly schools; what does matter is that each has worked out certain notions—for example, Turner's concept of liminality (93–111), or Geertz's analysis (*Interpretation* 360–411) of the ways that symbolic systems create meaning in particular cultures[6]—that provide new openings for the discussion of literature. It seems wholly appropriate that literary scholars should read anthropology, for the latter field is dedicated to the explanation of social practices that obviously have much in common with the practices out of which poems, plays, and novels are built. What the anthropologist offers the literary scholar are new theoretical frameworks to help make sense out of data that might otherwise come to seem chaotic, or, perhaps even more important, to find significance in data one might otherwise ignore.

If their interest in social practices has drawn literary scholars to anthropology, it has also attracted them to the work of social historians, for example the writing on early modern France and England, respectively, by Natalie Z. Davis and Lawrence Stone. Like the anthropologists, these historians pursue in detail the type of practice—riots, printing-house customs, methods of family planning within diverse classes—that feeds into literary works and that also characterizes the environment within which these works were created and received.[7] Similarly, an art historian such as Michael Baxandall demonstrates how a Florentine social practice such as the gauging of containers helped shape the way *quattrocento* painters saw and represented concrete objects (*Painting* 86–93), while, in extending this insight to national styles (*Limewood* 145–47), he links the differences in Italian and German methods of gauging to differences in artistic form within the two cultures. For the new literary historian all of these scholars within allied fields are paradigmatic for suggesting ways of bridging the historical and the aesthetic order, of locating the aesthetic forms shaping social phenomena as well as the social meanings inherent in aesthetic expression.

This need to find significant links between social and aesthetic forms has taken the new historians not simply to contemporary practitioners in neighboring fields, but to a variety of thinkers whose relevance to literary scholarship would scarcely have been acknowledged a few years before. It is no exaggeration to say that a literary education does not seem complete nowadays without a reading of the classical social theorists. For example, Max Weber's concept of bureaucratization (196–244) can prove a most useful tool for an understanding of the power relationships in literary works, while Emile Durkheim's analysis of the role of anomie in suicide (241–76) has a special suggestiveness for students of nineteenth-century novels. Moreover, Lewis Mumford's descriptions of the changing nature of cities in the course of history can help make explicit much that remains unspoken within novels about city life.

Any literary scholar reading Erving Goffman's detailed analyses of how people assume roles in everyday life would immediately note that these roles are not different in kind from those that characters in narratives play. In *Frame Analysis*, for example, Goffman focuses on how people create frames to interpret ordinary experience; like Geertz in *Negara*, Goffman selfconsciously uses theater as a means of approaching the supposedly "non-aesthetic" realm (see especially 124–55). The type of insight Theodor Adorno achieves in that discipline he called *Musiksoziologie*—for instance, the relationships he finds between Mahler's symphonic form, on the one hand, and Hegel's philosophy (13:155–63) and the European novel (13:209–29), on the other, or between operatic convention and the biases of the bourgeoisie (16:24–39)—provides a model for the juxtaposition of different orders of phenomena. Yet the new history can also find its models in certain figures we officially label literary critics, most notably perhaps in Walter Benjamin and Mikhail Bakhtin, both of whose major work was completed nearly half a century ago, but whose notions of technological "reproducibility" and "heteroglossia," respectively, to judge from the interest they are beginning to excite in American literary study, may well become the characteristic critical *topoi* of the 1980s.

It does not seem accidental that the issues the new history finds relevant are, more often than not, the issues with which recent critical theory has preoccupied itself. Yet as theory moves into historical investigation, concepts become embodied in real-life situations that extend the meaning and range of these concepts, indeed may well sometimes put these concepts to a test. Our contemporary concern with the process of reading finds ample embodiment in the study of how writers communicated with actual historical audiences, who in turn shaped not only the writer's development but the later reception of his writing. If I may cite the work of an art historian who has developed a following among literary scholars, Michael Fried's studies of how the changing role of the beholder can be linked to stylistic changes in eighteenth- and nineteenth-century French painting demonstrate the active part that audiences take in shaping art. Jerome McGann has shown that the problems readers have encountered interpreting an elusive work such as "The Ancient Mariner" (*Beauty* 135–72) can be understood by approaching the work through its critical history, while in another essay (*Beauty* 111–32), using examples from Byron, Blake, and Emily Dickinson, he demonstrates the often problematic relationship between a work's textual history and its later critical reception. As with the German practitioners of *Rezeptionsaesthetik* during the last decade, the study of a work's historical reception and textual history becomes a way of clarifying long-standing interpretive problems.

Similarly, our recent concern with intertextual relationships suggests a new approach to a work's sources—not simply, as in the older history, the study of a particular writer's reading habits, but the discovery of a larger network of texts that rethink and rewrite one another over considerable stretches of time. For example, a book such as Thomas M. Greene's recent study of translation and imitation in poets from Petrarch to Ben Jonson would not have achieved its characteristic insights without the theoretical perspectives on intertextuality of the last decade; yet Greene's discussions of how poets use their predecessors remain thoroughly rooted in a concrete historical world to a degree uncharacteristic of the discussions in which his own theoretical predecessors engaged. In a similar attempt to historicize a theoretical category, William Mills Todd III has utilized the celebrated communications model from Roman Jakobson's essay, "Linguistics and Poetics"; thus, to define the changing institutional nature of literary life in Russia from the late eighteenth through the mid-nineteenth century, Todd has fleshed out the six categories of Jakobson's chart with the various real-life addressers, codes, and addressees that flourished during this period (45–105).

Likewise, the selfconsciousness we have developed in recent years about the nature of interpretation has not only revealed the naïveté of the older history, which all too often refused to recognize the cultural biases and the interpretive conventions built into its method: it has also encouraged us to understand the historicity of all interpretation, to arouse our suspicions, for instance, toward the way we read contemporary concerns into earlier works and periods as well as toward the way we have unwittingly allowed elements of past interpretations to persist within later contexts. If I may cite an example from *Rezeptionsaesthetik,* a movement that anticipates (even if it has not significantly influenced) the recent turn to history in America, Peter Bürger prefaces an analysis of what he calls "distortions in human communication" (135–59) in *Le Rouge et le noir* with a detailed analysis of criticism on Stendhal since the beginning of this century. It is significant that Bürger's trenchant critique of earlier scholarship occupies more space than his discussion of the novel itself. Actually, as the title of his essay indicates, his subject is not simply the novel, or even a theme in this novel, but rather Stendhal's relation to historicity, a problem he finds he can best approach by examining the novel and its interpretive tradition at once; indeed, it seems appropriate that the new historical scholars in Germany should show a special concern for writers such as Stendhal, Heine, and Baudelaire, in whom historicity as a problem is thematized. A study of interpretive traditions qualifies our understanding not only of individual au-thors and works, but also of the way we depict whole periods of literary history. For example, Marjorie Perloff has recently demon-strated how historians of early twentieth-century American poetry divide into proponents of a Pound era and a Stevens era, that the two interpretive schools can in fact be differentiated through the sharply different literary tastes, ideological commitments, and moral values affirmed or implied in their respective writings (1–32).

Behind the various theoretical perspectives that are leaving their marks on the new history one can point to a larger attitude that the latter, as some of the preceding examples illustrate, has inher-ited from contemporary theory. I refer to that suspiciousness toward established authority—whether the authority of the writer, of lit-erary and interpretive traditions, or of society as a whole—that finds its embodiment in the strong social concerns within the new history. These concerns have manifested themselves most power-fully in the development of a feminist critical perspective—a devel-opment that took place at the same time, and sometimes in collab-oration with, the cultivation of theory that dominated the 1970s in American criticism. Although theory during this period often seemed

to lack historical concreteness, the new feminist critics were forced
to think in historical terms[8]—if only because the preeminently
masculine bias they saw shaping traditional literary history natu-
rally drove them to undertake the investigations needed for an
adequate rewriting of this history. Similarly, the criticism that
ethnical minorities in America have produced in recent years has
challenged many of the central assumptions that literary scholars,
whatever their critical orientation, had taken for granted for several generations. In view of the anti-authoritarianism behind both
the critical theory and the feminist and minority criticism of the
last decade, it seems natural that we are witnessing a return to
history and also that the aims and underlying assumptions of historical writing emerging today should differ strikingly from those
of the older history. The latter, for one thing, is rooted in the
German university of the late nineteenth century when literary
study, calling itself philology, sought to emulate the objectivity
that the natural sciences of that time saw in themselves. In his
modest role as scientific researcher the traditional literary historian viewed each of his contributions as a small building block,
perhaps just a dab of mortar, toward some temple of knowledge
that would presumably last into perpetuity.

With a century's distance we recognize that the model of science
upon which the older history fashioned itself has not endured, that
the objectivity of which it was so proud was compromised from the
start both by a characteristic late nineteenth-century view of science and by an equally characteristic nineteenth-century nationalist bias that motivated the organization of literary study into sharply
demarcated national units. Both of these time-bound views are
evident in a methodological pronouncement by Erich Schmidt, one
of the founders of the older literary history, in his inaugural lecture
at the University of Vienna in 1880: "Literary history should be a
segment of the history of the development of a people's intellectual
life with comparative views of other national literatures. It apprehends being from becoming and, like the newer natural science,
examines heredity and adaptation over and over again in a fixed
chain" (412).

Schmidt's allowance for "comparative views of other national
literatures" does not so much qualify as confirm the national literature as the center of the scholar's inquiry. If we have liberated
ourselves from the Darwinian chain that Schmidt holds up as a
model for literary history, even after a century his nationalist bias,

despite many changes in methodological fashion, remains anachronistically built into literary study through the continuing institutionalization of nationally organized units within the contemporary university. Not only do literary scholars still define themselves according to the national literature named on their academic degrees and on the doors of the department with which they are affiliated, but the period designations with which they are expected to complete their professional identity still reflect that attempt of the older literary history to chart the development, as Schmidt put it, of a people's intellectual life. Even the attempts in recent years to add courses and hire personnel in such newly created territories as critical theory and feminist criticism work to supplement existing arrangements rather than to alter the basic pattern by which departments are organized and graduate students are initiated into the profession. As in many other areas of life, the institutional arrangements within which we work long outlive the reasons that originally justified them. One wonders if the new history will succeed better than other recent critical paradigms in challenging these arrangements. Will it, for instance, be able to break down the barriers between the various national disciplines? Will it be able to find institutional forms to cope with the instabilities we have come to recognize in recent years—instabilities, for example, in what constitutes the literary canon, or in what precisely constitutes literature, the supposed object of our labors? Will these labors find the legitimation they need to sustain themselves long enough to produce a compelling body of work?

Whatever new shape these institutional forms may take, it is certain that we will not retain the self-images that the older historians cultivated about the nature of their work. We are no longer likely, for example, to justify the ways we organize our projects and achieve our insights with the word *objective*, to cite a characteristic term of honor with which most earlier forms of literary scholarship (not to speak of a multitude of other academic fields) sought to compliment themselves. Nor will we likely pride ourselves on the permanence of our endeavors. If even critical editions of great poets can wear out after a generation or two, what once was thought to be an enduring temple of knowledge begins to look more and more like a house of cards. Indeed, once we have questioned the objectivity of our endeavors or the permanence of our results, it seems only natural that we should see such terms as *objectivity* and *permanence* as themselves historical categories that, at their own appropriate historical moment, served specific and definable historical purposes.

Not that we have wholly abandoned the analogy to scientific inquiry that marked the older history. If the early literary historians obtained their notions of science from Comte, Spencer, and Darwin, the new historians are likely to obtain theirs from a figure such as Thomas Kuhn, for whom the historicity of science, with its paradigms shifting over time, remains primary to any generalizations one can draw from the scientific practices of a specific age. By the same token, the new historians remain aware of their own discipline's historicity: as this essay has tried to demonstrate, what we label "historical" assumes strikingly different shapes in different historical situations. Certainly it demands some historical imagination to recognize that what I have described as the older history was, in its early stages a century ago, a progressive form of scholarly practice.[9] Not, alas, in living memory, for in its later stages in North America and France it provided a negative model of pedantry and antiquarianism against which, in their quite varying ways, the early proponents of the New Criticism and the Nouvelle Critique could define and legitimate themselves. Those battles are long since past and the new cast of practitioners that has entered the critical scene is fast discovering that to call oneself historical is a badge of honor: it is, in fact, the most vital stance to take at this particular moment in history.

Afterword: From New Paradigm to Normal Science

Most of a decade has passed since I drafted this essay, a portion of which was presented before a 1983 Modern Language Association session enticingly titled "The Future of Criticism." Both of the other speakers, Edward Said and Jonathan Culler, predicted that the future direction lay in history, though each of them, as anybody familiar with their work could have predicted, foresaw a different set of emphases within that commodious realm that calls itself history. My own contribution concentrated on the type of work I saw being done around me as well as in neighboring fields such as anthropology, history, and art history, all of which have exercised an influence on what I referred to as the new history. I sought to call attention not only to examples of new historical work, but above all to point out some of the assumptions and conventions—for example, the refusal to build a narrative out of a cause-and-effect chain or the reluctance to organize one's presentation chronologically—underlying this work.

If these assumptions and conventions still seemed relatively new, even wrong-headed, to some listeners at the time,[10] they are fast becoming part of what Thomas Kuhn, describing the practices of a scientific community after a revolution in a particular field has become absorbed, has called "normal science" (10–42). Not that the younger literary scholars have uniformly embraced the new history. Unlike the communities analyzed by Kuhn, in which, at a given time, all significant work can be classified within that form Kuhn labels a "paradigm" (10–11, 43–51), literary study, even the study of a single national literature or a single genre, is by no means monolithic. Among the more recent arrivals on the critical scene, new history shares the field with Lacanian psychoanalysis, which, though it sometimes appears in a new historical guise (Fineman *Shakespeare's* 1–48), most often remains essentially ahistorical in orientation. Within literary study there is of course no single community, but rather a loose confederation of groups that Stanley Fish has dubbed "interpretive communities" (171–72). Thus, as one glances at the advertisements for new books or at the table of contents of journals, one will still note examples of the older history, the New Criticism, archetypical and phenomenological criticism, and 1970s-style deconstruction.

Like Freud's map of the human psyche (16–17), American criticism retains active memory traces from all critical schools that flourished during the lifetime of those practitioners still in the scholarly profession. Yet the new history today is the area within which the intellectual energy of many, perhaps even most graduate students and younger scholars is likely to be unleashed. Signs of its vitality, and, indeed, institutionalization are evident everywhere. A new monograph series by the University of California Press calls itself "The New Historicism: Studies in Cultural Poetics." One conference after another, as well as one panel after another at conventions, is sporting the name; it was for one such conference, called "Romanticism, Politics, and the New Historicism," held at UCLA in 1986, that I prepared the paper that became essay 3 of the present book. Journals, above all *Representations*, which started at the University of California, Berkeley, in 1983, have become associated with what is manifestly now a movement. A book of essays reflecting on the phenomenon has sought to cash in on all the curiosity by entitling itself simply *The New Historicism*. Indeed, the surest symptom that we are dealing with an institutionalized phenomenon is the fact that polemical essays attacking or defending new history have regularly begun to appear (Howard, Montrose, Pechter).

One can even speak of certain conventions that mark much newhistorical writing, for example the transfer of such deconstructive terms as "erasure," "transgression," and "rupture" from a timeless to a historical setting (the survival of these terms, in fact, attests to the strong deconstructive legacy inherited by the new history); or the habit—fast becoming obsessive—of opening an essay with a depiction of some seemingly obscure historical incident, as when Stephen Greenblatt introduces a study of gender perception in Renaissance life and theater with the following sentence: "In 1601 in a small town near Rouen, a 32-year-old widowed mother of two, Jeane le Febvre, had a very odd experience" ("Fiction" 30). If some are tempted to treat these opening anecdotes as affectations, they might note that one scholar has recently suggested a poetics of the anecdote (Fineman "History") to defend this new-historical practice. Behind and beyond these conventions lie some assumptions potentially threatening to most traditional notions governing literary study, for example, assumptions that genres, canons, and genders are not given by nature but rather are socially constructed, or that literary texts need not be accorded any status differentiating them from texts not customarily defined as "literary." The following statement in the introduction to a recent book on the social marginality of the English Renaissance stage provides a typically new-historical warning to readers with traditional expectations about the objects and materials of literary criticism: "In *The Place of the Stage*, literary analysis is conceived not as an end in itself but as a vehicle, a means of gaining access to tensions and contradictions less clearly articulated in other cultural forms but all the more powerful for their partial occlusion. Literature itself is conceived neither as a separate and separable aesthetic realm nor as a mere product of culture" (Mullaney x). To the extent that newhistorical scholars no longer focus primarily on literary texts in their own right or even on the standard literary canon, they have made a more radical move than scholars associated with deconstruction, which for the most part retained a commitment both to close readings and to canonical texts.

Thus far I have spoken of new history as a more or less monolithic enterprise, what we commonly refer to as a movement. Yet, as with any set of tendencies that we retrospectively label a movement, the individual practitioners to whom we attach the label often refuse to be lumped together and may instead assert the uniqueness of their own work or acknowledge only that they belong to some new-historical "sub-group" calling itself, say, gender studies, cultural studies, or Renaissance studies. Once one examines representative writings by those one labels new-historical, one becomes as aware of differences as much as of similarities. Moreover, practitioners have expended considerable energy on what precisely to label their endeavors. Greenblatt, who claims to have invented the term *New Historicism*, now opts for the term *cultural poetics* ("Towards"), though the book series he edits manages to include both terms in its title. British practitioners have opted for the term *cultural materialism*, and these practitioners can be described as more overtly Marxist, and less strongly influenced by deconstruction, than their American colleagues.[11] The replacement of the word *historical* by *cultural* may signal a desire to align oneself institutionally more with anthropology than with history, which as an academic discipline still remains too textually unselfconscious to suit those engaged in literary study. Moreover, the divergence of opinion about terminology has encouraged me to continue holding out for the term *new history*, which allows me to stress the historical dimension (whatever the alleged deficiencies of academic historians), and also avoids the implicit link with the German historicist tradition, which (note 9 above and essay 3) seems incongruent with the aims and, indeed, the whole ideological orientation, of contemporary new-historical scholars (Thomas 188–92).

New-historical studies differ not only in Britain and the United States, but also among specialists in various periods. Thus, studies of Renaissance literature are distinctly different in focus from those, say, on the romantics. One way to define this difference would be to note the varying roles played by writing within the culture of each period. During the Renaissance, for example, writing tells tales of power emanating from the royal courts of the newly consolidated national states, and the writer's role is shaped by his relation to this power; as a result, much new-historical writing on this period has centered on the nature, source, and dissemination of this power (Montrose 10–11). By the end of the eighteenth century, literary life and literature had become such powerful forces in their own right that writing itself came to organize and refigure power relationships within the new industrial culture; moreover, as Siskin has argued, the new forms of writing that developed during the romantic period themselves helped create the institutions for the definition and dissemination of literature that have remained with us to our own day.

Yet one can also go beyond the function of writing within a particular period to note that the more obvious political and social differences between periods would themselves necessitate quite distinct historical approaches to the texts produced. The fact that Elizabethan history was marked by the consolidation of the ruler's power and by fears surrounding her succession would itself suggest a historical focus for critical writing. John Bender, in an essay on new-historical approaches to eighteenth-century literature, speaks of such "naturalized presumptions" of the time as "the division of social life into private and public realms" and "the division of labor along lines of class, profession, and gender" ("A New"). Romantic new-historical studies cannot avoid the French Revolution and its ideological consequences,[12] while their Victorian equivalent, as anyone might have predicted even before these studies began to appear, would be concerned with such matters as the effects of industrialism and the imperialist enterprise.

Yet the differences between new-historical scholarship in various period specialities can also be attributed to the particular critical traditions within each period. However different in focus and method they may be, new-historical specialists in both Renaissance and romantic studies have reacted consciously to those earlier approaches that sought to depict the writing of these periods on its "own" terms, that is, on such overtly stated notions as the so-called Elizabethan world picture or the "internalization" of the French Revolution within the romantic psyche. In each of these instances the ideological analysis practiced by the new history has served to turn these notions on their heads. One might cite another, less specifically intellectual reason for these differences in approach between specialists in the various periods, namely the institutional fact that these specialists have found it suitable to their own careers to continue reproducing the bureaucratic period categories that I described in essay 1. What is now the oldest of the new-historical schools, that associated with the English Renaissance, has, through its journal and its monograph series mentioned above, as well as through the reputation of its leaders, established itself to the point that these leaders, like the functionaries of any patronage system, can help publish the writings and enhance the academic rank of those it designates as members of its guild.

If the new history, as I suggest in essays 6 and 7, has exercised a profound effect on the nature, indeed the very idea of literary canons, it has also begun to create its own canon of texts that, in the course of time, may come to seem as timeless as the long-canonical texts whose timelessness the new history has questioned. Not only has the new history unearthed a vast number of long out-of-print novels by women, but it has also given a renewed life to such once-famous forms as Renaissance pastoral, the Jacobean masque, and the condition-of-England novel. Moreover, its refusal to honor the demarcations developed during the last two centuries between "high" and "low" literature has called attention to—and perhaps will even help canonize—certain once-lowly texts such as sermons, Gothic romances, and working-class autobiographies. At least as important, many traditionally canonical works now sport both a higher ranking and a new guise. As I suggested in essay 6, a striking change of interpretation is itself a form of canon change. Thus, *The Tempest* has emerged as the characteristic new-historical Shakespearean play—just as *Hamlet* was central to romantic criticism and *King Lear* to existential (as well as to New) criticism. One need only survey such titles as "Caribbean and African Appropriations of *The Tempest*" (Nixon), "*The Tempest* and the New World" (Frey), "Prospero in Africa: *The Tempest* as Colonialist Text and Pretext" (Cartelli), " 'This Island's Mine': Caliban and Colonialism" (Griffiths), "Learning to Curse: Aspects of Linguistic Colonialism in the Sixteenth Century" (Greenblatt) to note that a play long celebrated as Shakespeare's final, conciliatory gesture has touched a special political nerve in our own time. These titles also reveal a new and increasingly powerful strain of historical scholarship initiated by Edward Said's book *Orientalism*, namely, the drive to rethink the canon of Western literature, indeed the very concept of "Western," from the perspective of those outside the so-called West.

However varied new-historical practices may be, the research they have produced will likely have long-term institutional consequences that we are only now beginning to foresee. To the extent that the traditional demarcations between literature and other forms of writing have broken down, the curricula of literature departments will no longer be grounded in a succession of long-acknowledged masterpieces neatly divided into courses according to equally long-acknowledged period concepts; and although the bureaucratically entrenched period categories I described in essay 1 do not show much promise of change, period specialists are at least likely to focus on texts that their predecessors often despised or ignored. To the extent that the new history has been nourished by ideas from other disciplines, some even outside the traditional boundaries of the humanities, literature departments will absorb methods and materials from areas such as anthropology, art history, and the history of science. Again, though the academic bureaucracy may retain traditional department structures, these may exist in name only, with literary scholars sometimes doing work not much different from that of, say, a cultural anthropologist. To the extent that the new history claims to redefine the scope, the content, the methods and the whole direction of literary study, courses in theory will share the curriculum with those devoted to what has traditionally been called literature—with the result that theoretical texts will likely come to exercise some of the functions and pleasures that were earlier thought to belong to literary texts alone. To the extent that we have come to see literature, to cite Mullaney's words, "as one realm among many for the negotiation and production of social meaning, of historical subjects, and of the systems of power" (x), we may even at some point discover that our century-old form of organization within the humanities no longer fits the type of knowledge we are producing—indeed, that if we work up the courage to act institutionally upon our present knowledge, the particular bureaucratic categories that have defined us professionally within the university may be rendered unrecognizable.

EPILOGUE

In the Form of an Interview

INTERLOCUTOR: So—what side is it you're on?

AUTHOR: That's a pretty blunt question.

INTERLOCUTOR: I'm simply asking what precisely your convictions are. Your vocabulary doesn't give out the verbal signals that readers normally need in order to place you properly. Although you discuss present-day issues, and sometimes even seem to take sides, your style is that of, shall I say, an older time.

AUTHOR: I think I see what you're getting at. My essayistic style probably gives me away as somebody shaped intellectually in the 1940s and '50s, when academics learned to cultivate a transparent, presumably jargon-free manner designed for the consumption of some common reader who, even during that time, as most of us well knew, had not existed in this country within living memory.

211

INTERLOCUTOR: You can tell me in any style you care to, but I'd like to know more about what your position is. You were so cagy about these matters in our last interview ("aFTER").

AUTHOR: Of course my general sympathies are with what the more historically minded people are doing.

INTERLOCUTOR: What are general sympathies? If you qualify sympathy, what kind of sympathy is *that?* Are you willing to call yourself a relativist?

AUTHOR: I'm a relativist whenever institutions impose demands on me that I'm not prepared to meet.

INTERLOCUTOR: A relative relativist, is that what you're saying? I see you feel the need to qualify whatever position someone might attribute to you. Perhaps you should put yourself in the place of your prospective readers: you might recognize they want to know where you stand so they can properly position *themselves* in relation to you.

AUTHOR: You scarcely need to remind *me,* of all people, that the conventions of modern critical writing dictate that authors be identified with particular positions, their own or, more commonly, those of whatever groups they may be identified with. Yes, I am perfectly willing to argue a position as long as I am also allowed to resist this perverse institutional demand by seasoning the brew with a measure of irony.

INTERLOCUTOR: You've put your finger on something. It's precisely this irony that prevents people from knowing what your position is, sometimes even from thinking you are serious about what you say.

AUTHOR: It's through this irony that I can say what I really mean.

INTERLOCUTOR: So you still believe there's still some stable meaning behind what people say.

AUTHOR: Sorry about that. I should have said it's through this irony that I can say what I really mean to say. But let me get to your remark about being taken seriously. I suspect there are many today who still take seriousness to be synonymous with solemnity. If I speak from my own experience as a reader, I can tell you that I for one don't read critics for their positions, which I am rarely interested in expounding either to myself or to others. It matters less to me that Jameson sought to perform the wedding ceremony of Marx and Freud or that Frye, a generation before, presided over the unification of that imperium he called *literature;* all this matters less to me than the fact that these theorists at their best can stimulate the reader to look at unfamiliar objects, situations, and problems or to see already familiar objects, situations, and problems in a strikingly new way. In the particular terms of this book, positions are less interesting for whatever they claim to say than for the group alignments they reveal and for the accommodations they are making to particular institutional needs and situations.

INTERLOCUTOR: There you go again, treating serious ideas as though they were material things.

AUTHOR: That's only if you set up one of those oppositions between, say, matter and spirit and relegate everything you term serious ideas to some spiritual realm. One of the points of my book is that ideas are mediated to us by institutions and that we might think differently about these ideas if we understood better how they got to us.

INTERLOCUTOR: Whenever you have a hard time explaining something, you blame it on those mysterious mediations you seem to see in institutions. It's the newest of the romanticisms, and I'm sure I'm not the only one who feels this is too easy a way out. When people have to stop short of a real explanation, they invent some god-term, and your god-term these days seems to be institutions.

AUTHOR: Then call it a devil-term. Institution-bashing's been an honored sport at least since Rousseau.

INTERLOCUTOR: You're getting a bit defensive, so let me put it another way. Am I right in sensing that your enthusiasm for what you call new history has waned a bit in the course of the decade?

AUTHOR: I suppose my enthusiasm for it was less compromised when I drafted "Toward a New History" in 1983. You may have gathered from the afterword that my feelings have aged a bit.

INTERLOCUTOR: Then let me ask, do you think this new history is a good thing?

AUTHOR: It's been the only viable career move the past ten years.

INTERLOCUTOR: You're giving me the easy institutional answer again.

AUTHOR: All right, we'll look at it from the point of view of the consumer, not the producer. Things tend to have about a ten-year shelf life in literary study. In a short time from now anecdotes about witchcraft or about the massacre of native innocents may no longer deliver the punch they did a few years ago.

INTERLOCUTOR: You are talking as though the most serious ideas circulating today can be discarded as easily as plastic containers.

AUTHOR: Canon change is as normal in criticism as in literature, and the two, we know, work in tandem with one another. If history was the key word during the 1980s, in the 1970s the word was text, together, of course, with its derivatives *textual, textualize, textuality*.

INTERLOCUTOR: And before text?

AUTHOR: During the sixties it was consciousness, though this one also had a subsidiary term, namely mind.

INTERLOCUTOR: And before that?

AUTHOR: In the fifties image and myth were the going thing. They curiously fed upon one another though for some people one of these two was superior to the other. Frye of course sought to join them together.

INTERLOCUTOR: You treat the history of criticism as a set of radical discontinuities.

AUTHOR: Not in the least. Each of these decades has shrewdly managed to absorb the key term of the last. Image and myth, for example, were relocated into the mind (whosever— yours, mine, many readers', the deity's) to become consciousness. Consciousness, in turn, was transformed (literally textualized) into text, and text, in turn, became historicized into history.

INTERLOCUTOR: That's a neat little Hegelian parable. Perhaps you are ready now to abandon your objections to the term *New Historicism*.

AUTHOR: Not in the least. I object to all the other baggage—inevitability, the grand march, and the like—that the term carries along with it. Treat this story as you just said—as a "little parable."

INTERLOCUTOR: So what's up for the 1990s? Pronounce the big word.

AUTHOR: *(after a pause):* Style.

INTERLOCUTOR: I never thought I'd hear you going formalist.

AUTHOR: Not at all. Remember that the new term always manages to absorb the old one in one way or another. If it really should take hold—and I make no guarantees to anybody—it'll be an entirely new way of dealing with style, not the stylistic features of what we have traditionally defined as literary works, but style in a much broader sense, the styles of particular cultures, of the institutions that frame and regulate the culture. If this should be where we're going, with our present knowledge we'd quickly recognize that the concept of style we impose on the phenomena we study would itself need to adapt itself to the particular cultural and historical situations we are observing. For this would be a stylistics that reeks of history as we've come to view history the past ten years, and it'd be thoroughly different from, though hopefully also in the spirit of the venerable stylistics of an Auerbach or a Spitzer.

INTERLOCUTOR: Is this New Stylistics of yours the same as the New Essentialism you announced in a recent paper ("Ideology" 407)?

AUTHOR: No connection. And I don't take the credit (or blame) for announcing it. I was simply reporting the words of a graduate student I'd briefly met who claimed that she and her friends were about to start a movement called the New Essentialism. She may well have meant it in jest for all I know—maybe, as I explained, half in jest, half seriously.

INTERLOCUTOR: Since you happened to report this where people are likely to see it, you must have thought it was at least fifty percent serious.

AUTHOR: Whether or not it was serious, it was symptomatic of the way new movements, new ideas get started—by being provocative, outrageous even, by challenging the pieties of the preceding generation so that a new generation finds some thinking space for itself. Who knows what might come of this even if it started as a joke? You raise money for a conference or two, send out some eye-catching posters. Then you put out a volume of essays by diverse hands with an alluring title (one of the conferences can easily supply the essays), and then you add a charismatic voice or two and you've got it launched.

INTERLOCUTOR: I'm still bothered by that word *essentialist*—not that it matters any to me, but for the last decade or so this has been about the worst possible thing you could say about a person.

AUTHOR: What were formerly terms of abuse make ideal names for movements and styles. Some of the most fashionable styles—baroque, impressionist, you name them—started just that way.

INTERLOCUTOR: Those were creative, not critical styles.

AUTHOR: You won't let go of those old distinctions.

INTERLOCUTOR: And you insist on confounding distinctions that everybody has long taken for granted.

AUTHOR: I thought we'd settled that matter in our last interview ("aFTER" 44–53).

INTERLOCUTOR: More like a stalemate, I suspect. What interests me more right now is not whether you were right or wrong, but the motives you may have for refusing to accept creativity as a special category.

AUTHOR: It's a historical, not a "special" category.

INTERLOCUTOR: Still, this refusal allows you and your cohorts to avoid acknowledging that there may be something inexplicable in great literature, something, say, that's left over after you think you've finished it off. I speak not only for myself but for a whole bunch of people who don't dare speak up for fear they'll be labeled old-fashioned, reactionary even, if they defend what they see as the traditional values on which their whole enterprise is built. Challenge these values and you may end up finding that none of us— you people plus all the rest of us—have anything left at all.

AUTHOR: History, I mean the field that's *really* history, has survived similar challenges. They called it "new history" there long before the literary folk took up the term.

INTERLOCUTOR: Yes, and you can find a multitude of historians who will tell you of the chaos that's been wrought in their field by people who insist the only real history is some sort of history from

"below." You know what they call the new history over there—
"history with the politics left out."

AUTHOR: Surely nobody's going to accuse us of doing literature
with the politics left out.

INTERLOCUTOR: I'll declare you innocent of any such charge. But
what you offer instead is something one might call "literature with
the greatness left out."

AUTHOR: That may be true, but then I prefer to treat the notion of
greatness as a historical category. I rarely use it in print. You may
have noticed there's only one spot in this book I used it to make
what seemed a value judgment: I was referring to Corneille's *Cinna*
and I called it a "great play" to indicate its special status within
the long tradition that it generated and that the essay happens to
deal with.

INTERLOCUTOR: But as a private person don't you often feel you
are experiencing something people call great?

AUTHOR: Of course. I've been conditioned my whole life to cultivate this sort of experience.

INTERLOCUTOR: And what criteria have you discovered to decide
whether this word is appropriate to your experience?

AUTHOR: Great is what you feel is great and you also believe you
have enough institutional support to back up this feeling.

INTERLOCUTOR: You've headed into that institutional deadend again.
Let me put it another way. Are you ever willing, in your most
private moments, I mean, to acknowledge that inexplicable quality
in literature I mentioned earlier?

AUTHOR: I suppose you mean something transcendent, magic, in-
effable.

INTERLOCUTOR: I'll go along with whatever you care to call it.

AUTHOR: You remind me of the lady in "Sunday Morning" who
keeps insisting on something transcendent out (or rather up) there
no matter how forcefully her companion tries to argue her out of it.

INTERLOCUTOR: And if I remember correctly, he argues in turn for
some immanence *in* there. Two sides of the same coin. You're still
skirting my question. How do you account for that shall-we-say

unnamable quality in literature that people have always had such a hard time accounting for?

AUTHOR: The whole game all this time was to set up one's explanatory system in such a way that the system would have some leftovers it could never adequately explain.

INTERLOCUTOR: And you really believe that serious professionals would deliberately create a system that could show up their inadequacies?

AUTHOR: Not at all. They've always been in it to win. And they can't lose with this particular system, for it legitimizes the object of their inquiry, namely literature, as something with magical attributes that they can almost but never quite fathom, and the status with which they've endowed this object in turn legitimizes their own bustling enterprise of always getting close to explaining what they see to it they will never wholly explain.

INTERLOCUTOR: Doubtless you think *you* are winning when you act so self-assured. But remember that people who break icons usually enjoy only short-term victories. In the long run it's the slicker arguments that get headed for trouble. But since you yourself brought up this business about the legitimacy of literature, I'll remind you that this legitimacy, acknowledged as it is by the legislators, the donors, the administrators and, yes, the very students who keep the system going, this legitimacy you make so much of has itself enabled you to pursue the activities by means of which you seek to destroy it. To put it bluntly, you are killing the goose that lays your golden eggs.

AUTHOR: They've never looked that golden to me.

INTERLOCUTOR: We are obviously not addressing one another in a rational way. But think back a bit, and if you're honest with yourself you may recognize that in the course of this interview the arguments of this book have been seriously undercut.

AUTHOR: That goes with the way interviews work. The interview is a genre quite distinct from the essay, which allows a single voice to dominate.

INTERLOCUTOR: *Genre*—that's another term, just like *institutions*, which you use to find easy explanations to get you out of potentially difficult, I might even say impossible, situations. It should be evident to you by now that you are standing on pretty thin ice.

AUTHOR: Those are the risks I choose to take.

INTERLOCUTOR: This does not address the concerns I just voiced. You are muddying the waters.

AUTHOR: And you are scurrying desperately from one threatening metaphor to another. Let my book simply speak for itself.

INTERLOCUTOR: With its warts showing.

NOTES

Prologue: Experiencing History in the Age of Historicism

1. See, for instance, Hayden White and Levin.

2. For a survey of this succession of period revivals, see Hitchcock.

3. For a well-known modern recapitulation of this distinction, see the detailed discussion of "primary" and "secondary" epic in Lewis 13–51.

4. For a more detailed treatment of these and related questions, see my *Historical* 54–72, 118–30.

5. See, for instance, the study of *Richard II* along these lines in Tillyard 287–99.

6. See, for instance, Renato Rosaldo's discussion of how one can define historical thought among the Ilongots in the Philippines (14–60). See also Marshall Sahlins's attempt to show that "different cultural orders have their own modes of historical action, consciousness,

and determination" in the chapter entitled "Other Times, Other Customs: The Anthropology of History" (32–72).

7. See Jauss ("Literary Process" 28–32) for a brief discussion of the term *posthistorical* and of what he calls the phenomenon of *postism* in contemporary critical discourse. Jauss claims *posthistorical* as the first of our *post* terms, and he traces its origin to Kojève's lectures on Hegel during the 1930s. Kojève actually uses the term as an adjective in his phrase "l'attitude post-historique" (597) to indicate that final stage in the Hegelian process called absolute knowledge. I use the term *posthistoricist* not to refer to a stage within any process but simply to signal my desire to avoid earlier historicist modes of thought.

1. Romantic Poetry and the Institutionalizing of Value

1. For a detailed discussion of this scene from a social-historical point of view, see Wellbery 232–36.

2. For a study of the poem's relative insignificance during the first half-century after its publication in 1850, see my article "Reception."

3. See, for example, the recent books by Klancher (*Making*), McGann (*Ideology*) and Siskin.

4. For a lucid description of the institutionalization of English studies in late nineteenth-century America, see Graff 55–80.

5. See, for example, Anne K. Mellor's recent collection, *Romanticism and Feminism*, which contains studies of canonical writers as well as of the not-yet-canonical Dorothy Wordsworth and Mary Lamb by specialists in romanticism who, for the most part, are also identified as feminist critics.

6. See Wagenknecht's collection, "How It Was," of brief memoirs by ten scholars about how it actually was to attempt writing about English romanticism during the 1950s.

7. It is significant that the poet chosen for this exercise was Shelley, the most firmly rejected member of the romantic pantheon during the first part of the century. Yet one might also note that the particular poem that these critics assigned themselves to write about is "The Triumph of Life," which, to judge from T. S. Eliot's generous comments on the poem (*Selected* 288, *To Criticize* 130–32), had more or less survived the anti-romantic assault. One could conclude from the latter instance that, in order for critics to maintain their credibility when knocking an established figure out of the canon, allowances need to be made for at least one poem. By the same token, the Yale group could

best make its case within an establishment of anti-Shelleyans by selecting a work that did not demand an uphill battle to sell.

2. Evaluation as Justification and Performance: The Leech Gatherer as Testing Ground

1. Discussions of "Resolution and Independence" as characteristically Wordsworthian do not necessarily culminate, as they do for Coleridge and Bradley, in a positive judgment of the poem. For example,
Georg Brandes in 1875 called it "one of Wordsworth's most characteristic, though certainly not one of his best poems" (4:57).

2. Among the few reviewers who comment on "Resolution and Independence," one might cite James Montgomery, who, though he has
nothing specific to say about the poem, calls it "the best in the volume"
(42); Francis Jeffrey, who, though praising "this fine distich: 'We poets
in our youth begin in gladness;/But thereof comes in the end despon-
dency and madness,' " paraphrases the rest with evident ridicule (222–
23); and the anonymous reviewer in *The Cabinet* who, in an otherwise
quite negative review of *Poems, in Two Volumes*, quotes the poem's
second stanza as something that can be read "with delight" (251).

3. The partially destroyed early version that the Hutchinson sisters
read, together with the version that Wordsworth composed in evident
response to their and Coleridge's criticisms, is reproduced in Curtis
186–95. The first published version, somewhat different from this first
revised version, is in the Cornell Wordsworth edition of *Poems, in Two
Volumes* 123–29; a facsimile of the early, partially destroyed version is
reproduced in this volume 316–23. The final version is in *Poetical
Works* 2:235–40. For studies of Wordsworth's process of revision, see
Curtis 97–113 and Brinkley.

4. See Curtis's commentary in Wordsworth, *Poems* 13, 20, 123n.

5. In retrospect this line displays an even more subtle use of Milton
than I believed at the time. The sublime moment consists simply in
the epithet "sable orbs," after which the language moves swiftly to the
more commonplace yet not quite conversational "yet-vivid eyes." The
shift from "mild surprise" to "sable orbs" and thence to "yet-vivid
eyes" leads the reader from one level of language to another with an
almost dizzying rapidity.

6. For a fine recent argument as to how we may hear Spenser (and
especially James Thomson's eighteenth-century Spenserizing) in "Resolution and Independence," see Schulman. Although he does not men-

tion the rejected stanza, Schulman cites Spenser's description of the old man Ignaro (in *FQ* 1.8.30–34) as an anticipation of Wordsworth's old man (Schulman 36–38).

7. For a more detailed description of the ways I (and presumably many other teachers of literature) have presented Wordsworth to students over the years, see my essay "Teaching Wordsworth" and my contribution to "How It Was" (Wagenknecht 566–69).

8. Leafing through my early book on *The Prelude*, I find a number of references to "Resolution and Independence" strewn throughout. See, for example, my defense of the essential dignity of the leech gatherer and of Wordsworth's other solitaries (219).

9. See, for example, the chapter entitled "The Two Voices" in Bateson 1–40. Note especially Bateson's claim: "In his most characteristic poems, like 'Resolution and Independence'— which A. C. Bradley rightly called 'the most Wordsworthian of Wordsworth's poems, and the best test of [our] ability to understand him'— the Two Voices turn out to be complementary instead of being contradictory" (4).

10. Heinzelman comes close to noting the performative aspects of this poem when, after commenting on Wordsworth's epistolary exchange with Sara Hutchinson, he writes, "If Sara Hutchinson had read with the feelings of the author, then her response to Wordsworth's poem would have been precisely what the poet himself had experienced in the encounter with the Leech-Gatherer. In other words, Wordsworth himself, as a 'reader' in the poem, acts out the exchanges which he hopes the poem might perpetuate in contracting the labor of *its* reader(s)" (215). What Heinzelman, in keeping with his book's argument, stresses as an economic exchange, I stress as a rhetorical exchange; we are both, of course, concerned with how literature articulates and disseminates values.

11. For a searching theoretical study of how values are created by and function within literature and literary study, see Smith.

3. Theories of Romanticism: From a Theory of Genre to the Genre of Theory

1. See, for example, de Man, *Allegories* 135–59, and Derrida 278–80. Derrida analyzes Rousseau's theory of linguistic origins primarily by way of the *Essay on the Origin of Languages* (164–268), but refers at various points to the Discourse to point out parallels and variations.

2. On the conflict, both in contemporary criticism and poetic prac-

tice, between present-day descendants of this subgenre and such competing postmodern forms as "collage" poems and "talk" poems, see Perloff 172–200.

3. Theories of romanticism, whether voiced by the romantics themselves or by their later expositors, characteristically employ texts both from the so-called romantic period and from earlier times to provide examples. Earlier texts such as Shakespeare's *Sonnets* and *Hamlet* have proved especially fertile for theorists of romanticism.

4. See, for example, the polemical books by Lasserre and Seillière. Lasserre entitles a section on Rousseau "Rousseau est le romantisme" (14–19), while Seillière entitles a chapter "J.-J. Rousseau principal inspirateur du mouvement romantique" (47–55). A large section of Lasserre's book (321–469) is devoted to connecting French romanticism with the liberal ideals of the French Revolution. Seillière links romanticism with utopian socialism and with what he calls "le mysticisme démocratique" (70, 113–20). Both writers treat romanticism as a phenomenon that has left what they see as adverse effects upon French culture down to their own day.

5. On the interpretive social sciences, see Geertz, *Local* 19–35. On history, see LaCapra.

6. On the integration of *Romantik* into the canon during the period of German unification, see Hohendahl 182–93.

7. It is significant, for example, that roughly half the essays in Benno von Wiese's two-volume anthology of model close readings of German lyric poems are on texts from the age of Goethe (1:185–429; 2:11–149).

8. For two significant "new historical" readings of some famous lines from Wordsworth as suppressions and sublimations of French political language and imagery, see Levinson on the immortality ode and Liu on the Simplon Pass (*Wordsworth* 3–31).

9. For a "new historical" reading of "The Rime of the Ancient Mariner" as thematizing the new Higher Criticism of the Bible and also as selfconsciously creating the interpretive framework with which it was later received by its readers, see McGann, *Beauty* 135–72.

10. On the history of historicism, especially on the roles of Vico and Herder, see Meinecke and Berlin, *Vico*.

11. On the intimate connections between historicism and romantic notions of the organic universe, see Thorslev 101–2.

4. The History in Opera: La clemenza di Tito, Khovanshchina, Moses und Aron

1. For some brief discussions of opera as a branch of historical drama, as well as of the operatic nature of much historical drama, see my study *Historical* 48, 50, 60–63, 66, 68, 80–81, 124. For discussions of historical drama as a branch of opera, see my study *Opera* 68, 256–84.

2. On crowd scenes in history plays, see my *Historical* 4, 146–53, 161–62. For crowd scenes in opera, see *Opera* 34–36.

3. Photographs of these productions are reproduced in the issue of *L'Avant-Scène* devoted largely to *Khovanshchina* (see Duault et al. 84, 92, 108, 160–61, 164–65). For photographs of the traditionally realistic Benois production, see Duault et al. 56, 65, 72, 97, 102.

4. Although he never experienced the performance of his opera during his lifetime, Schoenberg left detailed instructions for the work's scenic embodiment—instructions that show a desire for both realism, as in the scenic backdrop and the depiction of the miracles, and formal stylization, as in the ritualistic approach he takes to the configuration of characters on the stage and the relations they display to one another. See *Sämtliche* 3.A.8/1.5–6.

5. On the festiveness that permeates the overture, see Kunze 552–53.

6. On Marfa's priestess-like function not only in this scene but throughout the opera, see Vieulle. On the composer's intention to present Marfa as a realistically motivated character who uses prophecy for political ends, see Leyda and Bertensson 239–41.

7. For a superb analysis of the ceremonial nature of this opera, see Adorno's essay "Sakrales Fragment: Über Schönbergs *Moses und Aron*" (*Gesammelte* 16:454–75).

8. Well over thirty composers had set the libretto before Mozart got to it, while at least five settings, the last in 1839, were completed after Mozart's. For a list of these settings see the editorial apparatus in Metastasio 1:1498–99.

9. On the early reception of *La clemenza di Tito*, see A. Hyatt King 11–13 and Fellerer 139–49. Both sources provide statistics on the frequency of early performances and the publication of scores; in addition, Fellerer charts transcriptions and the publication of segments of the operas. All these findings attest to the great popularity of *La clemenza di Tito*.

10. For a discussion of the problems in attributing the composition of the recitatives, see Giegling ("Zu den Rezitativen"). The *secco* recitatives in Mozart's autograph of the opera are neither in Mozart's handwriting nor in Süssmayr's. Giegling argues against the possibility of Mozart's authorship of the recitatives by demonstrating a considerably greater musical sophistication in the recitatives that Mozart composed for two of his earlier *opere serie, Mitridate* and *Idomeneo*.

11. For comparisons of the various realizations of Musorgsky's piano score, see Lischke 110–19 and Reilly 19–21. A critical edition of Musorgsky's piano score is available in the fourth volume of Musorgsky, *Complete*.

12. Mozart's original intention to make a tenor out of Sextus, a part that in earlier settings of the opera had customarily been set for castrato, is evident from early sketches (see Moberly 291–92). The contract between the Bohemian authorities and Guardasoni is reproduced in Volek 281–82. The first Sextus was the castrato Domenico Bedini. Early studies of the opera, through a misunderstanding of the documents at hand, assumed that Bedini sang Annius. The misunderstanding is cleared up in Westrup 333–35.

13. For an analysis of Mazzolà's revisions to Metastasio's libretto, see Giegling ("Metastasios"). The dramatic and ceremonial elements that give Mozart's opera its peculiar character could not have manifested themselves if Mozart had set simply Metastasio's original text without Mazzolà's revisions; for example, the interchanges between the soloists and the chorus with which Mazzolà ended each act enabled Mozart to create climactic ensembles quite alien both to the letter and the spirit of the older *opera seria*. Heartz (in "Mozart"), through a demonstration of how closely the opera reflects changes in *opera seria* style among Italian composers of the 1780s, has challenged the long-standing notion that *Tito* is a "backward" work in its dramatic organization and musical style. Note especially Heartz's assertion that *Tito* "was the most modishly up-to-date work that he [Mozart] left" ("Mozart" 292). However "up-to-date" Mozart's upgrading of the *opera seria* form may have seemed during the 1790s, by the mid-nineteenth century, once the work of his Italian contemporaries had been forgotten, *La clemenza di Tito*, like Mozart's earlier *opere serie*, was automatically associated with a genre that not only had died out but also was associated with an extinct social order.

14. Wagner's comment appears in a late essay (1879), "Über die Anwendung der Musik auf das Drama." The whole sentence reads, "Mozart kannte [die tragische Muse] nur noch unter der Maske der

Metastasioschen *'Opera seria'*: steif und trocken,—*'Clemenza di Tito'* "
("Mozart knew [the tragic muse] only behind the mask of the Metasta-
sian *opera seria:* stiff and dry—*Clemenza di Tito."* [13:285]).

15. According to Teuber, these words appeared in the diary of a
Professor G. A. Meissner (2:268). But the same words appear in the
anonymously published memoir *Fantasien auf einer Reise nach Prag.* If
Teuber is correct in his attribution, for which he provides no documentation, the author of this memoir is Meissner. According to the Oester-
reichische Nationalbibliothek, a photograph of whose copy I have ex-
amined, the author is Franz von Kleist, uncle of the later-to-be-famous
dramatist.

16. On the history of Musorgsky's early experiments with speech
rhythms, above all in his early fragment *The Marriage,* see Taruskin,
Opera 307–25. On the composer's retreat, in the second version of *Boris
Godunov,* from the realistic speech rhythms of his early operatic fragments and the first *Boris,* see Taruskin, "Musorgsky" 251–53, 257–60.
On the peculiar accommodation of speech rhythms to melody that
Musorgsky achieved in *Khovanshchina,* see Emerson, "Musorgsky's"
252–53. On the relationship of *Khovanshchina* to earlier operatic form,
see Baroni.

17. For the continuity of the Wagnerian aesthetic down to Schoenberg, see Kerman. Adorno analyzes *Moses und Aron* as a Wagnerian
music-drama (*Gesammelte* 16:466–70). For some detailed descriptions
of how *Moses und Aron* builds upon nineteenth-century musical style
and organization, see Pamela White 118–29, 138–50, 160–234. White
stresses, for instance, Schoenberg's development of Wagnerian *Leit-
motive* as a means of musical narration as well as his way of finding
"equivalents" for modulation outside the tonal system.

18. "These other lines should serve as an eternal lesson for all kings
and as a spell for all mankind. . . . These two scenes, comparable, if not
superior, to all that was most beautiful in ancient Greece; these two
scenes, worthy of Corneille when he is not declaiming, and of Racine
when he is not thin" (4:491–92). Since the two passages praised by
Voltaire appear as recitatives, they were evidently not set to music by
Mozart, but by whichever assistant composed the recitatives; one might
note that Giegling singles out the setting of these very two passages as
examples of inferior musical writing ("Zu den Rezitativen" 123–24).

19. Wandruszka mentions analogies made between Leopold and
Titus during the former's lifetime (191); the portrait he presents of
Leopold, especially in relation to Joseph II, is more positive than most
historians accept.

20. The particular conspiracy that stands behind *Cinna*—if there was a single prototype at all—has long been a matter of scholarly conjecture. It has sometimes been thought that Corneille used the play as a means of asking for Richelieu's clemency toward those responsible for the so-called Va-Nu-Pieds rebellion in 1639 in the playwright's native city of Rouen. Since the play, like its eighteenth-century progeny, deals with an aristocratic conspiracy rather than with a popular revolt like the one in Rouen, a number of models have been suggested. For reviews of several theories, see Lancaster 3.2:312–14 and, more recently, Couton's commentary in his edition of Corneille (1:1582–86).

21. "Today who wouldn't rather be Mozart than Leopold, the monarch who was just crowned?"—attributed by Teuber (2:68) to the diary of the same Meissner who had praised the finale of the first act, as noted earlier in this essay. The same statement, though in slightly different wording ("Enough, at these moments I should rather be Mozart than Leopold") occurs in the anonymous *Fantasien* (91). It is likely an allusion to Mozart's comic song "Ich möchte wohl der Kaiser sein [I'd like to be the Emperor]" (K. 539), composed three years before while Joseph II was still on the throne.

22. For a brief description of the 1848 performance, see Teuber. After a detailed chronicle of the difficulties that the revolutionary activities of 1848 had created for the theatrical life of the city, Teuber describes the return to political stability that coincided with the coronation and the performance of the opera: "They performed Mozart's coronation opera *Titus*, and the occasion for this performance was the coronation of the youthful Emperor Franz Josef. A festival play by Hickl, *Austria's Stars*, opened the celebration; the grand Sextus of Fehringer and the sympathetic Vitellia of Grosser were worthy of the festive presentation with which the theater season of 1848, one of the most significant and precarious years in the history of the Prague theater, to a certain degree achieved a happy conclusion. The venerable institution had averted catastrophe" (3:387–88).

23. The theme associated with Peter the Great appears near the end of act IV and was also used by Rimsky-Korsakov to provide an ending for the uncompleted last act. Shostakovich used this, but, as I indicated earlier, provided an alternative ending as well, while Stravinsky created a quite different ending, without fanfares, for a Diaghilev production in 1913. The fragmentary act as printed in Lamm's critical edition gives no evidence that Musorgsky intended to end the opera with a fanfare. Without the fanfare Peter's ultimate triumph would no longer have the prominence in Musorgsky's scheme that it achieves in

most present-day performances. For a convenient chart on the differ-
ences between the piano score, the Rimsky version, and a libretto that
Musorgsky apparently wrote after composing most of the opera, see
Emerson, "Musorgsky's" 266–67.

24. On the controversies among Soviet scholars as to where Musorgsky's sympathies lay, see Emerson, "Musorgsky's" 245–50. Emerson's own interpretation stresses the composer's musical and dramatic
identification with the Old Believers (250–64).

25. In his study of the differences between the first and second
versions of *Boris Godunov*, Taruskin claims that the strong populist
sentiments we note in Musorgsky's treatment of the populace did not
enter the opera until the latter version (1871), that, whereas the first
version (1869) deviated relatively little from Pushkin's text, the new
version, above all in the Kromy scene that the composer added to the
end of the opera, deviates from Pushkin at the same time that it
postulates a more positive view of the populace than before; Taruskin
attributes this new view to the influence of Musorgsky's contemporary
Nikolai Kostomarov ("Musorgsky" 256). For a study of the generic
changes that both Pushkin and Musorgsky worked on the Boris theme,
see Emerson, "Bakhtin."

26. In a letter Musorgsky indicates his need to keep Peter and the
regent offstage: "(But Peter and Sofia are kept off stage— this is decided; better without them), and I am eager to do a people's drama—
I am so eager" (Leyda and Bertensson 224).

27. See Volpé, Ternovsky, and Billington 412–14. As Volpé and
Ternovsky point out, within the new populist historiography the Old
Believers were seen as models for resistance against the centralized
state. Ternovsky mentions the popularity of the Old Believers in other
forms such as historical fiction and painting during Musorgsky's time
(151). For a history of the Old Believer schism from its origins in the
religious reform of the 1650s through the revival of interest in the
schism that took place during Musorgsky's time, see Cherniavsky.

28. For the historical background, see Venturi 501–6 and Walicki
222–35. For a survey of Musorgsky's relation to populism, see Hoops,
who stresses not only how *Khovanshchina* reflects populist hopes but
also the dashing of these hopes during the later years of its composition
(293–96).

29. On the relation of representation to the divine prohibition of
concrete images, see Adorno 16:458–59.

30. "In the realization of this scene, since it affects the center of my
conception, I went quite far, and at this spot my piece is probably also

most 'opera'— which indeed it should be" (*Briefe* 188). The "operatic" nature of this scene was a cause of some embarrassment to Schoenberg, as we note in the apologetic tone with which he describes the scene to Anton von Webern: "You know that I do not much care for the dance [around the Golden Calf]. Its expressive power in general is on no higher a level than the most primitive program music; and in its petrified mechanical quality its 'beauty' seems hateful to me" (*Briefe* 165). In view of the musical style of the disciple to whom he was writing, it is no wonder that Schoenberg should seek to excuse the relative opulence of the Golden Calf scene. One might also note that the closer Schoenberg got to what might be construed as a musical representation of some "real" world, the more nervous he evidently became about lapsing into an older aesthetic mode.

31. "Everything I have written bears a certain inner resemblance to me" (*Briefe* 154). Schoenberg insists on the autobiographical element in response to Berg's inquiry about other depictions of Moses— for example, Strindberg's posthumous play *Moses*—that Schoenberg might have had in mind as models. But Schoenberg was equally insistent on the religious nature of the work, as when, shortly before his death, he wrote to his disciple Josef Rufer: "The content and its treatment are purely religious-philosophical" (*Briefe* 298). The latter remark was occasioned by what Schoenberg viewed as the wrong kind of biographical approach—in particular, an entry in *Grove's Dictionary of Music* by Gerald Abraham, who had attempted to connect the conflict between the spiritual and the material in the opera with what he called "the inner conflicts of Schoenberg's tortured and enigmatic mind" (6:573).

32. For a comprehensive treatment of Schoenberg's relation to Judaism and to the Jewish people, see Mäckelmann.

33. For detailed comparisons of *Der biblische Weg* and *Moses und Aron*, see Mäckelmann 157–67 and my article "Arnold Schoenberg's." Although *Der biblische Weg* has not yet been published in German, it is available in an Italian translation (*La via biblica*).

34. Adorno briefly mentions the political setting in the following terms: "*Moses und Aron* was composed just before the outbreak of the Third Reich, doubtless as a defense against what was dawning" (460). Mäckelmann also suggests parallels between the political situation and the composition of the opera (140–48).

35. This handwritten document, entitled "The Jewish Government in Exile," is described in Ringer 45–46, with this excerpt quoted by Ringer (46). Note, for example, the following sentence (not quoted by

Ringer), in which Schoenberg imagines himself exercising a world-leadership role: "The authority thus bestowed upon me enables me and my collaborators and advisers to take the destiny of our nation firmly and conscientiously [sic] in hand and to make such arrangements and agreements with other nations which this government deems suitable for a lucky solution of the 2000 years old Jewish problem" ("Jewish Government" 3–4). If one is to take Schoenberg literally, this document would raise certain questions about the composer's mental stability at the time.

36. For a fine recent study that *does* take operas seriously for what they can tell us about their times, see Robinson. Writing as an intellectual historian, Robinson presents Berlioz's *Les Troyens*, for example, as an embodiment of Hegelian historical process (103–54) and Verdi's *Don Carlos* as a critique of mid-nineteenth-century *Realpolitik* (155–209).

5. *The Literature in History:* Danton's Death *in the Texts of Revolutions*

1. On the relation of the fatalism letter to what in France was called the "éole fataliste" of historians— Thierry, Guizot, Mignet and Thiers, the last two of whom were principal sources for *Danton's Death*— see Jancke 130–35.

2. For a cautionary note on the applicability of Mayer's extensive findings, see Wetzel. For a critique of Mayer's failure to account for the religious dimension of the play, see Rey 24–26, 65–66.

3. I do not mean to imply an ideological one-dimensionality to Carlyle's great history. As Rosenberg has demonstrated in his distinguished recent study of *The French Revolution*, Carlyle's narrative contains within its ample borders a generous array of diverse voices that jostle against one another throughout the book. See above all Rosenberg's Bakhtin-influenced chapter entitled "Narrative Voices" (76–90). Yet Rosenberg also stresses the narrative control that Carlyle exercises throughout: "Although the narrator avoids the first person, the reader everywhere senses his controlling presence, the covert 'I' directing our attention to times and places far removed from the field of action" (59). In the role of epic poet that he has so consciously assumed, Carlyle, like Milton before him, can impose a unity upon the multiplicity he has unleashed—in a way that a dramatist such as Büchner refuses to do.

4. See, among other studies of the Büchner-Heine relationship, Poschmann 203–28; Mayer, "Büchner und Weidig" 69, 126–34, and "Eine kurze Chronik" 390–91; and Dedner 345–53.

5. For a modern assessment of the role of Mignet and Thiers in the development of historiography in early nineteenth-century France, see Stadler 121–28. On the "liberal version" of the Revolution that they and other historians of the 1820s propagated, see Mellon 5–30. For an assessment of Mignet's and Thiers' views of the Revolution with Büchner's play particularly in mind, see Zöllner 17–59. On the continuity of their "fatalism" through Büchner and Marx (including their notions of class conflict), see Görlich and Lehr 50–54.

6. For an easy-to-follow, line-by-line compilation of Büchner's borrowings from these three narrative sources, see Büchner, *La Mort* 35–52. This edition presents the source material in the order in which it appears in the play. For a line-by-line analysis of Mignet and Thiers that starts from these sources and then moves to the play, see Zöllner 60–91. On Büchner's ability to distance himself on occasion from Strahlheim in the very act of borrowing from him, see Mayer, "Zur Revision" 316–17.

7. On Büchner's use of these sources from the early 1790s, see Beck. Mayer argues that a number of sources that Beck and others before him had attributed to French documents of the 1790s could have been found by Büchner in German in a supplementary volume of Strahlheim's *Unsere Zeit* ("Zur Revision" 297–317). Since the version in Strahlheim is a translation of these documents, one can still attribute them to the decade of the Revolution.

8. For a list of reception studies, some of them full-length monographs, up to the late 1970s, see Gerhard Knapp 453–54. Several have appeared since this bibliography, including the long section entitled "Wirkungsgeschichte" in Hauschild 161–288. For an analysis of recent reception studies, see Grimm 115–35. For a list of stories and dramas about Büchner himself, see Gerhard Knapp 454–55. For some early reviews of the play, followed by a study of how these reviews anticipate recent conflicts in the play's interpretation, see "Dokumente" and Bohn.

9. For lengthy accounts, including quotations from contemporary newspaper reviews, see Strudthoff 52–56, 105–9, 125–31 respectively. For additional descriptions, including a list of the extensive cuts and changes that Reinhardt made to maintain his focus on the crowd, see Viewweg 56–68, 188–90, 213–16 respectively. Viewweg also analyzes the influence of the German revolution of 1918 on various productions of the play during the Weimar Republic (69–98).

10. From the point of view of this essay, it seems significant that at one spot Ozouf employs a classic literary text partially about the Revolution, Wordsworth's *Prelude,* in the same way that she uses the archival materials on which her study is based, that is, as an eyewitness account of a festival, in this instance the Festival of the Federation (described in book 6 of the poem) that the English poet experienced while traveling across France in the summer of 1790 (56–57). Thus, a work that has traditionally been treated as "literature" here serves as the raw material of "history."

11. Hunt stresses the relation between conspiratorial and literary plots. For an earlier application by a historian of Frye's (as well as other literary theorists') categories to historical discourse, if not precisely to "history itself," see Hayden White.

12. For a detailed study of Büchner's use of classical analogy in the play, see Koopmann.

7. *On the Sacrality of Reading Lists: The Western Culture Debate at Stanford University*

1. Professor Cavalli-Sforza has informed me he was not responsible for the headline. For a balanced analysis written well after the completion of the debate and emanating from a British source, see Reed.

2. For a history of this and subsequent courses in Western Civilization in the United States, see Allardyce, whose article has supplied some of the historical detail in the present essay.

3. Much has been written in recent years on the shaping power that Arnold exercised on humanistic study down to this day. See, among many others, Baldick 18–57, Graff 3–7, and Arac 117–38.

8. *From Opera to Postmodernity: Institutions as Frames*

1. For an analogous comparison, see DiMaggio's detailed study of the development of the Boston Museum of Fine Arts and the Boston Symphony Orchestra during the late nineteenth and early twentieth centuries. DiMaggio uses Boston as a case study to describe such phenomena of the period as the separation of high and popular culture and the development of a cultural elite.

2. On the development of professionalism in the administration of the various arts during the last century, see Peterson.

3. For statistics on the dramatic difference in governmental support for the arts in the United States and most European countries, see the tables in Montias 299, 300, and 303. For example, whereas government support for arts organizations during the early 1970s comprised .13% of national income in Germany, it comprised only .008% of national income in the United States (303). In the United States, arts organizations are dependent on foundations and on private donors to a far greater degree than they are in European countries. Philip Glass remarks wrily on the difference (especially before the 1980s) between support for new works in Europe and the United States (*Music* 46–47).

4. For some interesting remarks on how operas are commissioned by smaller companies and how they fare at the box office, see Duffy and Blassingham. One might note that nearly all the contemporary operas discussed in these articles, which seek to encourage the composition and production of new works, are musically and often also theatrically conservative. For a discussion, with telling statistics, of the paucity of contemporary operas (even of a conservative sort!) in the repertory of the major American companies, see Martorella 83–114.

5. On conscious attempts during the later nineteenth century to "strengthen boundaries between the performer and the audience, the former transported, the latter receptive and subdued," see DiMaggio 312. DiMaggio describes a process of audience training applicable not only to music listeners but also to museum-goers and, I might add, to readers of literature. Challenging this process is central to postmodernist aesthetics.

6. See Nagler. For a recent debate on the subject, see Graubard, ed. 49–59.

7. For a discussion of how the term *anti-aesthetic* can be useful in understanding postmodernist art, see Foster (xv-xvi), who defines the term as, among other things, "signaling a practice . . . sensitive to cultural forms . . . that deny the idea of a privileged aesthetic realm" (xv). As I have argued in this paper, the opera house for at least the past century has identified itself with such a realm.

8. For a brief discussion of *Einstein on the Beach* (and also *Satyagraha*) in relation to Glass's earlier music and to that of other minimalist composers, see Martins 11–17, 79–86. For Glass's own account of the genesis of the opera and for an analysis of the music, see *Music* 27–62.

9. For a description of the rationale and method of *Europeras 1 & 2*, see Durner, on whom my own brief account is dependent. I have been

unable to secure an audio- or videotape of a performance. The composer himself reports he knows of no such record—appropriately enough for the patron saint of a movement that has questioned the notion of an imperishable work of art.

9. *Toward (and After) a New History in Literary Study*

1. For a searching study of the American appropriation of Auerbach, see Bové 79–208. Bové treats Auerbach "as a master who helps overcome the troubling battles between literary historians and New Critics," but argues that this appropriation "trivializes Auerbach" (129).

2. For a classic critique of how the evolutionary model compromised the attempt of Chambers and other older historians to present "objective" history, see Hardison 1–34. For a later, structuralist attack on Hardison for not breaking away sufficiently from the evolutionary model to see discontinuities in literary history, see Warning 125–26.

3. The occasion for Steinberg's citation was the publication, almost two decades after its completion, of his dissertation on the trinitarian symbolism that he claimed had shaped Borromini's Roman church San Carlo alle Quattro Fontane. According to Steinberg, the idea behind the dissertation had seemed uncommonly daring during the 1950s, for no documents existed to prove that Borromini explicitly intended to express the trinity in the form that the architect gave the church. From the point of view of the present essay, one could say that the evidence Steinberg submitted was strictly of the circumstantial sort. Circumstantial evidence had long been introduced by the older historical scholars in English literature, especially those working on Shakespeare, who left embarrassingly little evidence about his intentions. Such distinguished traditional historical studies of Shakespeare such as Campbell's and Elton's supply abundant documentary information to recreate the intellectual milieu from which we are expected to draw conclusions about what the dramatist's intentions must have been. Although this type of evidence might not have passed muster in an early twentieth-century scholarly court, by mid-century it had come to seem quite acceptable.

4. For a recent study of the new history's relation to various forms of Marxism, see Gallagher.

5. Nearly all recent descriptions of the new history mention Foucault's pervasive influence. For a sharp critique of Foucault and his

new-historical followers for the political passivity to which his ideas supposedly lead, see Lentricchia.

6. For a recent critique of the political implications of Geertz's work and the legacy of Geertz's politics on the literary scholars who have used him, see Pecora.

7. Davis points out the paucity of theoretical framing in earlier social historians when she writes that "most books on 'everyday life' in the late Middle Ages and early modern period do not help us very much, for they merely describe the curious charivaris and carnivals and stop short of analysis" (100–101). When writing about ceremonies of misrule, she tells us, she consulted not only Renaissance sources and the older literary historians such as E. K. Chambers, but such theoreticians of play as Roger Caillois and Mikhail Bakhtin (101–3).

8. For a recent study of the new history's relationship to feminism, see Newton.

9. The older literary history, as I describe it here, remained the dominant mode within German literary scholarship for a relatively short period, for it had largely spent its force by the turn of the century, when it was replaced by that mode called *Geistesgeschichte*, which represented a return to and a further development of German historicist thought. Auerbach's *Mimesis* counts in Germany as one of the great monuments of *Geistesgeschichte* (see "Epilegomena" 15–18) and was not a product of what I describe as the older history. Since the latter, which the Germans call "positivist," was not essentially historicist in its orientation, I have deliberately avoided the word *historicism* in this paper—despite the fact that Americans often use the term loosely to refer to any sort of historical method. One might also note that when Americans spoke disparagingly of "German" scholarship during the New Critical period, they were referring to a mode that had not been dominant in Germany for half a century, yet which maintained its hold on literary scholarship in most other European countries and in America throughout this time.

10. The editor of the conservative *New Criterion*, Hilton Kramer, though complimenting me for "a remarkably clear and coherent analysis of the subject," claimed that he "found much to disagree with in Professor Lindenberger's conclusions—he [Lindenberger] looked with particular pleasure on what he called 'the social concerns of the new literary history' " (7). Kramer's comment is a reminder that, however diverse the political affiliations of new-historical scholars may be, these affiliations must all look disconcertingly leftish from a right-wing point of view.

11. For a searching comparison between British and American new-historical practice, see Wayne, who emphasizes the relevance of British political events of the 1980s to critical writing:

> In reading through some of the most recent work on Shakespeare by British scholars, one is struck by the number of references to the present political scene. Essays on Shakespearean subjects by British contributors to the two above-mentioned collections are filled with allusions to the Thatcher government's domestic policies, to the 1984/5 coalminers' strike, to the Falklands campaign, to the persistence of colonialist and patriarchal ideologies, and to the role of Shakespeare as the central ideological figure in a national culture. (49)

12. For a comparison of new-historical work in Renaissance and romantic studies, see Liu, "Review" 180–81. On its effects on romantic studies, see Klancher, "English."

WORKS CITED

Abraham, Gerald. "Schönberg, Arnold." In Henry Cope Colles, ed., *Grove's Dictionary of Music*, 4:573–74.

Abrams, M. H. *The Mirror and the Lamp: Romantic Theory and the Critical Tradition*. New York: Oxford University Press, 1953.

—— *Natural Supernaturalism: Tradition and Revolution in Romantic Literature*. New York: Norton, 1971.

—— "Structure and Style in the Greater Romantic Lyric." In Hilles and Bloom, eds., *From Sensibility to Romanticism: Essays Presented to Frederick A. Pottle*, pp. 527–60.

Abrams, M. H. et al., eds. *Norton Anthology of English Literature*. 1st ed. New York: Norton, 1962.

—— *Norton Anthology of English Literature*. 5th ed. New York: Norton, 1986.

Adams, Hazard, ed. *Critical Theory Since Plato*. New York: Harcourt, Brace, 1971.

Adams, John. *Nixon in China*. San Francisco Concert Opera. Herbst Theater, Veterans Building, San Francisco. May 21–22, 1987.

Adorno, Theodor W. *Gesammelte Schriften*. Rolf Tiedemann, ed. 20 vols. to date. Frankfurt: Suhrkamp, 1970–.

Allardyce, Gilbert et al. "The Rise and Fall of the Western Civilization Course." In *American Historical Review* (1982), 87:695–743.

Arac, Jonathan. *Critical Genealogies: Historical Situations for Postmodern Literary Studies*. New York: Columbia University Press, 1987.

Arnold, Heinz Ludwig, ed. *Georg Büchner I/II*. Munich: text + kritik, 1979.

—— *Georg Büchner III*. Munich: text + kritik, 1981.

Arnold, Matthew. *Complete Prose Works*. R. H. Super, ed. 11 vols. Ann Arbor: University of Michigan Press, 1966–77.

—— *Poetry and Criticism of Matthew Arnold*. A. Dwight Culler, ed. Boston: Houghton Mifflin, 1961.

—— "President's Report." In *Transactions of the Wordsworth Society* (1883), no. 5, pp. 4–9.

Auerbach, Erich. "Epilegomena zu *Mimesis*." In *Romanische Forschungen* (1953), 65:1–18.

—— *Mimesis: The Representation of Reality in Western Literature* (1946). Willard Trask, tr. Princeton: Princeton University Press, 1953.

Bakhtin, M. M. *The Dialogic Imagination*. Caryl Emerson and Michael Holquist, trs. Austin: University of Texas Press, 1981.

Baldick, Chris. *The Social Mission of English Criticism, 1848–1932*. Oxford: Clarendon Press, 1983.

Baran, Henryk, ed. *Semiotics and Structuralism: Readings from the Soviet Union*. White Plains, N.Y.: International Arts and Sciences Press, 1976.

Barber, Samuel. *Antony and Cleopatra*. Metropolitan Opera. Metropolitan Opera House, New York. September 16, 1966.

Baroni, Mario. "*Chovanscina*." In *Musik-Konzepte* (September 1981), no. 21, pp. 69–94.

Bate, Walter Jackson. *The Burden of the Past and the English Poet*. Cambridge: Harvard University Press, 1970.

Bateson, F. W. *Wordsworth: A Re-interpretation*. 2d ed. London: Longmans, 1956.

Baxandall, Michael. *The Limewood Sculpture of Renaissance Germany*. New Haven: Yale University Press, 1980.

—— *Painting and Experience in Fifteenth Century Italy*. New York: Oxford University Press, 1972.

Beal, Graham, curator. *A Quiet Revolution: British Sculpture Since 1965.* San Francisco Museum of Modern Art. Veterans Building, San Francisco. June-July 1987.

Beck, Adolf. "Unbekannte französische Quellen für 'Dantons Tod' von Georg Büchner." In Lüders, ed., *Jahrbuch des freien deutschen Hochstifts,* pp. 489–538.

Bender, John B. *Imagining the Penitentiary: Fiction and the Architecture of Mind in Eighteenth-Century England.* Chicago: University of Chicago Press, 1987.

—— "A New History of the Enlightenment." To be published in a forthcoming book on eighteenth-century scholarship edited by Leopold Damrosch, Jr., at the University of Wisconsin Press.

Benjamin, Walter. *Illuminations.* Harry Zohn, tr. New York: Schocken, 1969.

Bennett, William and Donald Kennedy, interviewees. MacNeil/Lehrer NewsHour. Public Broadcasting System. April 19, 1988.

Berlin, Isaiah. *"Khovanshchina."* In San Francisco Opera program (November 1984), pp. 34–40.

—— *Vico and Herder: Two Studies in the History of Ideas.* London: Hogarth Press, 1976.

Billington, James H. *The Icon and the Axe: An Interpretive History of Russian Culture.* New York: Knopf, 1966.

Blassingham, Ellen. "Marketing Opera: Is There an Audience for New Works?" In Blassingham, ed., *Perspectives,* pp. 127–35.

Blassingham, Ellen, ed. *Perspectives: Creating and Producing Contemporary Opera and Musical Theater: A Series of Fifteen Monographs.* Washington, D.C.: Opera America, 1983.

Bloom, Allan. *The Closing of the American Mind.* New York: Simon and Schuster, 1987.

—— "Educational Trendiness." In *The Wall Street Journal,* January 26, 1989, p. A15.

Bloom, Harold. *The Anxiety of Influence: A Theory of Poetry.* New York: Oxford University Press, 1973.

Bloom, Harold, ed. *Deconstruction and Criticism.* New York: Seabury Press, 1979.

Bohn, Volker. " 'Bei diesem genialem Cynismus wird dem Leser zuletzt ganz krankhaft pestartig zu Muthe': Überlegungen zur Früh- und Spätrezeption von *Dantons Tod.*" In Arnold, ed., *Georg Büchner III,* pp. 104–30.

Bohn, Volker, ed. "Dokumente der Frührezeption von *Dantons Tod.*" In Arnold, ed., *Georg Büchner III,* pp. 99–103.

Bolelli, Tristano. "I Classici banditi." In *La Stampa*, January 30, 1988, p. 3.

Bovè, Paul A. *Intellectuals in Power: A Genealogy of Critical Humanism.* New York: Columbia University Press, 1986.

Bradley, A. C. *Oxford Lectures on Poetry* (1909). Bloomington: Indiana University Press, 1961.

Brandes, Georg. *Main Currents in Nineteenth-Century Literature.* 6 vols. New York: Macmillan, 1901–1905.

Brecht, Bertolt. *Brecht on Theatre.* John Willett, tr. New York: Hill and Wang, 1964.

Brinkley, Robert. "*The Leech-Gatherer* Revisited." In *The Wordsworth Circle* (1985), 16:98–105.

Brook, Peter. *La tragédie de Carmen.* Vivian Beaumont Theater, New York. 1983.

Brown, Malcolm Hamrich, ed. *Musorgsky: In Memoriam 1881–1981.* Ann Arbor: UMI Research Press, 1982.

Büchner, Georg. *La Mort de Danton.* Richard Thieberger, ed. Paris: Presses Universitaires de France, 1953.

—— *Sämtliche Werke und Briefe.* Werner R. Lehmann, ed. 2 vols. Hamburg: Christian Wegner, 1967–71.

—— *Werke und Briefe.* Fritz Bergemann, ed. Wiesbaden: Insel, 1958.

Burckhardt, Jakob. *The Civilization of the Renaissance in Italy.* S. G. C. Middlemore, tr., rev. Irene Gordon. New York: New American Library, 1960.

Bürger, Peter. *Actualität und Geschichtlichkeit: Studien zum gesellschaftlichen Funktionswandel der Literatur.* Frankfurt: Suhrkamp, 1977.

Cage, John. *Europeras 1 & 2.* Oper Frankfurt, Frankfurt. December 1987.

—— "*Europeras 1 & 2:* Synopses." In *Sulfur* (Fall 1988), 8(2):162–68.

Campbell, Lily B. *Shakespeare's "Histories": Mirrors of Elizabethan Policy.* San Marino, Calif.: Huntington Library, 1947.

Carlyle, Thomas. *The French Revolution: A History.* New York: Modern Library, n.d.

Carroll, Lewis. *Alice in Wonderland.* Donald J. Gray, ed. New York: Norton, 1971.

Cartelli, Thomas. "Prospero in Africa: *The Tempest* as Colonialist Text and Pretext." In Howard and O'Connor, eds. *Shakespeare Reproduced*, pp. 99–115.

Cavalli-Sforza, Luca. "Alla ricerca di un Dante nero." In *La Stampa*, March 31, 1988, p. 3.

Césaire, Aimé. *Une tempête.* Paris: Editions du Seuil, 1969.

Chambers, E. K., *The Mediaeval Stage.* 2 vols. Oxford: Clarendon Press, 1903.

Chéreau, Patrice, dir. *Der Ring des Nibelungen.* Bayreuth Wagner-Festspiele, Bayreuth. August 1976.

Cherniavsky, Michael. "The Old Believers and the New Religion." In *Slavic Review* (1966), 25:1–39.

Chiapelli, Fredi, ed. *First Images of America: The Impact of the New World on the Old.* 2 vols. Berkeley: University of California Press, 1976.

Coleridge, Samuel Taylor. *Biographia Literaria.* James Engell and W. Jackson Bate, eds. 2 vols. Princeton: Princeton University Press, 1983.

Colles, Henry Cope, ed. *Grove's Dictionary of Music.* 4th ed. 6 vols. London: Macmillan, 1940.

Corneille, Pierre. *Oeuvres complètes.* Georges Couton, ed. 3 vols. Paris: Gallimard, 1980–1987.

Court, Franklin. "The Social and Historical Significance of the First English Literature Professorship in England." In *PMLA* (1988), 103:796–807.

Cragg, Tony. *Axehead (mixed materials).* San Francisco Museum of Modern Art. Veterans Building, San Francisco. June-July 1987.

Curtis, Jared R. *Wordsworth's Experiments with Tradition: The Lyric Poems of 1802 with Texts of the Poems Based on Early Manuscripts.* Ithaca: Cornell University Press, 1971.

Curtius, Ernst Robert. *European Literature and the Latin Middle Ages* (1948). Willard R. Trask, tr. New York: Pantheon, 1953.

Dahlhaus, Carl. "Musorgskij in der Musikgeschichte des 19. Jahrhunderts." In *Musik-Konzepte* (September 1981), no. 21, pp. 7–22.

Davis, Natalie Z. *Society and Culture in Early Modern France.* Stanford: Stanford University Press, 1975.

Dedner, Burghard. "Legitimationen des Schreckens in Georg Büchners Revolutionsdrama." In *Jahrbuch der deutschen Schillergesellschaft* (1985), 29:343–80.

de Man, Paul. *Allegories of Reading.* New Haven: Yale University Press, 1979.

—— "The Rhetoric of Temporality." In Singleton, ed., *Interpretation: Theory and Practice,* pp. 173–209.

Derrida, Jacques. *Of Grammatology* (1967). Gayatri Chakravorty Spivak, tr. Baltimore: Johns Hopkins University Press, 1976.

Dickman, Stephen. *Real Magic in New York.* Film Makers' Cinematique, New York. January 1971.

—— *Tibetan Dreams.* John Drew Theatre of Guild Hall, East Hampton, New York. April 1988 (act 1), and April 1990 (full opera).

DiMaggio, Paul. "Cultural Entrepreneurship in Nineteenth-Century Boston." In *Media, Culture and Society* (1982), 4:33–50, 303–22.

DiMaggio, Paul, ed. *Nonprofit Enterprise in the Arts: Studies in Mission and Constraint.* New York: Oxford University Press, 1986.

Duault, Alain et al. Special issue on *Khovanshchina* of *L'Avant-Scène* (November/December 1983), 57/58.

Duffy, John. "Commissioning Operas." In Blassingham, ed., *Perspectives*, pp. 121–25.

Durkheim, Emile. *Suicide: A Study in Sociology.* John A. Spaulding and George Simpson, trs. New York: Free Press, 1951.

Durner, Leah. "Past and Future in John Cage's Europeras 1 & 2." In *EAR Magazine* (April 1988), 13(2):10–13.

Dutschke, Rudi. "Georg Büchner und Peter-Paul Zahl, oder: Widerstand im Übergang und mittendrin." In Mayer, ed., *Georg Büchner Jahrbuch 4/1984*, pp. 10–75.

Eagleton, Terry. *Literary Theory: An Introduction.* Minneapolis: University of Minnesota Press, 1983.

Eliot, T. S. *Complete Poems and Plays 1909–1950.* New York: Harcourt, Brace, 1971.

—— *Selected Essays.* 3d ed. London: Faber and Faber, 1951.

—— *To Criticize the Critic and Other Writings.* London: Faber and Faber, 1965.

—— *The Use of Poetry and the Use of Criticism* (1933). London: Faber and Faber, 1964.

Elton, William. *King Lear and the Gods.* San Marino, Calif.: Huntington Library, 1966.

Emerson, Caryl. "Bakhtin and Intergeneric Shift: The Case of Boris Godunov." In *Studies in Twentieth Century Literature* (1984), 9:145–67.

—— "Musorgsky's Libretti on Historical Themes: From the Two *Borises* to *Khovanshchina*." In Groos and Parker, eds., *Reading Opera*, pp. 235–67.

Fantasien auf einer Reise nach Prag. [No author on title page.] Dresden und Leipzig: Richtersche Buchhandlung, 1792.

Fellerer, Karl Gustav. "Zur Rezeption von Mozarts Oper um die Wende des 18./19. Jahrhunderts." In *Mozart-Jahrbuch 1965–1966*, pp. 39–49. Salzburg: Zentralinstitut für Mozartforschung, 1967.

Fineman, Joel. "The History of the Anecdote: Fiction and Fiction." In Veeser, ed., *The New Historicism*, pp. 49–76.

—— *Shakespeare's Perjured Eye: The Invention of Subjectivity in the Sonnets*. Berkeley: University of California Press, 1985.

Fish, Stanley. *Is There a Text in This Class? The Authority of Interpretive Communities*. Cambridge: Harvard University Press, 1980.

Foster, Hal. "Preface." In Foster, ed., *The Anti-Aesthetic: Essays on Postmodern Culture*, pp. ix-xvi.

Foster, Hal, ed. *The Anti-Aesthetic: Essays on Postmodern Culture*, Port Townsend, Wash.: Bay Press, 1983.

Foucault, Michel. *The Order of Things: An Archaeology of the Human Sciences* (1966). [Alan Sheridan-Smith, tr.] New York: Random House, 1970.

Francisco, William, dir. *Titus*. By Wolfgang Amadeus Mozart. San Francisco Spring Opera. Curran Theater, San Francisco. March 1971.

Freud, Sigmund. *Five Lectures on Psycho-Analysis* (1910). James Strachey, tr. New York: Norton, 1977.

Frey, Charles. "*The Tempest* and the New World." In *Shakespeare Quarterly* (1979), 30:29–41.

Fried, Michael. *Absorption and Theatricality: Painting and Beholder in the Age of Diderot*. Berkeley: University of California Press, 1980.

—— "Painter into Painting: On Courbet's *After Dinner at Ornans* and *Stonebreakers*." In *Critical Inquiry* (1982), 8:619–49.

—— "The Structure of Beholding in Courbet's *Burial at Ornans*." In *Critical Inquiry* (1983), 9:635–83.

Friedrich, Götz, dir. *Aida*. Berlin Komische Oper, East Berlin. 1969.

Frye, Northrop. *Anatomy of Criticism: Four Essays*. Princeton: Princeton University Press, 1957.

—— *Fearful Symmetry: A Study of William Blake*. Princeton: Princeton University Press, 1947.

Furet, François. *Interpreting the French Revolution*. Elborg Forster, tr. Cambridge: Cambridge University Press, 1981.

Gabel, John B. and Charles B. Wheeler. *The Bible as Literature*. New York: Oxford University Press, 1986.

Gadamer, Hans-Georg. *Truth and Method* (1960). No translator named. New York: Crossroad, 1988.

Gallagher, Catherine. "Marxism and the New Historicism." In Veeser, ed., *The New Historicism*, pp. 37–48.

Gates, David with Tony Clifton. "Say Goodnight Socrates: Stanford University and the decline of the West." In *Newsweek*, February 1, 1988, p. 46.

Geertz, Clifford. *The Interpretation of Cultures*. New York: Basic Books, 1973.

—— *Local Knowledge: Further Essays in Interpretive Anthropology.* New York: Basic Books, 1983.

—— *Negara: The Theatre State in Nineteenth-Century Bali.* Princeton: Princeton University Press, 1980.

Giegling, Franz. "Metastasios Oper 'La clemenza di Tito' in der Bearbeitung durch Mazzolà." In *Mozart-Jahrbuch 1968–70*, pp. 88–94. Salzburg: Zentralinstitut für Mozartforschung, 1970.

—— "Zu den Rezitativen von Mozarts Opera 'Titus.' " In *Mozart-Jahrbuch 1967*, pp. 121–26. Salzburg: Zentralinstitut für Mozartforschung, 1968.

Glass, Philip. *Music by Philip Glass.* New York: Harper and Row, 1987.

—— *Satyagraha.* Netherlands Opera, Rotterdam. September 1980.

Glass, Philip and Robert Wilson. *Einstein on the Beach.* Byrd Hoffman Foundation in cooperation with Metropolitan Opera. Metropolitan Opera House, New York. November 21, 1976.

Goethe, Johann Wolfgang. *Dichtung und Wahrheit.* Erich Trunz, ed. Hamburg: Christian Wegner, 1955.

—— *The Sorrows of Young Werther and Selected Writings.* Catherine Hutter, tr. New York: New American Library, 1962.

Goffman, Erving. *Frame Analysis.* New York: Harper, 1974.

Gombrich, E. H. *Art and Illusion: A Study in the Psychology of Pictorial Representation.* New York: Pantheon, 1960.

Görlich, Bernard and Anke Lehr. "Materialismus und Subjektivität in den Schriften Georg Büchners." In Arnold, ed., *Georg Büchner III*, pp. 35–62.

Grab, Walter, ed. *Georg Büchner und die Revolution von 1848.* Königstein: Athenäum, 1985.

Graff, Gerald. *Professing Literature: An Institutional History.* Chicago: University of Chicago Press, 1987.

Graubard, Stephen R., ed. "The Future of Opera." In *Daedalus* (1986), 115(4):2–92.

Greenblatt, Stephen. "Fiction and Friction." In Heller et al., eds., *Reconstructing Individualism: Autonomy, Individuality, and the Self in Western Thought*, pp. 30–52.

—— "Learning to Curse: Aspects of Linguistic Colonialism in the Sixteenth Century." In Chiapelli, ed., *First Images of America: The Impact of the New World on the Old*, 2:561–80.

—— *Renaissance Self-Fashioning: From More to Shakespeare.* Chicago: University of Chicago Press, 1980.

—— "Towards a Poetics of Culture." In Veeser, ed., *The New Historicism*, pp. 1–14.

Greene, Thomas M. *The Light in Troy: Imitation and Discovery in Renaissance Poetry*. New Haven: Yale University Press, 1982.

Griffiths, Trevor R. " 'This Island's Mine': Caliban and Colonialism." In *Yearbook of English Studies* (1983), 13:159–80.

Grimm, Reinhold. *Love, Lust, and Rebellion: New Approaches to Georg Büchner*. Madison: University of Wisconsin Press, 1985.

Groos, Arthur and Roger Parker, eds. *Reading Opera*. Princeton: Princeton University Press, 1988.

Habermas, Jürgen. *Strukturwandel der Öffentlichkeit: Untersuchungen zu einer Kategorie der bürgerlichen Gesellschaft*. Neuwied: Hermann Luchterhand, 1962.

Hall, Spencer and Jonathan Ramsey, eds. *Approaches to Teaching Wordsworth's Poetry*. New York: Modern Language Association, 1986.

Hardison, O. B., Jr. *Christian Rite and Christian Drama in the Middle Ages*. Baltimore: Johns Hopkins University Press, 1965.

Harrison, Gary. "Wordsworth's Leech Gatherer: Liminal Power and the 'Spirit of Independence.' " In *ELH* (1989), 56:327–50.

Hartman, Geoffrey. *Wordsworth's Poetry: 1787–1814*. New Haven: Yale University Press, 1964.

Hauschild, Jan-Christoph. *Georg Büchner: Studien und neue Quellen zu Leben, Werk und Wirkung*. Königstein: Athenäum, 1985.

Heartz, Daniel. "Mozart and his Italian Contemporaries: 'La clemenza di Tito.' " In *Mozart-Jahrbuch 1978–79*, pp. 275–93. Kassel: Bärenreiter, 1979.

—— "Mozart's Overture to *Titus* as Dramatic Argument." In *Musical Quarterly* (1978), 64:29–49.

Hegel, G. W. F. *Reason in History*. Robert S. Hartman, tr. Indianapolis: Bobbs-Merrill, 1953.

Heinzelman, Kurt. *The Economics of the Imagination*. Amherst: University of Massachusetts Press, 1980.

Heiss, Christine. "Die Rezeption von *Dantons Tod* durch die deutsch-amerikanische Arbeiterbewegung im 19. Jahrhundert." In Mayer, ed., *Georg Büchner Jahrbuch 4/1984*, pp. 248–63.

Heller, Thomas C., Morton Sosna, and David E. Wellbery, eds. *Reconstructing Individualism: Autonomy, Individuality, and the Self in Western Thought*. Stanford: Stanford University Press, 1986.

Hilles, Frederick W. and Harold Bloom, eds. *From Sensibility to Romanticism: Essays Presented to Frederick A. Pottle*. New York: Oxford University Press, 1965.

Hirsch, E. D. *Cultural Literacy: What Every American Needs to Know*. Boston: Houghton Mifflin, 1987.

Hitchcock, Henry-Russell. *Architecture: Nineteenth and Twentieth Centuries.* 3d ed. Harmondsworth: Penguin, 1969.

Hofkosh, Sonia. "The Writer's Ravishment: Women and the Romantic Author—The Example of Byron." In Mellor, ed., *Romanticism and Feminism,* pp. 93–114.

Hohendahl, Peter Uwe. *Building a National Literature: The Case of Germany 1830–1870.* Ithaca: Cornell University Press, 1989.

Hoops, Richard. "Musorgsky and the Populist Age." In Brown, ed., *Musorgsky: In Memoriam,* pp. 271–306.

Howard, Jean E. "The New Historicism in Renaissance Studies." In *English Literary Renaissance* (1986), 16:13–43.

Howard, Jean E. and Marion F. O'Connor, eds. *Shakespeare Reproduced: The Text in History and Ideology.* New York: Methuen, 1987.

Huet, Marie-Hélène. *Rehearsing the Revolution: The Staging of Marat's Death 1793–1797.* Robert Hurley, tr. Berkeley: University of California Press, 1982.

Hume, David. "Of the Standard of Taste" (1757). In Adams, ed., *Critical Theory Since Plato,* pp. 314–23.

Hunt, Lynn. *Politics, Culture, and Class in the French Revolution.* Berkeley: University of California Press, 1984.

Huxley, Aldous. "Wordsworth in the Tropics." In *Yale Review* (1929), n.s. 18:672–83.

Ibsen, Henrik. *Letters and Speeches.* Evert Sprinchorn, ed. New York: Hill and Wang, 1964.

Imbrie, Andrew. *Angle of Repose.* San Francisco Opera. War Memorial Opera House, San Francisco. November 1976.

Introduction to Contemporary Civilization in the West: A Source Book. 2 vols. New York: Columbia University Press, 1946.

Jakobson, Roman. "Linguistics and Poetics." In Sebeok, ed., *Style in Language,* pp. 350–77.

Jancke, Gerhard. *Georg Büchner: Genese und Aktualität seines Werkes.* Kronberg: Scriptor Verlag, 1975.

Jauss, Hans Robert. "The Literary Process of Modernism from Rousseau to Adorno." Lisa C. Roetzel, tr. In *Cultural Critique* (1988–89), no. 11, pp. 27–61.

—— *Toward an Aesthetic of Reception.* Timothy Bahti, tr. Minneapolis: University of Minnesota Press, 1982.

Jeffrey, Francis. Review of Wordsworth, *Poems, in Two Volumes.* In *Edinburgh Review* (October 1807), 11:214–31.

Johnson, Samuel. *Lives of the English Poets.* George Birkbeck Hill, ed. 3 vols. Oxford: Clarendon Press, 1905.

Keats, John. *Letters*. Hyder Edward Rollins, ed. 2 vols. Cambridge: Harvard University Press, 1958.

Kerman, Joseph. "Wagner: Thoughts Out of Season." In *Hudson Review* (1960), 13:329–49.

Kermode, Frank. *The Romantic Image* (1957). New York: Random House, 1964.

King, A. Hyatt. *Mozart in Retrospect: Studies in Criticism and Bibliography*. London: Oxford University Press, 1955.

King, Bill. "Don't compromise on CUS proposal, BSU spokesman says." In [Stanford] *Campus Report*, February 10, 1988, p. 14.

Klancher, Jon P. "English Romanticism and Cultural Production." In Veeser, ed., *The New Historicism*, pp. 77–88.

—— *The Making of English Reading Audiences, 1790–1832*. Madison: University of Wisconsin Press, 1987.

Knapp, Gerhard P. "Kommentierte Bibliographie zu Georg Büchner." In Arnold, ed., *Georg Büchner I/II*, pp. 426–61.

Knapp, Steven. *Personification and the Sublime: Milton to Coleridge*. Cambridge: Harvard University Press, 1985.

Kojève, Alexandre. *Introduction à la lecture de Hegel*. Paris: Gallimard, 1947.

Koopmann, Helmut. "*Dantons Tod* und die antike Welt: Zur Geschichtsphilosophie Georg Büchners." In *Zeitschrift für deutsche Philologie* (Sonderheft 1965), 84:22–41.

Kramer, Hilton. "The MLA centennial follies." In *The New Criterion* (February 1984), 2:1–8.

Kuhn, Thomas S. *The Structure of Scientific Revolutions*. Chicago: University of Chicago Press, 1962.

Kunze, Stefan. *Mozarts Opern*. Stuttgart: Reclam, 1984.

LaCapra, Dominick. *History and Criticism*. Ithaca: Cornell University Press, 1985.

Lancaster, Henry C. *A History of French Dramatic Literature*. 5 vols. Baltimore: Johns Hopkins University Press, 1929–1942.

Lasserre, Pierre. *Le romantisme français*. 3d ed. Paris: Mercure de France, 1907.

Leavis, F. R. *Revaluation: Tradition and Development in English Poetry* (1936). New York: Norton, 1947.

Lentricchia, Frank. "Foucault's Legacy: A New Historicism?" In Veeser, ed., *The New Historicism*, pp. 231–42.

Levin, David. *History as Romantic Art*. Stanford: Stanford University Press, 1959.

Levinson, Marjorie. *Keats's Life of Allegory: The Origins of a Style*. Oxford: Basil Blackwell, 1988.

—— "Wordsworth's Intimations Ode: A Timely Utterance." In Mc-Gann, ed., *Historical Studies and Literary Criticism*, pp. 48–75.

Lewis, C. S. *A Preface to* Paradise Lost. 1942. New York: Oxford University Press, 1962.

Leyda, Jay and Sergei Bertensson, eds. and trs. *The Musorgsky Reader.* New York: Norton, 1947.

Lindenberger, Herbert. "aFTER sAUL's fALL: An Interview with the Author." In *New Literary History* (1989), 21:37–57.

—— "Arnold Schoenberg's *Der biblische Weg* and *Moses und Aron:* On the Transactions of Aesthetics and Politics." In *Modern Judaism* (1989), 9:55–70.

—— *Georg Büchner*. Carbondale: Southern Illinois University Press, 1964.

—— *Historical Drama: The Relation of Literature and Reality*. Chicago: University of Chicago Press, 1975.

—— "Ideology and Innocence: On the Politics of Critical Language." Special issue of *PMLA* (1990), 105:398–408.

—— *On Wordsworth's "Prelude."* Princeton: Princeton University Press, 1963.

—— *Opera: The Extravagant Art*. Ithaca: Cornell University Press, 1984.

—— "The Reception of *The Prelude*." In *Bulletin of the New York Public Library* (1960), 64:196–208.

—— "Teaching Wordsworth from the 1950s to the 1980s." In Hall and Ramsey, eds., *Approaches to Teaching Wordsworth's Poetry*, pp. 32–38.

Lischke, André. "Les versions de la Khovanshchina." In Duault et al., pp. 110–19.

Liu, Alan. Review of Simpson, *Wordsworth's Historical Imagination*. In *The Wordsworth Circle* (1988), 19:172–82.

—— *Wordsworth: The Sense of History*. Stanford: Stanford University Press, 1989.

Lotman, Jurij. "Theater and Theatricality in the Order of Early Nineteenth Century Culture." In Baran, ed., *Semiotics and Structuralism: Readings from the Soviet Union*, pp. 33–63.

Lovejoy, Arthur O. *Essays in the History of Ideas*. Baltimore: Johns Hopkins University Press, 1948.

Lowes, John Livingston. *The Road to Xanadu: A Study in the Ways of the Imagination* (1927). New York: Vintage, 1959.

Lüders, Detlev, ed. *Jahrbuch des freien deutschen Hochstifts*. Tübingen: Max Niemeyer Verlag, 1963.

Lukács, Georg. *Deutsche Realisten des 19. Jahrhunderts*. Berlin: Aufbau-Verlag, 1952.

—— *The Historical Novel.* Hannah and Stanley Mitchell, trs. Boston: Beacon Press, 1963.

—— *Theory of the Novel* (1916). Anna Bostock, tr. Cambridge: MIT Press, 1971.

McGann, Jerome J. *The Beauty of Inflections: Literary Investigations in Historical Method and Theory.* Oxford: Clarendon Press, 1985.

—— *The Romantic Ideology: A Critical Investigation.* Chicago: University of Chicago Press, 1983.

McGann, Jerome J., ed. *Historical Studies and Literary Criticism.* Madison: University of Wisconsin Press, 1985.

Mack, Maynard, ed. *An Essay on Man* (1950). Volume III, part 1 of Alexander Pope, *Poems,* Twickenham ed. 6 vols. London: Methuen, 1939–1954.

—— "The World of *Hamlet.*" In *Yale Review* (1952), 41:502–23.

Mäckelmann, Michael. *Arnold Schönberg und das Judentum.* Hamburg: Karl Dieter Wagner, 1984.

Marsch, Edgar, ed. *Über Literaturgeschichtsschreibung: Die historisierende Methode des 19. Jahrhunderts in Programm und Kritik.* Darmstadt: Wissenschaftliche Buchgesellschaft, 1975.

Martins, Wim. *American Minimal Music: La Monte Young, Terry Riley, Steve Reich, Philip Glass.* J. Hautekiet, tr. London: Kahn and Averill, 1983.

Martorella, Rosanne. *The Sociology of Opera.* New York: Praeger, 1982.

Marx, Karl. *Selected Writings.* David McLellan, ed. Oxford: Oxford University Press, 1977.

Mayer, Thomas Michael. "Büchner und Weidig—Frühkommunismus und revolutionäre Demokratie: Zur Textverteilung des 'Hessischen Landboten.' " In Arnold, ed., *Georg Büchner I/II,* pp. 16–298.

—— "Georg Büchner: Eine kurze Chronik zu Leben und Werk." In Arnold, ed., *Georg Büchner I/II,* pp. 357–425.

—— "Zur Revision der Quellen für *Dantons Tod* von Georg Büchner." In *Studi germanici* (1969), 7:287–336.

Mayer, Thomas Michael, ed. *Georg Büchner Jahrbuch 4/1984.* Frankfurt: Europäische Verlagsanstalt, 1986.

Meinecke, Friedrich. *Historism: The Rise of a New Historical Outlook.* J. E. Anderson, tr. London: Routledge and Kegan Paul, 1972.

Mellon, Stanley. *The Political Uses of History: A Study of Historians in the French Restoration.* Stanford: Stanford University Press, 1958.

Mellor, Anne K. "On Romanticism and Feminism." In Mellor, ed., *Romanticism and Feminism,* pp. 3–9.

Mellor, Anne K., ed. *Romanticism and Feminism.* Bloomington: Indiana University Press, 1988.

Metastasio, Pietro. *Tutte le opere*. 2d ed. Bruno Brunelli, ed. 5 vols. Milan: Mondadori, 1947–1954.

Michelet, Jules. *Histoire de la révolution française*. Gérard Walter, ed. 2 vols. Paris: Gallimard, 1952.

Mill, John Stuart. *Autobiography and Other Writings*. Jack Stillinger, ed. Boston: Houghton Mifflin, 1969.

—— *Essays on Poetry*. F. Parvin Sharpless, ed. Columbia: University of South Carolina Press, 1976.

Moberly, R. B. "The Influence of French Classical Drama on Mozart's 'La clemenza di Tito.' " In *Music and Letters* (1974), 55:286–98.

Montgomery, James. Review of Wordsworth, *Poems, in Two Volumes*. In *Eclectic Review* (January 1808), 4:35–43.

Montias, John Michael. "Public Support for the Performing Arts in Europe and in the United States." In DiMaggio, ed., *Nonprofit Enterprise in the Arts*, pp. 287–319.

Montrose, Louis. "Renaissance Literary Studies and the Subject of History." In *English Literary Renaissance* (1986), 16:3–12.

Morosan, Vladimir. "Musorgsky's Choral Style." In Brown, ed., *Musorgsky: in Memoriam*, pp. 95–133.

Mühlher, Robert. In *Dichtung und Krise: Mythos und Psychologie in der Dichtung des 19. und 20. Jahrhunderts*. Vienna: Herold, 1951.

Mullaney, Steven. *The Place of the Stage: License, Play, and Power in Renaissance England*. Chicago: University of Chicago Press, 1988.

Mumford, Lewis. *The Culture of Cities*. New York: Harcourt, Brace, 1938.

Musorgsky, Modest. *Complete Works*. Paul Lamm, ed. 18 vols. New York: Edwin F. Kalmus, n.d.

Nagler, A.M. *Misdirection: Opera Production in the Twentieth Century*. Hamden: Archon, 1981.

Nemoianu, Virgil. *The Taming of Romanticism: European Literature and the Age of Biedermeier*. Cambridge: Harvard University Press, 1984.

Newton, Judith Lowder. "History as Usual? Feminism and the 'New Historicism.' " In Veeser, ed., *The New Historicism*, pp. 152–67.

Nietzsche, Friedrich. *Werke*. Karl Schlechta, ed. 3 vols. Darmstadt: Wissenschaftliche Buchgesellschaft, 1966.

Nixon, Rob. "Caribbean and African Appropriations of *The Tempest*." In *Critical Inquiry* (1987), 13:557–78.

Oliver, William I., dir. *Danton's Death*. By Georg Büchner. Department of Dramatic Art, University of California, Berkeley. University Theater, Berkeley. February-March 1971.

Ozouf, Mona. *Festivals and the French Revolution*. Alan Sheridan, tr. Cambridge: Harvard University Press, 1988.

Pater, Walter. *Selected Writings.* Harold Bloom, ed. New York: New American Library, 1974.

Peacock, Ronald. "A Note on Georg Büchner's Plays." In *German Life and Letters* (1956–57), 10:189–97.

Pechter, Edward. "The New Historicism and Its Discontents." In *PMLA* (1987), 102:292–303.

Pecora, Vincent. "The Limits of Local Knowledge." In Veeser, ed., *The New Historicism,* pp. 243–76.

Perloff, Marjorie. *The Dance of the Intellect: Studies in the Poetry of the Pound Tradition.* Cambridge: Cambridge University Press, 1985.

Peterson, Richard A. "From Impresario to Arts Administrator: Formal Accountability in Nonprofit Cultural Organizations." In DiMaggio, ed., *Nonprofit Enterprise in the Arts,* pp. 161–83.

Pinkert, Ernst-Ullrich. "Langer Marsch, aufrechter Gang, Schmerzen verschiedener Art: *Editorischer Kommentar* zu Rudi Dutschke's Büchner-Zahl-Essay." In Mayer, ed., *Georg Büchner Jahrbuch 4/1984,* pp. 76–153.

Plato. *Dialogues.* Benjamin Jowett, tr. 2 vols. New York: Random House, 1937.

Ponnelle, Jean-Pierre, dir. *Cavalleria rusticana.* By Pietro Mascagni. San Francisco Opera. War Memorial Opera House, San Francisco. November 1980.

—— *La clemenza di Tito.* By Wolfgang Amadeus Mozart. Unitel film. Broadcast on BBC-2, July 11, 1981.

—— *Der fliegende Holländer.* By Richard Wagner. San Francisco Opera. War Memorial Opera House, San Francisco. September-October 1975.

Poschmann, Henri. *Heinrich Heine und die Zeitgenossen: Geschichtliche und literarische Befunde.* Berlin: Aufbau-Verlag, 1979.

Pound, Ezra. *Literary Essays* (1954). T. S. Eliot, ed. London: Faber and Faber, 1960.

Ranke, Leopold von. *Sämmtliche Werke.* 54 vols. Leipzig: Duncker und Humblot, 1867–90.

Rauschenberg, Robert. *Retroactive I.* Wadsworth Atheneum, Hartford.

Reed, Chris. "Reform and rage." In the *Guardian,* September 27, 1988, p. 21.

Reilly, Edward R. *The Music of Mussorgsky: A Guide to The Editions.* New York: Musical Newsletter, 1980.

Rey, William H. *Georg Büchners 'Dantons Tod': Revolutionstragödie und Mysterienspiel.* Berne: Peter Lang, 1982.

Richards, I. A. *Practical Criticism: A Study of Literary Judgment* (1929). New York: Harcourt, Brace, n.d.

Rigney, Ann. "Toward Varennes." In *New Literary History* (1986), 18:77–98.

Ringer, Alexander L. "Arnold Schoenberg and the Politics of Jewish Survival." In *Journal of the Arnold Schoenberg Institute* (1979), 3:11–48.

Robbins, Jerome, chor. *Moves: A Ballet in Silence.* New York City Ballet. New York State Theater, New York. May 2, 1984.

Robinson, Paul. *Opera and Ideas: From Mozart to Strauss.* New York: Harper and Row, 1985.

Rosaldo, Renato. *Ilongot Headhunting: 1883–1974.* Stanford: Stanford University Press, 1980.

Rosenberg, John D. *Carlyle and the Burden of History.* Cambridge: Harvard University Press, 1985.

Rothman, Andrea. "Trouble Is, Someone Keeps Erasing Certain Lines from the Libretto." In *The Wall Street Journal,* July 22, 1987, p. 25.

Rousseau, Jean-Jacques. *Dictionnaire de musique.* Paris: Chez la Veuve Duchesne, 1768.

—— *Discourse on Inequality* (1755). In *The Essential Rousseau,* pp. 143–201. Lowell Bair, tr. New York: New American Library, 1974.

—— *Essay on the Origin of Languages* (around 1750). John H. Moran and Alexander Gode, trs. New York: Frederick Ungar, 1966.

Sahlins, Marshall. *Islands of History.* Chicago: University of Chicago Press, 1985.

Said, Edward W. *Orientalism.* New York: Pantheon, 1978.

Salvatore, Gaston. *Büchners Tod.* Frankfurt: Suhrkamp, 1972.

Schiller, Friedrich von. *Naive and Sentimental Poetry* (1795). Julius A. Elias, tr. New York: Frederick Ungar, 1966.

—— *On the Aesthetic Education of Man* (1794). Elizabeth M. Wilkinson and L. A. Willoughby, eds. and trs. Oxford: Clarendon Press, 1967.

Schlegel, August Wilhelm. *Kritische Schriften und Briefe.* Edgar Lohner, ed. 5 vols. Stuttgart: W. Kohlhammer, 1962–1967.

Schlegel, Friedrich. *Kritische Schriften.* Wolfdietrich Rasch, ed. Munich: Karl Hanser, 1964.

Schmidt, Erich. "Wege und Ziele der deutschen Literaturgeschichte" (1880). In Marsch, ed., *Über Literaturgeschichtsschreibung: Die historisierende Methode des 19. Jahrhunderts in Programm und Kritik,* pp. 400–419.

Schoenberg, Arnold. "Der biblische Weg." Unpublished manuscript.

—— "Brief über die jüdische Frage." In Stuckenschmidt, *Schönberg: Leben, Umwelt, Werk,* pp. 495–96.

—— *Briefe.* Erwin Stein, ed. Mainz: B. Schott's Söhne, 1958.

—— "A Four-Point Program for Jewry." In *Journal of the Arnold Schoenberg Institute* (1979), 3:49–67.

—— "The Jewish Government in Exile." Unpublished manuscript.

—— *Sämtliche Werke*. 23 vols. to date. Mainz: B. Schott's Söhne, 1966–.

—— *Testi poetici e drammatici*. Luigi Rognoni, ed. Emilio Castellani, tr. Milan: Feltrinelli, 1967.

—— *La via biblica*. In *Testi poetici e drammatici*, pp. 77–150.

Schulman, Samuel E. "The Spenserian Enchantments of Wordsworth's 'Resolution and Independence.' " In *Modern Philology* (1981), 79:24–44.

Schulz, Caroline. "Bericht über Georg Büchners Krankheit und Tod." In Grab, ed., *Georg Büchner und die Revolution von 1848*, pp. 132–38.

Schulz, Wilhelm. "*Nachgelassene Schriften* von G. Büchner." In Grab, ed., *Georg Büchner und die Revolution von 1848*, pp. 51–127.

Sebeok, Thomas A., ed. *Style in Language*. Cambridge: MIT Press, 1960.

Seillière, Ernest. *Le romantisme*. Paris: Stock, 1925.

Shelley, Percy Bysshe. *Poetry and Prose*. Donald H. Reiman and Sharon B. Powers, eds. New York: Norton, 1977.

Simpson, David. *Wordsworth's Historical Imagination: The Poetry of Displacement*. New York: Methuen, 1987.

Singleton, Charles, ed. *Interpretation: Theory and Practice*, Baltimore: Johns Hopkins University Press, 1969.

Siskin, Clifford. *The Historicity of Romantic Discourse*. New York: Oxford University Press, 1988.

Smith, Barbara Herrnstein. *Contingencies of Value: Alternative Perspectives for Critical Theory*. Cambridge: Harvard University Press, 1988.

Stadlen, Peter. "Schoenberg's Speech-Song." In *Music and Letters* (1981), 62:1–11.

Stadler, Peter. *Geschichtsschreibung und historisches Denken in Frankreich: 1789–1871*. Zurich: Verlag Berichthaus, 1958.

"The Stanford Mind." Editorial. In *The Wall Street Journal*, December 22, 1988, p. A12.

"Stanford Slights the Great Books for Not-So-Greats." In *The Wall Street Journal*, December 22, 1988, p. A12.

Steck, Odil Hannes. "*Moses und Aron*": *Die Oper Arnold Schönbergs und ihr biblischer Stoff*. Munich: Kaiser, 1981.

Steinberg, Leo. *Borromini's San Carlo alle Quattro Fontane: A Study in Multiple Form and Architectural Symbolism*. New York: Garland, 1977.

Stone, Lawrence. *The Crisis of the Aristocracy: 1558–1641.* London: Oxford University Press, 1967.

Strindberg, August. *Queen Christina, Charles XII, Gustav III.* Walter Johnson, tr. Seattle: University of Washington Press, 1955.

Strudthoff, Ingeborg. *Die Rezeption Georg Büchners durch das deutsche Theater.* Berlin: Colloquium Verlag, 1957.

Stuckenschmidt, H. H. *Schönberg: Leben, Umwelt, Werk.* Zurich: Atlantis, 1974.

Syberberg, Hans-Jürgen, dir. *Parsifal.* By Richard Wagner. Corinth Video, 1982.

"Synopsis." *La forza del destino.* In San Francisco Opera Program (September-October 1986), p. 42.

Taruskin, Richard. "Musorgsky vs. Musorgsky: The Versions of *Boris Godunov.*" In *Nineteenth Century Music* (1984–85), 8:91–118, 245–72.

—— *Opera and Drama in Russian: As Preached and Practiced in the 1860s.* Ann Arbor: UMI Research Press, 1981.

Ternovsky, Eugène. "Le Raskol, composant historique d'une querelle idéologique." In Duault et al., pp. 148–51.

Teuber, Oscar. *Geschichte des Prager Theaters.* 3 vols. Prague: A. Haase, 1883–1888.

Thomas, Brook. "The New Historicism and other Old-fashioned Topics." In Veeser, ed., *The New Historicism,* pp. 182–203.

Thorslev, Peter L. *Romantic Contraries: Freedom Versus Destiny.* New Haven: Yale University Press, 1984.

Tillyard, E. M. W. *Shakespeare's History Plays* (1944). New York: Collier, 1962.

Todd, William Mills, III. *Fiction and Society in the Age of Pushkin.* Cambridge: Harvard University Press, 1986.

Treitschke, Heinrich von. *Deutsche Geschichte im neunzehten Jahrhundert.* 5 vols. Leipzig: S. Hirzel, 1886–1889.

Trilling, Lionel. *Matthew Arnold* (1939). Cleveland: World, 1955.

Turner, Victor. *The Forest of Symbols.* Ithaca: Cornell University Press, 1967.

Vasari, Giorgio. *Lives of the Artists* (1568). George Bull, tr. Harmondsworth: Penguin, 1965.

Veeser, H. Aram, ed. *The New Historicism.* New York: Routledge, 1989.

Venturi, Franco. *Roots of Revolution: A History of the Populist and Socialist Movements in Nineteenth Century Russia.* Francis Haskell, tr. New York: Knopf, 1964.

Viehweg, Wolfram. *Georg Büchners 'Dantons Tod' auf dem deutschen Theater*. Munich: Laokoon-Verlag, 1964.

Viëtor, Karl. "Die Tragödie des heldischen Pessimismus: Über Büchners Drama *Dantons Tod*." In *Deutsche Vierteljahrsschrift für Literaturgeschichte und Geistesgeschichte* (1934), 12:173–209.

Vieulle, Marie-François. "Marfa ou la flamme à la question." In Duault et al., pp. 124–31.

Volek, Tomislav. "Über den Ursprung von Mozarts Oper 'La clemenza di Tito.' " In *Mozart-Jahrbuch 1959*, pp. 274–86. Salzburg: Zentralinstitut für Mozartforschung, 1960.

Volpé, Ruth. "L'intérêt du XIX siècle russe pour la culture nationale." In Duault et al., pp. 135–37.

Voltaire. *Oeuvres complètes*. Louis Moland, ed. 52 vols. Paris: Garnier, 1877–1885.

Wagenknecht, David, ed. "How It Was." In *Studies in Romanticism* (1982), 21:553–71.

Wagner, Richard. *Gesammelte Schriften*. Julius Kapp, ed. 14 vols. Leipzig: Hesse und Becker, n.d.

Walicki, Andrzej. *A History of Russian Thought from the Enlightenment to Marxism*. Hilda Andrews-Rusiecka, tr. Stanford: Stanford University Press, 1979.

Wandruszka, Adam. "Die 'Clementia Austriaca' und der aufgeklärte Absolutismus: Zum politischen und ideellen Hintergrund von 'La clemenza di Tito.' " In *Österreichische Musikzeitschrift* (1976), 31:186–93.

Warhol, Andy. *Twenty-five Colored Marilyns*. Fort Worth Art Museum, Fort Worth.

Warning, Rainer. *Funktion und Struktur: Die Ambivalenzen des geistlichen Spiels*. Munich: Wilhelm Fink, 1974.

Wayne, Don E. "Power, Politics, and the Shakespearean Text: Recent Criticism in England and the United States." In Howard and O'Connor, eds., *Shakespeare Reproduced*, pp. 47–67.

Weber, Max. *From Max Weber: Essays in Sociology*. H. H. Gerth and C. Wright Mills, eds. and trs. New York: Oxford University Press, 1946.

Wellbery, Caroline. "From Mirrors to Images: The Transformation of Sentimental Paradigms in Goethe's *The Sorrows of Young Werther*." In *Studies in Romanticism* (1986), 25:231–49.

Wellek, René. *Concepts of Criticism*. Stephen G. Nichols, Jr., ed. New Haven: Yale University Press, 1963.

Westrup, J. A. "Two First Performances: Monteverdi's 'Orfeo' and Mozart's 'La clemenza di Tito.' " In *Music and Letters* (1958), 39:327–35.

Wetzel, Heinz. "Ein Büchnerbild der siebziger Jahre: zu Thomas Michael Mayer: 'Büchner und Weidig—Frühkommunismus und revolutionäre Demokratie.' " In Arnold, ed., *Georg Büchner III*, 247–64.

White, Hayden. *Metahistory: The Historical Imagination in Nineteenth-Century Europe.* Baltimore: Johns Hopkins University Press, 1973.

White, Pamela. *Schoenberg and the God-Idea: The Opera "Moses und Aron."* Ann Arbor: UMI Research Press, 1985.

Wiese, Benno von. *Die deutsche Lyrik.* 2 vols. Düsseldorf: Bagel, 1957.

Wilson, Robert et al. Record brochure. *Einstein on the Beach.* CBS Records, M4 38875, n.d.

Wimsatt, W. K. *Hateful Contraries: Studies in Literature and Criticism.* Lexington: University of Kentucky Press, 1965.

—— *The Portraits of Alexander Pope.* New Haven: Yale University Press, 1965.

Winkler, John. *Rehearsals of Manhood.* Princeton: Princeton University Press, forthcoming.

Winters, Yvor. *Forms of Discovery.* [Chicago]: Alan Swallow, 1967.

Wordsworth, Jonathan, ed. "Waiting for the Palfreys: The Great *Prelude* Debate." In *The Wordsworth Circle* (1986), 17:2–38.

Wordsworth, William. *The Letters of William and Dorothy Wordsworth: The Early Years 1787–1805.* Ernest de Selincourt, ed. 2d ed., rev. Chester Shaver. Oxford: Clarendon Press, 1967.

—— *Poems, in Two Volumes.* Jared R. Curtis, ed. Ithaca: Cornell University Press, 1983.

Review of *Poems, in Two Volumes.* In *The Cabinet* (April 1808), 3:249–52.

—— *Poetical Works.* Ernest de Selincourt and Helen Darbishire, eds. 2d ed. 5 vols. Oxford: Clarendon Press, 1940–54.

—— *The Prelude, 1798–1799.* Stephen Parrish, ed. Ithaca: Cornell University Press, 1977.

—— *The Prose Works of William Wordsworth.* W. J. B. Owen and Jane Worthington Smyser, eds. 3 vols. Oxford: Clarendon Press, 1974.

Workman, Bill. "Stanford Puts an End to Western Civilization." *San Francisco Chronicle*, April 1, 1988, p. A7.

Zöllner, Bernd. "Büchners Drama 'Dantons Tod' und das Menschen- und Geschichtsbild in den Revolutionsgeschichten von Thiers und Mignet." Ph.D. diss., University of Kiel, 1972.

INDEX

Abraham, Gerald, 231
Abrams, M. H., *The Mirror and the Lamp*, 189-90; *Natural Supernaturalism*, 65, 80
Adams, John: *Nixon in China*, 185, 186, 187
Adorno, Theodor, 199; on *Moses und Aron*, 226, 228, 230, 231
Aeschylus, 137
Allardyce, Gilbert, 153, 234
Arac, Jonathan, 234
Archaeology, 5, 6, 10
Architecture, 5, 145
Ariosto, Lodovico, 63
Aristotle, 137, 140, 157; *Ethics*, 155, 158; *Politics*, 158
Arnim, Achim von, 7
Arnold, Matthew: on Chaucer, 38; as cultural spokesman, 34, 76, 80, 139-40, 146, 154; as influence on humanistic study, 234; on romantics, 29-30, 32, 34, 51; "Dover Beach," 29, 75-76, 77; "Memorial Verses," 74-75
Auerbach, Erich, 215; *Mimesis*, 190, 236, 237
Austen, Jane, 81, 132

Babeuf, François-Émile, 112, 118
Bacon, Francis, xiv
Bakhtin, Mikhail, xviii, 199, 232, 237
Balanchine, George, 174, 182
Baldick, Chris, 234
Balzac, Honoré de, 141; *Séraphita*, 9
Barber, Samuel: *Antony and Cleopatra*, 171

259